MW00736305

"Alex Factor's book is a must-read for anyone who is contemplating, or currently engaged in any part of the ASP business. It's a unique book, a soup-to-nuts description of everything from ASP technology to ASP economics. I strongly recommend it."

John Gay, CTO, NCS Pearson

"The past few years have seen considerable hype and confusion around the term ASP. Alexander Factor's *Analyzing Application Service Providers* provides clarity in this constantly evolving and rapidly growing market space by describing the fundamentals and economics of the application outsourcing model."

Jessica Goepfert, Senior Analyst, ASP Services, IDC

"This book provides the most comprehensive assessment of ASP economics, architectures, and technologies that I've seen. Service providers, as well as their customers, stand to benefit from applying Factor's analytical frameworks."

Paul Hodgetts, Director of Product Development
Chief Architect, Escrow.Com

Analyzing Application Service Providers

Alexander Factor

Sun Microsystems Press
A Prentice Hall Title

The publisher offers discounts on this book when ordered in bulk quantities. For more information, contact: Corporate Sales Department, Phone: 800-382-3419; Fax: 201-236-7141; E-mail: corpsales@prenhall.com; or write: Prentice Hall PTR, Corp. Sales Dept., One Lake Street, Upper Saddle River, NJ 07458.

Editorial/production supervisor: *Carol Wheelan*
Cover design director: *Jerry Votta*
Cover designer: *Kavish & Kavish Digital Publishing & Design*
Manufacturing manager: *Alexis R. Heydt*
Marketing manager: *Debby vanDijk*
Acquisitions editor: *Gregory G. Doench*

Sun Microsystems Press
Marketing manager: *Michael Llwyd Alread*
Publisher: *Rachel Borden*

10 9 8 7 6 5 4 3 2 1

ISBN 0-13-089425-7

Sun Microsystems Press
A Prentice Hall Title

Table of Contents

Foreword

A fundamental shift is occurring in the way businesses are using information technology to gain operational efficiencies and strategic advantages. A new information-processing paradigm called Application Service Provider (ASP) is changing the dynamic of business application delivery and management. ASP offers businesses reliable and secure access to every conceivable application via the Internet. ASP diminishes, or eliminates altogether, businesses' needs to operate their own information resources and manage hired staffs. ASP substitutes usage fees for businesses' capital outlays for technology, facilities, and staff. Finally, ASP provides higher levels of service allowing businesses to focus more on their core competencies rather than running their own IT.

This book doesn't pretend to be "scientific" about ASP. The ASP industry is young and novel, and little knowledge has been accumulated about it to suffice for a scientific inquiry. Thus, the book is more qualitative than quantitative. Focusing more on spotting trends than on measuring them, it pursues a common-sense correctness over scientific accuracy. Over time, however, this situation is bound to change and other books should be written on the quantitative effects of ASP. This author only timidly hopes to participate in that process.

ASPs are complex, both in a business sense and technologically. Along with their high potential comes ample confusion. This book attempts to alleviate some of this confusion by defining the ASP terminology and frameworks to address what ASP really is, who is involved, and how to build it. This book provides:

- ASP definition, genesis, economics; current trends, future directions, problems
- Types of ASP services, their competitive advantages, value propositions
- ASP designs, architectures, methodologies, and enabling technologies

The business models, technical architectures, methodologies, tools, and other ideas described in this book should help different ASP stakeholders to design their ASP strategies. These stakeholders include computer and communications hardware vendors, software publishers, systems integrators, service providers, value-added resellers, and other companies participating in the business IT value chain. The book should also appeal to potential ASP users as it shows how ASP can help their businesses meet numerous business challenges such as these:

- Reduce the investment and operational costs of IT computing.
- Provide a greater ease of use and improved user productivity.
- Support connectivity, portability, and utility of computing.
- Build for flexibility, scalability, reliability, and availability of computing.

The book draws heavily from the author's own experience building "first-comer" ASPs. This experience—combined with the collective knowledge of his respective organization, Sun Professional Services, and numerous colleagues in the Internet services industries—is distilled into the pages of this book.

Preface

The explosion of interest in the Internet and electronic business is creating a myriad of new business opportunities. Every day, more and more businesses seek new solutions involving the Internet and Web-based technologies. These businesses realize that the new technologies can enable them to more effectively transact business with customers, suppliers, and internal departments, and more efficiently run their operations by leveraging the capabilities offered by the nascent Internet technologies. While many ISVs[1] and solution providers still believe that their customers would purchase hardware, COTS,[2] and tools and then customize/develop them for their use, increasing technological complexities and overhead make these propositions ever more taxing or simply economically impossible for all but a few very large companies.

Why a Book Analyzing ASP?

Recently, a group of IT[3] market players pioneered the concept of application outsourcing. The key premise for application outsourcing is that a business application doesn't have to be owned, run, and maintained by businesses themselves but can be provided by an out-

---

1. ISV- Independent Software Vendor.
2. COTS – Commercial Off-the-Shelf Systems (applications!).
3. IT – Information Technology.

side party. Like many services bought and consumed by businesses, IT services can also eventually be bought and consumed. Some promising results have already been achieved in application outsourcing with some application outsourcing models.

This book attempts to define application outsourcing, understand its genesis, and develop rationale for its future growth and evolution.

Application outsourcing enables businesses to economize on facilities, software, hardware, and staff by either fully or partially eliminating their IT functions. It is especially advantageous to medium and small companies[4] for whom application outsourcing can provide access to application functionality that up until now has been unavailable or simply not affordable.

The outside parties that offer application outsourcing services—that is, application outsourcers, or application service providers—can achieve major operational efficiencies and higher quality of services by leveraging built-in ASP economies of scale, scope, and learning inherent in a shared outsourcing model. For example, economies of scale can arise from the sharing of networks, servers, systems, and application software or from shared customer care, data centers, support, and maintenance. Economies of scope can result from standardization, version control, reuse, and focused training. Over time, as ASPs learn how to do their business, new efficiencies attributable to the economies of learning (as in a learning curve) will accrue and make ASP even more efficient.

This book attempts to formalize diverse economies inherent in ASP and apply them to ASP-related decision processes, models, and architectures.

Application outsourcing (or ASP) is more than just a collection of multiple IT departments. Service improvements cannot come from simply duplicating and multiplying traditional systems and operations. ASP must leverage the scale and scope of its systems and networks, and it must thrive on synergies of experience and refined policies and processes to offer services that are superior to those an individual IT department could ever provide. To achieve this, there must be something special about ASP, the technologies it uses, how it designs its architectures, the skills of people running it, and its operating policies and processes.

---

4. The author uses the following size criteria averaged from similar breakdowns and used by numerous ISVs, SIs, and market analysts:

Large $1 billion or more in annual sales
Medium   ($300 to $500 million) to $1 billion in annual sales
Small   ($20 to $50 million) to ($300 to $500 million) in annual sales

This book attempts to define ASP architectures, applicable technologies, and specific ASP services to be offered to ASP business customers.

ASP is a new phenomenon. If the logic of ASP services becoming commodities and utilities described in this book should prevail in real life, current ASPs will, over time, undergo major metamorphoses.

This book attempts to peek into the future, so to speak, by projecting some of the currently observable and sustainable trends to paint a believable and probable view of tomorrow's ASPs.

What's in the Book

This book is an analytical assessment of the phenomena of ASP. The hallmark of its approach is the introduction of various analytical frameworks applied to ASP. Frameworks are used throughout the book to categorize, classify, or simply organize an understanding of what ASPs are and where they are going.

Thus, the book introduces frameworks for customer ASP economics, ASP services definitions, ASP technologies, ASP architectures, ASP ecosystems, ASP value propositions, ASP investment decision processes, and some others.

The book is written in a business-like language focusing on the business impact of ASP on its customers, ecosystem, and overall economy. Words like value propositions, cost/benefits, time-to-market, capital preservation, capital and expenses, service quality, and other business-related terms are used extensively.

This book is a modest attempt to understand ASP. It leaves a lot of questions open to further analysis and discussion. It hopes to explore and analyze, posit and argue, provoke and challenge. While the book may contain some contestable statements, either explicit or not, they are intended to incite debate, not controversy.

What Is Not in this Book

This book is not about ASP markets and their trends, even though some references to market research are provided. This book is not about rating and comparing already available ASP services, their pricing, delivery channels, and support, although some elements of ASP's marketing mix are mentioned to define ASP's competitive advantages. The book alludes to ASP's drivers and enablers but doesn't study them in depth. This book is not about competition and selection of best of breed services and providers.

No book on technology or business can ever provide a complete account of its subject. Some things are always left out. Some other things, however, may be excluded from the book, or disclaimed, by design. Here are some of them:

Products and Vendors. While the book mentions certain products and vendors, such references are not endorsements. Technologies, products, and business requirements change rapidly and endorsements become time-dependent judgments inappropriate for a book. Products and vendors are mentioned in the book mostly to illustrate the state of technologies for the time when the book was written or, perhaps, to illustrate or support a certain point made in the text.

Market Research and Statistics. As was indicated above, this book doesn't focus on marketing. Still, some market research, published articles, and government statistics are provided and referenced in the book. Normally, such references are used to substantiate the author's logic and conclusions and should only be trusted for the time and space for when they are applied.

Recipes and Frameworks. The book avoids all kinds of technical and business recipes. It does, however, emphasize the frameworks. While some frameworks may have a cross-business applicability, there are no one-size-fits-all frameworks. It is up to the reader to decide how to apply each to their case and then fill in the blanks accordingly. Note that no framework is ever final and complete, and that other, better frameworks will inevitably arrive. Still, if readers should find some frameworks in this book helpful, the author will consider this book a success.

A Word on Terminology

Vision, business needs, and new technologies drive the creation of a new marketplace. Uncertainty, doubt, and limited knowledge rule its early stages. And it doesn't help when the players in the marketplace also add to the confusion by creating too many definitions and nomenclatures. Yet, this is exactly what is happening in the ASP marketplace.

As of this writing, more than 2,000 providers offer ASP types of services. There are ASPs, Business Service Providers (BSPs), Network Information Service Providers (NISPs), Solutions Service Providers (SSPs), Commerce Service Providers (CSPs), Business Process Outsourcers (BPOs), ASP Aggregators, and others, just to name a few. Add to them Internet Service Providers (ISPs), Independent Software Vendors (ISVs), Value-Added Resellers (VARs), Systems

Integrators (SIs), Vendor Integrators (VIs), Managed Services Providers (MSPs), and Network & Systems Management (NSMs) Outsourcers and others—many of them also dreaming to be providers—and figuring out who's who gets very depressing, very fast. So, to simplify terminology, the previous definition is limited to the providers of network-delivered applications services only. Thus, the three major terms used in the book are Service Providers (SPs), ASPs and Application Outsourcers. SPs are more generic than ASPs as they provide services supporting ASP. The terms ASP and Application Outsourcers are used interchangeably.

Additionally, it is assumed that the ASP (or an SP or an Application Outsourcer) is built as a network-computing (NC) environment. Therefore, the term NC is also used extensively throughout the book.

Audience and Technical Level Required

All participants in the ASP business model are the book's targeted audience:

- ASP Entrepreneurs—investigating ASP markets and business opportunities
- ISVs—seeking new markets for their products
- Service Providers—looking for new use of bandwidth and portal services to retain customers
- Technology Providers—adjusting to new market demands and looking for new markets
- Systems Integrators (SIs and VIs)—seeking new/replacement revenue sources
- VARs—seeking new/replacement revenue
- Investors—seeking new markets and companies to invest in

Most executives, managers, and business/technical analysts of potential ASP customers can also benefit from this book as it can tell them, among others things, how to choose an ASP.

While this book is *not* intended for purely technical professionals, some things about the readers are assumed. They include:

- Some understanding of computing and communications technologies and terminology, especially the Internet
- Basic knowledge of the most significant technological and business developments in the computing and communications industries over the last five to ten years
- A familiarity with the names of certain trend-setting companies and their products

Organization of this Book

Figure I.1 depicts the titles of the book's chapters and their relationships. The book consists of two informal parts and the last summary chapter. Part 1 covers the ASP basics and consists of three chapters.

- Chapter 1 offers simple definitions of ASP.
- Chapter 2 explores why businesses outsource and how an evolution of business needs forced traditional outsourcing to become ASP.
- Chapter 3 provides a deeper analysis of the ASP phenomenon—its salient business and technical characteristics, its ecosystem, and its drivers and enablers.

Figure I.1   *The book's chapters and their relationships.*

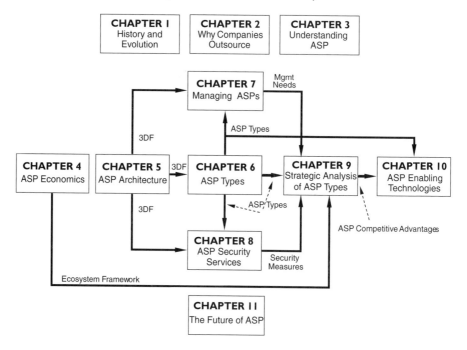

Part 2 of the book consists of seven chapters. It combines the architectural, technological, and business aspects of ASP.

- It first defines the economic framework (Chapter 4) for the analysis of distributed network computing architectures, which, at the end of Part 2, in Chapter 9, is applied to ASP to derive its competitive strategies.
- In the meantime, the intermediate Chapters 5 through 8 are dedicated to defining network computing and ASP architectures (Chapter 5), the requirements for ASP types and services (Chapter 6), ASP management disciplines (Chapter 7), and ASP security requirements (Chapter 8).
- The last chapter in Part 2, Chapter 10, is dedicated to ASP enabling technologies that both support the ASP technical, management, and security requirements and provide the foundation on which future ASPs will be built.

The last chapter in the book, Chapter 11, provides insights into ASP's future.

ACKNOWLEDGEMENTS

It all started with Rachel Borden, Sun Microsystems' Publisher, an inveterate optimist, who first encouraged and then supported me throughout the entire writing and publishing process. Thank you, Rachel!

I am forever indebted to Greg Doench, my Prentice Hall Acquisitions Editor, and Carol Wheelan, Production Editor, for their patience, experience, and a unique ability to make the complicated process of publishing seem fun and easy. They also were very instrumental in prerelease promotion and marketing, together with Sun's Pat Spencer, who was indispensable in helping with endorsements and promotion.

Very special thanks belong to my technical editors, Corinne Gregory of Prentice Hall and Dr. Brad Blumenthal of Sun. Thank you, Corinne, for your cool common sense that spared me an exposure of overlooked mistakes and convoluted logic. Thank you, Brad, for your perceptive critique and invaluable suggestions which helped improve the book immeasurably.

I am especially grateful to Mark Bauhaus, a Sun Professional Services VP, for making me a member of his outstanding team of true professionals who authored, among many other great things, the three-dimensional framework (3DF) for designing network computing architectures. The 3DF gave me a comprehensive construct and a point of departure for developing my own ideas about ASP architecture, its features, ASP types, and ASP economics. My many thanks go to the key members of Mark's team: Dr. Jim Baty, Stu Stern, Ed Schwarz, and Dan Berg.

The market and technology research companies referenced in the book—Gartner, Meta, Ovum, Forrester, IDC, and others—perform an extremely valuable service for their customers of tracking the ASP industry, its trends and offerings. Their insights and predictions (especially those of ASP's impending future) instilled in me a strong belief in the "destiny" of ASP and persuaded me to research and write. My special thanks go to Dean Davison of Meta and Audrey Apfel of Gartner.

I owe my understanding of the basic principles of operational economics to Professor Richard Langlois of the University of Connecticut. His writings on the subject helped me create an economic framework for ASP used in the book.

And finally, this book could not happen if it were not for many clients with whom I had a privilege to work. It was only through my interactions with them, by understanding their visions, learning their needs, and working together to resolve their challenges that I learned enough to write this book.

Alexander Factor, September 2001

Chapter 1

The History and Evolution of Outsourcing and ASP

IT outsourcing is defined as a "turning over of information systems and/or communications functions, as a whole or in part, to a third-party contractor" as a "solution to the challenge, problem, and expense of creating and running a corporate information enterprise."[1] Outsourcing is legitimately considered a forerunner of the new service dubbed Application Service Provider (ASP) or, as some call it, Application Solution Provider, which is the subject of this book.

This chapter starts with the discussion of outsourcing's legacy—exploring its broad history from a basic division of labor to an outsourcing of business services. It further defines ASP, analyzes its various "personalities," compares it with traditional outsourcing, and finally presents the currently hot outstanding issues.

Outsourcing: Historical Insights

Division of Labor and Specialization

The modern languages deal with an increasing number of new concepts and ideas. To cope with an ever-evolving vocabulary, languages

---

1. Daniel Minoli, *Analyzing Outsourcing*, New York: McGraw-Hill, Inc. 1995. p 1.

use abstraction to help create the new terms conjuring up the new concepts and ideas. Yet an unpleasant consequence of abstraction is that it tends to obscure the historical context of these ideas and concepts, erasing the potential for a better understanding of their true legacy and nature. Outsourcing is one such abstracted term that has, over time, amassed considerable positive momentum as well as negative baggage.

Outsourcing has been around since the times of hunters and gatherers. Those who were strong hunters hunted, those who were strong gatherers gathered. Simply put, the primitive society, perhaps subconsciously, recognized the importance of specialization and "outsourced" certain functions to those who excelled at them or, in economic terms, performed them more efficiently.

This concept of specialization progressed and evolved over time. In a homestead economy, the owners of "home and land" performed every chore themselves—planted and harvested, herded and fed, butchered and preserved, wove and sewed, logged and built. Spreading time and energy over many different activities didn't help to improve efficiency. It was the emergence of communities, communications, and markets enabling people to specialize and excel at their trades that led to increased productivity and improved livelihoods. Thus came the farmers and builders, cowboys and traders, tailors and cobblers, smiths, butchers, bakers, fishermen, foresters, bankers, pharmacists, and many others. As time went on, further divisions of labor and further specialization occurred.

It does not take a big leap of faith to start equating outsourcing with specialization (or division of labor). The main difference lies in the domain in which these terms are used. Specialization is an economic concept. It explains how the market forces stipulate the need for and drive the "division of labor," how this "division of labor" is structured, and how it leads to societal wealth. Outsourcing is a utilitarian concept used in business and accounting. From the accounting point of view, it is defined as "the transfer of an internal service function to an outside vendor."[2]

Since outsourcing tends to lower costs as a result of specialization it is widely encountered in business and everyday life. Examples of outsourcing in business may include parts manufacturing in the auto industry, the prefabrication of building blocks in civil engineering and home construction, and the gathering of financial information by banks and brokerage houses. For consumers, outsourcing is even more evident, although it may not be immediately recognized. Consumers are both end users and providers of outsourced services

---

2. J.L. Wagner, "Issues in Outsourcing," 1992 IRMA Conference Proceedings, Idea Group Publishing, 1992, p. 214.

and products. Indeed, most people don't grow their own wheat to make bread; they simply buy it in a grocery store. Likewise, people don't drill wells for fresh water, don't grow cotton to weave clothes, don't make bricks and mortar, don't dig for oil and ore, don't assemble home appliances and cars, and so on and so on.

Business Services

In business, outsourcing can be found everywhere. Big or small, simple or complex, businesses have historically outsourced numerous support functions such as food preparation, janitorial work, and MROs.[3] More complex outsourced support functions include those in legal, accounting (e.g., payroll check printing), financial audits, communications, transportation, advertising and promotion, employee recruitment and relocation, insurance, health care, and investment management.

Why is it advantageous to buy services from the outside rather than conduct them from within the company? Because the service providers who specialize in these services have developed efficiencies and learned how to offer high quality and competitive pricing. As a result, many of these providers—advertisers, executive recruiters, insurers, and CPA firms—are booming; even a new term to describe such services was born: *business services.*

To be effective and efficient in business services, providers eventually resorted to the help of networks and computers to automate many of their functions. Running service applications on behalf of many customers (some performed remotely) further improved providers' efficiencies, increased their investment leverage, and made them, for all practical purposes, bona fide utilities.

Information Technology (IT) is one of the most common business services available today. Indeed, if a power utility company can build its plant, install generators, develop distribution networks, and provide power to many customers, why can't an IT utility company build computing facilities, buy and install computers, deploy application software, and provide application services to their customers? Yes, it is possible, and, in fact, many companies have been doing this for a long while.

IT Service as a Utility

In the early days of industrialization businesses developed their own sources of energy: water, sun, steam. Over time, however, specialized

---

3. MRO—Maintenance, Repair, and Operational functions.

providers of energy emerged, offering cheaper sources and easy access to them. This process culminated in the invention of electricity, the most versatile energy form known to man. With electricity, companies could consume all the energy they wanted, when they needed it, and pay only for what they used. Energy became a commodity and its producers became utilities.

A similar metamorphosis awaits IT. Except for those who use IT as their core competency or a product, most businesses may eventually treat IT as a utility service. Since the new forms of outsourcing promise comprehensive IT services with potential economic advantages, these outsourcers stand a good chance of becoming IT service utilities. Like other established utility providers, the new outsourcers would assume the responsibility, on behalf of its customers, for managing the delivery of new services while ensuring its availability, performance, and scalability.

Here are two simple examples of advanced IT outsourcing services that can be perceived as IT utilities. An office manager connects online to a service provider to check the catalogs for office supply products she wants to buy, makes selections, and places the order. The service provider she uses already knows her purchase preferences, style, and even approval processes and uses workflow engines to follow the rules to complete the approval for a fast and efficient purchase. In another example, a sales manager wants to view reports summarizing the activities of his distributed sales force. He can do so by dialing a secure remote Web site to run a sales force automation application. This application tallies up sales numbers, reports on the effectiveness of sales incentives or promotions, and recommends the next activity. This is a pretty advanced application, using data mining techniques against the database of products, services, sales data, actions, and policies. Incidentally, the sales manager's company is relatively small and could not afford to buy this application, but it still benefits from it by renting it from its service provider.

Traditional IT Outsourcing

IT outsourcing has existed for a long time, yet it has suffered from some limitations in the breadth of offerings, service quality, flexibility, and most importantly, enabling technologies. Timesharing was one of the first types of IT outsourcing services introduced in the 1950s. Computers were expensive then and even large companies opted to buy processing cycles in lieu of computers. Timesharing was popular for almost 25 years. But as technologies evolved, other outsourcing ideas emerged. In the late 1980s, large consulting firms like Andersen Consulting, CSC, EDS, SHL Systemhouse and vendors like IBM invented remote management services. A customer's systems, networks, and applications were monitored and managed remotely from a Network Operations Center (NOC), and the customer was assured high service guarantees through the implementation of so-called Service Level Agreements (SLAs). Customers liked these services and bought them mostly to ensure availability for their systems and networks.

Business Process Outsourcing (BPO) was originated by consultants too. It offered customers professional assistance for streamlining and managing their operational business processes. Finally, IT outsourcing—which was almost a total takeover of a customer's IT environment—emerged as an offering around 1990. IT outsourcing found its customers among those who wanted, for whatever reason, to divest themselves of their own IT facilities, operations, and personnel and focus on other aspects of their businesses. The advent of network computing in the late 1980s, the Internet in the early 1990s, and the new software development tools and techniques, combined with the profound changes in global economies, gave rise to the totally new models of outsourcing, such as ASP.

The transition from timesharing, BPO, Network and System Management (NSM), IT outsourcing, and other legacy forms of outsourcing to the Service Providers of today, especially ASPs, was evolutionary. However, the current state of outsourcing is vastly different from its traditional forms. Table 1.1 provides a simple comparison.

Table 1.1 *Legacy and Modern Outsourcing*

Legacy Outsourcing	*Modern Outsourcing*
Numerous computer platforms	Converging computing platforms
Proprietary (mostly incompatible) architectures	Open architectures
Domination by the mainframes	Distributed computing
High cost, low quality networking	Low cost, high quality networking
In-house software development and limited availability of packaged software	Mostly packaged software

Selective Outsourcing

IT outsourcing is exciting and promising, both as an economic and utilitarian concept. Yet its evolution has been imperfect and it has had some negative press. Still, it is possible to make a case here that whatever the reports of IT outsourcing's failings, they frequently had little to do with the outsourcing's fundamentals, but rather with how IT outsourcing had been used and by whom.

Numerous market research papers and books have tackled IT outsourcing but few have provided empirical evidence of outsourcing successes (or failures) in terms of economic measures such as Economic Value Added (EVA).[4] Most conclusions from published works were either based on secondary data or obtained from sources not very close to real business. One researcher, Paul Strassmann,[5] made a thorough inquiry into the rationale for outsourcing and the types of companies who took out big IT outsourcing contracts. The key word here is "big," implying large-scale outsourcing (as opposed to selective) of mission-critical applications, functions, processes, and roles.

Strassmann successfully tested numerous hypotheses of EVA from IT outsourcing, using extensive empirical databases of his own primary research and arrived at some illuminating conclusions. He wrote:

> Those corporations that outsourced more than sixty percent of their IT budget were economic losers when they began outsourcing. They were probably shedding IT resources along with other corporate functions because they were in financial trouble. I could not find any corporation with a consistently large economic value-added and rising employment that outsourced its information technology despite claims of synergy or the advantages of getting rid of commodity work. The losers were casting off IT because they were already shrinking their firm anyway.

Thus, most big outsourcing contracts were taken out by those companies whose EVA was already falling, or in simple terms, the companies whose business was already in decline. Other independent researchers, namely, Brynjolfsson and Hitt,[6] echoed Strassmann's findings by stating that:

> Companies that try to jump on the outsourcing bandwagon may be chasing a parked car. We found no association between outsourc-

---

4. EVA—Economic Value Added is a metric most commonly used in the business world for setting and tracking financial goals and for executive compensation. EVA is extensively studied both by academia and business. A simple description of EVA is provided in "All about EVA" by D. Christinat, *CFO Magazine*, November 1996.

5. Paul A. Strassmann, "The Squandered Computer," *The Information Economics Press*, pp. 181-204, 1997.

6. E. Brynjolfsson and L. Hitt, "The Productive Keep Producing," *Information Week*, September 18, 1995.

ing and success. If anything, companies that outsourced more of information system work tend to have lower productivity and profitability. The only performance measure the heavy outsourcers did well on was stock market returns. In the short term, the market reacts favorably to outsourcing.

So, was it outsourcing in and of itself that pushed these failing companies further down the spiral of decline? Or was it because the outsourcing contracts were too big, making them fundamentally wrong? Perhaps selective outsourcing was better? To cast off the IT outsourcing's misplaced culpability, Strassmann gave answers to these three questions in one simple comment.

> The high performance companies do selective outsourcing, ranging anywhere from three to eleven percent of their total budget, but retain most of their information management capabilities as an important ingredient of their overall managerial competency.

Thus, Strassmann stated that IT outsourcing still remained a viable business concept, albeit with a caveat about the advantages of selective outsourcing. The elements of "modern outsourcing" (Table 1.1)—the Internet, open architectures, distributed computing, and many other technology developments such as high capacity storage and bandwidth—are all driving IT outsourcing's improved capabilities and lower costs.

While most legacy IT outsourcing was an "all or nothing" service, modern outsourcing offers selectivity, both in terms of application functions as well as infrastructure services offered to its customers.

xSP and ASP

From the late 1990s, with the developments of new business drivers and technological enablers (see Chapter 3), outsourcing has re-emerged as one of the most viable business propositions for the future of IT. At the time of this writing, there are many different outsourcers, yet a solid taxonomy of their services, let alone business terminology, are still lacking.

To identify and differentiate themselves, the new outsourcing providers have added one to two letters in front of the letters "SP" to designate their specific function. Thus, there is an MSP (Managed Service Provider), an IPP (Internet Presence Provider), a CSP (either a Commerce, or Content, or Capacity Service Provider), an ASP (Application Service Provider), and many others.

To generalize, the service provider industry invented the term xSP, where the "x" connotes any type of a service provider. This book could also use this term. However, since the supreme goal of all providers is to enable the *ultimate* consumer to get *application* services, this book will apply the term Application Service Provider or ASP to all service providers *involved* in delivering such application services. Thus, the term ASP will epitomize, in this book, the next generation of outsourcing as a point of convergence of multiple technological and economic trends.

An ASP can be described in a number of different ways:

- as a business
- as a substitute for a customer's IT
- as a member of a new ecosystem of other businesses.

Every definition from this list offers a unique perspective and helps with a deeper understanding of ASP phenomenon, its legacy, and its future directions.

ASP as a Business

ASP provides the services and possesses the characteristics of a typical IT organization, at least for what it offers. But an ASP itself is also a bona fide business. Besides providing the services, an ASP must operate as a business. It must devise the business models (e.g., services, markets, pricing, support), develop and run effective sales and marketing, handle finances, run PR, execute proper corporate governance, and perform many other functions typical of a business yet not present in a company's IT department.

Basic Definition of ASP

An ASP is a business that offers multiple customers access to business applications over the network (e.g., the Internet) while charging rental or subscription-based fees for services used. Or, deciphering this definition, ASP is a business that:[7]

- delivers application services over *the network*
- delivers services to *many* customers with a wide range of requirements
- charges *rental* or subscription-based fees
- provides customer-specific *service guarantees.*

---

7. The author has researched this book since early 2000 and has independently arrived at this four-point ASP definition. It is similar to, and hence validated by, the IDC publication #24024 in February 2001.

The delivery of application services over the network (the Internet, VPN,[8] dedicated facilities, etc.) is more than just servicing customer requests online. These services are delivered with comprehensive service guarantees requiring a lot more behind-the-scenes ASP activities than a typical IT department would ever have to do. This may include, but is not limited to, management of partnerships with networking and network management service providers; implementation of sophisticated security and intercustomer privacy measures; additional forms of customer care and support; network service usage tracking, metering, and billing.

The ASP must efficiently support multiple customers (as opposed to one) all coming with different sets of application needs and varied service quality requirements. However, ASP customers usually demand higher quality or lower cost from the ASP than they would normally get from their own IT. Otherwise, why outsource at all? Yet, supporting multiple customers is not an easy feat. Besides the technical difficulties of hosting multiple customers' systems and applications while striving for business efficiencies (see Chapter 9), many ASP-unique operational and management challenges also arise. These include the per-customer service usage tracking, metering, and billing as well as customer-specific fault isolation, management, and recovery, just to name a few. The theme of multiple customers and related concepts of multiple tenants will be analyzed in greater detail in subsequent chapters of this book.

The ASP business model is a rental model, meaning that unlike an internal IT department, the ASP business depends on the collection of user fees rather than pre-ordained IT budgets. Further, the ASP is always under customer scrutiny and the threat of customer departures if it does not live up to the terms of its customer service delivery. All this exerts extreme pressure on ASPs to offer better, quicker, and cheaper services.

The ASP must manage its operational environment and services both holistically, i.e., within certain pre-established boundaries of qualities for the entire ASP, and also by individual customer, according to each customer's contractual service level guarantees stipulated in the contracts called SLAs. Chapter 6 offers more details on SLAs and their role in the management of services provided to ASP customers.

Finally, though not in the aforementioned definition, the ASP must operate in Internet time, under the pressure of increasing competi-

---

8. VPN—virtual private network.

tion, rapidly evolving technologies, and continuously changing customer needs, coupled with the decreases in business cycle times and shrinking latency intervals. The order is very tall. Yet, it is exactly this Internet time—plus increasing technological complexity, dearth of talent, and other drivers—that motivate business customers to consider ASPs in lieu of their own IT in the first place.

It should be noted here that some very large corporations' IT departments behave in the manner similar to the above description. They build shared computing and networking infrastructures, service multiple (internal and even external) customers, compute usage-based charge-backs, and operate on the basis of SLAs. They effectively operate as internal ASPs, and are referred to as HSPs, for Home Service Providers.

The Rental Model

The rental model is the hallmark of ASP and its most recognized business characteristic. ASPs charge their customers fees for services—by user seats, applications, transactions, usage term (e.g., a month), or other unitary measures, or combinations thereof. These fees serve as proxies of all costs the customers would incur if they bought, installed, and managed all the applications they rent from ASPs themselves. Add to that the time-to-market factor—another ability ASPs strive to excel at—and ASP services (e.g., application renting) become an even more attractive proposition to potential customers.

It should be noted, though, that a rental model for services is not new in the world of network computing. The familiar Internet Service Providers (ISPs) have used it for years. In their model, a customer signs up for an ISP service comprised of email, Web access, chat, news, and other Internet applications and pays monthly or hourly fees. ASPs simply expand this model to business applications.

ASP as a Substitute for a Customer's IT

For customers, ASPs may become a partial (selective) or a complete substitute for their company's IT organization, effectively assuming some or all IT functions. This creates a substitution effect that applies to whole systems or just their components, to processes and procedures, and to the roles and relationships comprising the entire corporate IT's business. Just like an IT department, an ASP plans its environment, systems, applications, and services. It designs and performs the processes for systems, software, and services procurement and for the installation, development, operation, and management.

Further, it deals with equipment vendors, telephone companies, software publishers, systems integrators, consultants, and most importantly, with the customer's internal user communities. All these functions that used to be done by the customers themselves now become the prerogative of ASPs. Figure 1.1 juxtaposes a customer's typical roles with and without an ASP.

A customer's decision to use an ASP changes the paradigm of IT management. In a typical enterprise, an IT department is a cost center. Defensive about its budget, it always longs for budget increases, always needs more money, and despite the best and sincere efforts by management to contain the budgets, the budget's long-term trend has always been upward.

The ASP holds the potential to change that. With multiple ASP offerings, businesses can use their budgets to seek better quality services from the competing ASPs. Over time, the "invisible hand"[9] of free markets will improve the quality of such services and lower their costs, possibly reducing the IT budgets in the process. And eventually these IT services may even become commodities traded in the open market. The "invisible hand" of open markets for IT services has already begun to shape the ASP industry, promising customers more options, higher quality, and lower costs.

Figure 1.1 *IT roles and ASP customer roles.*

IT's Typical Roles

- Plan investments
- Build facilities
- Hire and train people
- Budget and track expenses
- Select and procure systems
- Select, procure, and test software
- Work with vendors and providers
- Hire integrators and consultants
- Organize and define processes
- Install systems and software
- Develop software
- Customize packages
- Maintain systems and applications
- Provide user support
- Run the data center
- Plan for the future

ASP Customer's Roles

- Specify application services needs
- Budget service costs and return on investment
- Contract for services
- Focus on your business, not IT

---

9. The term was introduced by Adam Smith in his historic work, *The Wealth of Nations* published in 1777.

ASP as a New Ecosystem

The ASP is a complex arrangement. It has personalities of multiple businesses. It can be in part a Web portal and an ISP; a technology provider and a packaged application vendor (an Independent Software Vendor [ISV]); a Systems Integrator (SI) and a specialized consultant (e.g., systems management, database, operations); and a platform and operations outsourcing business.

The ASP is the intersection of relationships between the customers and their suppliers. It steps in between them and effectively becomes a surrogate provider of products and services, otherwise delivered by these suppliers. In doing so, the ASP assumes many new roles and responsibilities. It can be a marketing channel and support organization as well as a conduit for information flows between customers and suppliers. The ASP thus becomes a complex ecosystem thanks to its assumption of multiple business personalities, including the roles listed below:

- ISPs for end user access
- Telephone Company providing network access
- ISVs who provide packaged applications
- Enabling Technology Providers: vendors of hardware and OS, LAN and WAN equipment, management and operations tools, and so forth.
- Business consultants
- Technology consultants
- Systems integrators
- Value-added resellers, and many others.

Chapter 11 provides a more detailed description of the members of the ASP ecosystem and how they are impacted by it.

IT Outsourcing and ASP - Differences and Similarities

By all accounts, printed or verbal, the ASP is the heir apparent of traditional IT outsourcing. In the name of progress, one should then expect the ASP to *be more* than IT outsourcing, *do more*, and *do it better, faster, and cheaper.* Table 1.2 attempts to add clarity to the imprecise statement of "more and better." This table has been partially borrowed from the Meta Group's report[10] and has been expanded by the author.

10. Dean Davison, "Service Management Strategies," Meta Group, File 819, September 29, 1999.

Table 1.2 *Outsourcing and ASP: Differences and Similarities*

	Traditional In-House	*Traditional Outsourcing*	*Application Service Provider Model*
Software Licenses	Customer owns and manages licenses.	Outsourcer can, yet mostly the customer owns and manages licenses.	ASP usually owns and manages.
Hardware Ownership	Customer must purchase, install, and finance infrastructure.	Outsourcer or customer can own infrastructure.	ASP's infrastructure. Customers may never know what powers their applications.
Infrastructure Location	Customer's data center.	Outsourcer's location or Customer's location.	ASP's location or third-party collocation.
Physical Infrastructure Management	Customer manages everything.	Outsourcer manages physical infrastructure either from its own facility or remotely.	ASP or collocation vendor does all HVAC, power, and physical security management and administration.
Computing Infrastructure Management	Customer manages everything.	Outsourcer manages infra-structure either from its own facility or remotely.	ASP does (or manages others that provide) all systems and network (e.g., routers and switches) configuration, management, tuning, administration, and even application management.
Implementation	Customer company customizes software to its own business processes.	Third parties customize software to customer's busi-ness processes usually paid for separately and coordinated by the customer company.	Implementation costs—for application customization and/or personalization—are factored into monthly rental charges.

Table 1.2 *Outsourcing and ASP: Differences and Similarities (Continued)*

Contract Terms and Pricing	Yearly budget cycles.	Long, often 7 to 10 year contracts.	Three to five years but getting shorter.
Billing	Internal auditing and assessment.	Annual fees.	Per-user per-month fees, plus subscription charges, etc.

The "more and better" aspect of ASP becomes more obvious from Table 1.2 emphasizing the Operational (i.e., Infrastructure Management) and Implementation skills. If the ASP industry is to succeed, these skills will be acquired and practiced. However, ASPs are currently facing major challenges. The same Meta Group's report previously mentioned offered the following insights:

> As they (ASPs) now attempt to become providers of core, mission-critical applications, few have the proper operational disciplines—change management, security architectures, data centers, disaster recovery strategies—or the rigor of traditional outsourcers. With their current structure, ASPs differ from traditional outsourcing only in minor ways... After removing the market hype, most ASPs have little or no operational or implementation skills . . .

Further, while implementation and operational abilities are essential for the ASP success, there is another issue that, in the author's mind, must be addressed by ASPs. It is leverage. Let's explain it. ASPs host and manage multiple applications, for multiple customers, and with multiple sets of service level guarantees. To be successful, ASPs must leverage their resources: hosting and communications infrastructures, operational skills, professional services, management structures and processes and, finally, the ASP's own business practices. All these "musts" are called upon to ensure that ASPs deliver quality service and operational savings which, when passed to customers, create competitive advantages. The issue of leverage is addressed in detail in Chapters 4 and 9.

Unresolved/Open Issues

Major and still unresolved issues remain with the ASP. Some are related to business, some to technology. A "T" is used to label technical issues, while "B" is used for business issues. Wherever applicable, this book addresses them or simply states the need to address them in the future. Some of these issues are listed here:

Standardization (T). This relates to the application program interfaces (APIs) between applications from different vendors, on different systems, and so forth, to achieve economies of scale and scope and improved time to market. One might also talk about deeper technical issues such as overall interoperability of industry de facto standards (e.g., DNS/LDAP and Active Directory), diversity of router protocols, numerous variants of UNIX, the use of Extended Markup Language (XML), and so forth.

Sharing (T). Resource sharing in the ASP model is mired in controversies related to security and accounting. The former is both a technology and customer education issue. The latter is about monitoring and management of events of resource consumption by each customer's application instance.

Legal and Commercial Terms (B & T). These issues concern mostly ISVs and Technology Vendors (e.g., of computing and network hardware) and are related to how to sell to ASPs, how to price products and compensate sales, how to support products, how to account for their use, how to audit ASPs, and how to collect revenue.

Ethics and Law (B). This is the degree to which ASPs should be responsible for customers' applications, data, and performance, and the consequences of their use to customers' businesses as well as the consequences of customers' uses of ASP equipment and services (common carrier free speech issues, for example).

Economics (B). A deep understanding of the ASP's economics should contribute to its overall success and survival. Serendipitously, despite the significance of IT to the overall U.S. and world economies, very little has been researched and published on the subject of IT economics.

Summary

This chapter shows the historical inevitability of outsourcing for achieving improved efficiency and productivity that lead to increased societal wealth. It associates the historical trends in division of labor and specialization with the concept and philosophy of outsourcing and shows how outsourcing has evolved over time and permeated every aspect of contemporary life.

The chapter also provides the basic definition of the ASP, a major point of reference used throughout this book. Additionally, for a better understanding of the ASP, this chapter offers other definitional ramifications of the ASP, showing it as a bona-fide business, as a substitute for a customer's IT, and as a powerful proxy for the relationship between the customer and a large ecosystem of ASP suppliers and service providers.

Some key conclusions related to ASP are as follows:

Defining IT as a Utility. The ASP should be looked upon as the vehicle to migrate outsourced IT services to an information utility that is priced as a commodity.

Substituting ASP for IT. The ASP is similar to a corporate IT, yet offers improved application services to multiple customers on a rental basis.

ASP and its Ecosystem. The ASP is a complex ecosystem and assumes numerous customer-facing roles and responsibilities of its ecosystem's members: ISPs, technology (hardware and software) vendors and suppliers, ISVs, SIs, and various consultants.

A Transition From Cost to Investment. For a business customer, employing ASPs heralds a change in its IT's funding and management. Formerly provided by a cost center, services provided by a singular IT application or a bundle thereof become the targets of investment decisions with a clearly identified Return On Investment (ROI) and the "invisible hand" of free markets shaping their future.

The implications of the ASP to business are a massive impact on finance, organizational structure, personnel, and varied business philosophies, processes, and policies.

Chapter 2

Why Companies Outsource

This brief chapter offers the analytical support to Chapter 1's ideas about xSPs, in general, and ASPs, in particular. The chapter consists of three sections. The first section develops an economic rationale for outsourcing. It explores the anecdotal evidence of business outsourcing practices and shows the rationale for outsourcing decisions and their evolution.

The second section examines an ASP substitution effect via the analysis of activities and costs within a typical corporate IT department that the ASP promises to replace. The analysis shows the types of costs the ASP can or cannot replace, drawing the boundaries and limitations of ASP's total substitution abilities in the process. The last section is a summary.

The Big Question

To outsource or not to outsource? Many IT and corporate executives face this big question. As was mentioned earlier, per Strassmann's analysis, some rationale for outsourcing had been seriously misplaced in the past. However, things are now changing. New computing technologies—the Internet, new business models, and most importantly, new business and market realities—are creating both the powerful drivers and potent enablers for this renaissance of outsourcing, albeit under a different name of xSP. Still, the big question "Why Do Companies Outsource?" remains. It begs a more formal analysis using various analytical frameworks. Two such frameworks are applied below: one to peak into an economic rationale for outsourcing decisions, and another to model an ASP cost substitution effect.

Weeding Costs and Maximizing Value

Every business is a complex web of myriad transactions. These transactions are exchanged among integral parts of the business or with its outside constituencies: customers, suppliers, partners, governments, and so forth. There are many examples of business transactions: material purchases, invoices and payments, job orders, financial transactions, payroll payments, personnel record updates, order entries, purchase orders, sales receipts, promotional activities, internal email, and many, many others. All transactions have value and costs associated with them. Value is a transaction's contribution to the business' bottom line; cost is what the business spends to obtain this value. If a transaction's value is greater than cost, the transaction is productive. Conversely, if its value is less than its cost, the transaction is *un*productive. For a business to survive, the total of productive transactions must exceed the total of the unproductive ones. Or, in other words, the total value of all transactions must exceed their total costs.

Every business has numerous unproductive transactions. Some contribute absolutely nothing to the bottom line while others cost more than they bring. Examples of the former are government reporting and tax payment transactions; examples of the latter are payroll transactions, among many others. It is not surprising that from the early days of outsourcing, businesses recognized these unproductive transactions and included them among the first ones to be outsourced to those who could process them more efficiently. Such transactions included payroll, tax reporting, recruiting, and legal services.

The four simple diagrams depicted in Figure 2.1 are based on a simple postulate that it is in a business' general interest to weed out unproductive transactions and maximize the value of productive ones. These diagrams show the logic of weeding costs and maximizing value demonstrating, in the process, the implicit rationale for using outsourcing and the ASP.

Figure 2.1   *Business transactions as functions of costs and values.*

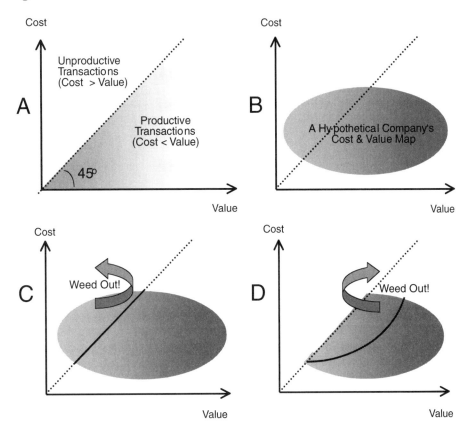

Diagram A in Figure 2.1 shows a Cost/Value chart with a 45° line. The space above 45° is where the unproductive transactions reside; the space below is for productive transactions. Diagram B shows a Cost/Value transaction space for a hypothetical company. Similar to Diagram A, all transactions above a 45° angle line are unproductive and must be "weeded out," which is shown in Diagram C.

Next, Diagram D depicts the second round of transaction weeding. Now, transactions being weeded out are those below 45°. Yet, the business' management has decided to weed them out as less productive and reassign their resources to the more productive ones located further to the right of the 45° line.

Examples of transactions in the first round of weeding may be business support activity transactions, such as recruiting, advertising, payroll-check printing, legal work, accounting audits, and so forth. When the costs of conducting these transactions within the business are higher than, or begin to exceed, their value, they are outsourced.

Information processing activities are candidates for the second round of weeding. Most such transactions are productive, yet should their costs rise—for instance, due to increasing complexity of new technologies—their value to cost ratio would decrease. The business may decide to outsource these information-processing transactions and reinvest the released resources in the more productive, core-competency related activities. This constitutes an economic rationale for businesses to look toward the ASP.

The Boundaries of Outsourcing

If outsourcing is just another term for "division of labor," it must always lead to higher efficiencies. Hence, all forms of IT outsourcing (e.g., Application Outsourcing or ASP) also hold the promise of higher efficiencies. If not, how can one explain the emergence, and rapid growth, of the new ASP industry?

A lot of anecdotal information has been published on the economic benefits of the ASP. The analyst TeleChoice of Boston[1] estimates the savings from the ASP, as compared to running the same applications in-house, in the 40% to 60% range. US Internetworking, a major ASP itself, places the numbers in the range[2] between 20% and 40%. Oracle-On-Line executives[3] claim to have achieved a bottom-line savings of about 50%. All these numbers are pretty convincing. If only they could be substantiated? Only if the numerous questions about how, when, and under what circumstances these numbers were achieved could be answered as easily. For now, these questions can be viewed in four groups:

- **Measuring**. How long does it take for the IT outsourcing efficiencies to start kicking in? How are they being observed and measured? Against what costs are they evaluated? Over what period of time? Were they communicated to all involved parties—end users, providers, suppliers, investors, etc.—and how?

- **Consistency.** Were these IT outsourcing (or ASP) efficiency figures consistent and repeatable or simply the results of one-off lucky deals or unique circumstances?

1. TeleChoice, Inc., a Boston Consultancy, 1999.
2. See US Internetworking, Inc.'s Web site.
3. See http://www.internetwk.com/story/INW19990507S0003 for quotes by Chris Russell, president of Oracle Business Online.

Even if all the answers to these questions are provided, the answers will still be provisional, subjective, and empirical, leading to further questions, as provided here.

- **Planning**. How could end users compute their potential (e.g., future) benefits from outsourcing for planning purposes? Or, how can a budding IT outsourcer (e.g., ASP) build its business models, write business plans, and project the financials to convince its bankers to invest?

- **Impact Analysis**. How will the changing business environment—economics, laws, and regulations—as well as applications and underlying technologies impact these outsourcing effects? Is there a way to forecast the impact of these changes on IT outsourcing, the ASP, and its customers?

One approach to answering these questions is to analyze a so-called phenomenon of ASP substitution. Or, more specifically, develop a methodology to analyze how the business functions performed by business itself can be replaced, or *substituted* for, by the services of IT outsourcers (or ASP). An attempt to develop such a methodology, along with simplifying assumptions and the necessary disclaimers, is described as follows.

The ASP Substitution Effect

To compute the ASP substitution effect requires the taxonomy of costs and their distribution within a corporate IT group combined with a thorough understanding of the specific functions IT outsourcing or ASP are capable of replacing. By analyzing the substitution for each IT cost category and tallying the results, it is possible to arrive at the total ASP substitution effect. Naturally, the result will be dependent on a number of (implicit) assumptions.

Modeling the Substitution Effect

First of all, the taxonomy of costs will be dependent on incumbent practices. For instance, if an organization is dependent on off-the-shelf applications fully supported by ISVs (for example, standard small-business accounting packages), neither personnel for application customization nor development and testing equipment may be needed. Second, a cost distribution structure will vary from business to business, by industry, business size, practices, strategies, and finally, technologies. Both of these considerations will also change over time (e.g., as a business grows). Finally, answering the question about what the ASP can substitute, and how much of it, will always remain a subjective matter. It will again depend on the type of business, its application requirements, the type of ASP, the knowledge and experience of the analysts, and so forth.

The following analysis uses the material on cost taxonomy and distribution derived from Forrester Research.[4] It also assumes that IT infrastructure costs represent 50% of the IT budget. The rest of the costs are spent on a wide range of labor, products, and services, most of them expenses, such as payroll and personnel, training, facilities (e.g., real estate, utilities, administration, security), and outside services (e.g., legal, recruiting, printing, postal, disaster recovery, taxes, fees, etc.). It is these first 50% that are described in Table 2.1 and the following analysis. Also, it should be noted that the real numbers provided in the table and analysis here are less important than the logic behind their use. For this reason, the age of the Forrester report, published in 1998, is less relevant than its format.

Table 2.1 *Taxonomy of IT Costs and ASP Substitution Effect*

Cost Categories	% of IT Budget	Who Pays What Costs

Business Applications
  Application Licensing
  Customization
	52%	ASP pays all costs.

Data
  Web Content
  Databases
  Data Warehousing
  Applications
	5%	ASP pays for hosting of apps and all data management software licenses.
		
		Company pays for design, population, updates, and processing of all data.

Core Systems Software
  Email, Directories, Backup, Archival, Web, etc.
  Distributed Systems Middleware (e.g., RMI, CORBA, DCE)
  Systems and Network Management
	8%	ASP pays for hosting all core systems.

4. R. Shevlin, W. Deutsch, M. Walker, and L. Helmsdorf, *Infrastructure Pending Strategies,* Forrester Research, November 1998.

Table 2.1   *Taxonomy of IT Costs and ASP Substitution Effect (Continued)*

Computing Hardware	26%	ASP pays for all costs.
Equipment (servers, data storage, workstations, PC, hubs, routers, switches, NSM equipment, etc.) Equipment Deployment (installation, tuning, and testing) Incidentals (facility preparation, documentation, and cabling)		
Communications LAN WAN Internet Services	9%	Company pays all costs which may be higher with the ASP than without. More LANs and LAN equipment (hubs, routers, cabling, net management, etc.) are needed to link existing LANs to the Internet and WAN via routers. Most communications previously done over LANs (e.g., internal email, file transfers, printing) will be conducted over WAN and the Internet.

The following formula can then be used:

$$ICR = \Delta A + \Delta D + \Delta S + \Delta H + \Delta C - \Delta T$$

Let Infrastructure Costs Replaced (ICR) be the IT budget costs substituted for by the ASP. It consists of five components, each corresponding to the cost category from Table 2.1 less the total costs of training, ΔT.

Let ΔA be the percentage of the IT budget related to the selection and implementation of business application surrendered to the ASP, excluding training costs. This delta cost corresponds to category 1, Business Applications, in Table 2.1. Assuming that the price of Commercial Off-the-Shelf products (COTS), which the ASP pays for, stands[5] at 15.7% of IT budget, and that the company and ASP equally share the responsibility for COTS selection, piloting and reviews, installation, integration, and policy/processes establishment, the ASP substitution effect on applications is:

$$\Delta A = 15.7\% + (52\text{-}15.7\%)/2 = 33.85\%$$

Let ΔD be the percentage of the IT budget related to data management surrendered to ASP, excluding training costs. This delta cost corresponds to category 2, Data, in Table 2.1. To be on the conservative side, the costs of design, population, updates, and processing of all data are considered sunk. Hence,

$$\Delta D = 0\%$$

Let ΔS be the percentage of the IT budget related to the selection, installation, and operations of core systems surrendered to the ASP, excluding training costs. This delta cost corresponds to category 3, Core Systems Software, in Table 2.1. Since all of these core systems operations are run by ASP:

$$\Delta S = 8\%$$

Let ΔH be the percentage of the IT budget related to hardware acquisition, installation, and maintenance surrendered to the ASP, excluding training costs. This delta cost corresponds to category 4, Computing Hardware, in Table 2.1. Since all of the hardware needed to run applications is paid for by the ASP:

$$\Delta H = 26\%$$

Let ΔC be the percentage of the IT budget related to communications costs surrendered to the ASP, less training costs. This delta cost corresponds to category 5, Communications, in Table 2.1. Since the company pays all communications costs plus some extra, ΔC_1 is used to designate those extra costs that the company incurs as a result of using the ASP.

$$\Delta C = -\Delta C_1$$

---

5. Daniel Minoli, *Analyzing Outsourcing*, New York: McGraw-Hill, Inc., 1995.

If ΔT is the company's total training cost, attributable to different categories from Table 2.1, its total is as follows:

$$\Delta T = (\Delta T_A + \Delta T_D + \Delta T_S + \Delta T_H + \Delta T_C)$$

Thus, the total substitution effect by ASP is:

$$ICR = \Delta A + \Delta D + \Delta S + \Delta H + \Delta C - \Delta T$$

$$ICR = 33.85\% + 0\% + 8\% + 26\% - \Delta T - \Delta C_1$$

$$\text{Or:}\quad ICR = 67.85\% - \Delta T - \Delta C_1$$

The aforementioned calculations provide insights into the limits on the ASP's ability to substitute infrastructure outsourcing for a company's infrastructure. Thus, based on the assumption discussed earlier, the ASP can only substitute for about two-thirds of a company's overall IT infrastructure budget—less increases in communications expenses due to the ASP. There is a caveat, however. These numbers apply to the entire IT infrastructure budget, including all built-in overhead and hidden economies. When only one or several applications are hosted by an ASP, a more careful attribution of IT infrastructure costs to applications will be needed to more adequately assess the ASP substitution effect.

Another caveat has already been mentioned. The numbers used to calculate the approximately two-thirds may and will change. While it should not invalidate the computational logic, when these numbers change the formulas above can be recomputed.

ASP Substitution Rules

Following are two powerful rules flowing from the aforementioned analyses. They should be considered when designing the ASP value proposition to customers and when calculating bases for an ASP substitution effect. The rules are as follows:

ASP Cost Substitution Rule 1: The upper limit on the ASP's infrastructure cost substitution will always be less than 100%, less training costs, less communications costs attributed to the need to connect customers to the ASP.

ASP Cost Substitution Rule 2: Since the ASP substitution effect is always less than 100%, the ASP's efficiencies must always be measured against ICR, not the whole IT budget.

Summary

So, why do companies outsource? The answer is relatively simple. First of all, since a business' operations can be envisioned as a collection of transactions, outsourcing invites the process of "weeding" out inefficient transactions (costs higher than value) first and less efficient ones later. Second, strong and compelling reasons arising from the substitution effect could convince many companies to consider the ASP in lieu of their internal IT. These reasons are as follows:

- Substitution effect analysis helps identify the types of costs relevant to the companies' outsourcing decisions and advises them which costs must be analyzed, measured, and planned. It narrows down the search for cost economies with a clear vision as to how these economies can be achieved (i.e., via the ASP). Since substitution analysis uses empirical research already based on certain simplifying assumptions, randomness of this analysis is largely curbed.

- Next, substitution effect analysis is a valuable tool for financial planning to be used either by incipient ASPs or their customers. This effect helps ASPs to define value propositions to their customers, design marketing strategies (e.g., services, pricing), and even make technical investment decisions. The customers, in turn, can learn what to ask of and what to expect from ASPs.

- Finally, the substitution analysis is grounded in the "here and now." Its foundation—cost taxonomy and distribution—is firmly latched to the current, incumbent circumstances. As those circumstances change, so does the foundation and, consequently, the analysis may then produce different results.

Chapter 3

Understanding ASP

Chapter 1 reviewed the historical evidence underlying the concept of outsourcing, introduced the term xSP, and provided a comprehensive definition of the ASP, an important member of an xSP family of providers. Chapter 2 further explored the ASP, showing its economic rationale and limitations.

This chapter picks up where Chapter 1 left off. It outlines the ASP's most salient business and technical characteristics, defines its business ecosystem, and inventories its major business and technology trends, drivers, enablers, and barriers to success.

ASP Characteristics

Many articles and research papers have been written about the ASP and its salient business and technical characteristics. While most focus on end customers, some address ASPs themselves and/or the members of their ecosystem: ISVs, SIs, Value Added Resellers (VAR), ISPs, Telcos, and so forth. As a result, important characteristics of

ASPs (outlined in Table 3.1) can be distilled from all this work. They are the so-called four C's: Application-Centricity, Convergence, Complexity, and Control.

(Application) Centricity. ASPs are application-centric. This means that they exist for one and only one purpose: to provide their customers access to business applications. ASPs host these applications, help adapt them to customer needs, and then manage their operations, evolution, maintenance, and support. ASPs host these applications in their many Data Centers that are normally networked together.

Convergence. As a business, the ASP is a point of convergence of diverse enabling technologies, implementation and management disciplines, and professional and technical skills used to develop, deploy, manage, and service hosted applications for ASP customers.

Complexity. The ASP's complexity arises from the convergence characteristic as it relates to multiple technologies and skills mentioned earlier. To simplify the definition, it helps to compare the ASP with enterprise IT. An ASP is similar to an enterprise IT department, except it is *more*. It deals with the same inputs—hardware, software, applications, networks, add-on outside services, end-user demands, and so forth—except there are more of them. An ASP's relationships with technology and service providers are also more complex, with synergistic partnerships and long-term contracts replacing one-off arms-length buy-sell transactions. An ASP may also have to run multiple applications on multiple platforms for multiple customers. To meet customers' varied demands and expectations, an ASP must also build varied business practices that are more complex than those used in an IT department. These include formal application and service definitions, operating policies, performance metrics, costing models and pricing schemes, audits, reporting, and others.

Still, there is *more*. While in most organizations an IT department is a cost center, an ASP is a profit center. Bona-fide business as it is, it must develop its own business plans and strategies, build marketing channels, promote and sell, manage partners, train customers, and ultimately answer to investors or shareholders. Add to that the novelty of ASP, its new and untested business models, and the strength of the claim of the ASP complexity increases.

Control. Finally, the ASP's characteristic of control flows from complexity. By taking on a portion or the entire customer's IT functions, the ASP effectively assumes some, or all, of its customer's IT responsibilities. For one, the ASP substitutes its own relationship with the customer for the relationships the customer has with its technology vendors, service providers, systems integrators, and business consultants, to name just a few. In this new role, the ASP establishes partnerships with all these suppliers in order to be able to speak to its customers in one voice on behalf of them all.

Table 3.1 *ASP Characteristics*

CHARACTERISTIC	DESCRIPTION
(Application) Centricity	Built to provide application services Central management of applications/infrastructure
Convergence	Technological convergence Skills convergence
Complexity	Multiple applications/multiple customers Dynamic environment (new applications, customers, needs, etc.) New business models/new business challenges
Control	Assumption of vendor/provider relationships New realities of account control

ASP Ecosystem

Chapter 1 offered a sneak preview of the ASP Ecosystem. Figure 3.1 draws a more detailed view of a typical ASP Ecosystem. The materials that follow analyze the members of the ASP ecosystem and their legacies and roles.

The pre-ASP model of providing IT services required businesses to deal with multiple suppliers (e.g., ISVs, Technology Suppliers, SIs, Vendor Integrators [VIs], VARs) in order to build a portfolio of applications needed by their business. In contrast, when an ASP begins to offer IT services, it assumes the roles and responsibilities of many suppliers, effectively reducing the number of points of contact for the customer from many to one.

What used to be a "retail product and services purchase model" practiced by many a corporate IT has been replaced by a "retail product and services rental model." Instead of dealing with multiple suppliers, the business leaves this to the ASP's "wholesale product and services purchase model" and enjoys a single point of contact with the ASP itself.

ISVs

ISVs are publishers of business application software. Ideally, their offerings can cover all conceivable business functions for different vertical markets and business sizes, domestically and internation-

Figure 3.1 *How ASP changes the roles of traditional suppliers of IT products and services.*

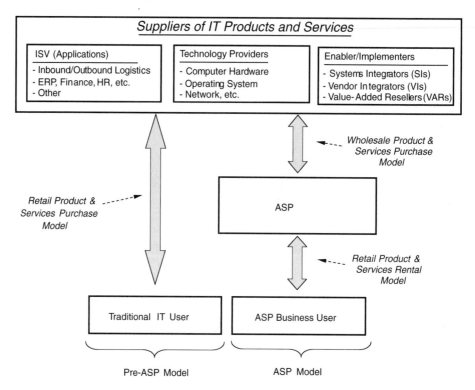

ally. If modeled against a traditional value chain,[1] their offerings range from the Inbound Logistics applications (procurement, supply chain, logistics, etc.), to those supporting Business Processes (e.g., Enterprise Resource Planning [ERP], Manufacturing Resource Planning [MRP], Operating Resource Management [ORM], finance, and human resources), to those on the Outbound-Logistics side (e.g., order entry, customer care, distribution, sales force automation, marketing analysis, and others).

Major application vendors have focused both on the Business Process applications (e.g., SAP, Oracle, BAAN, J.D. Edwards) and the Outbound and Inbound Logistics. Mostly mainframe based, therefore requiring considerable resources, these applications are complex and need long deployment cycles. However, since these applications are functionally stable, businesses believe they could afford the long

---

1. Michael Porter of Harvard University invented the traditional value chain in the mid-1970s. Chapter 6 offers more detailed insights into how Porter's value chain works for ASP.

deployment cycles. Because they are expensive and mostly big, only wealthy business customers could afford them.

While these traditional vendors prospered, a new breed of companies emerged capitalizing on new technologies and nascent market trends. They started building applications on the "periphery" of the value chain, for the Inbound and Outbound Logistics applications (Manugistics, i2, Siebel, etc.), addressing the needs of the small and medium-size companies. And finally, with the further development of the Internet, these new competitors began to promote the electronic means of conducting business, for example, a so–called e-commerce space (Netscape, OpenMarket, Broadvison, Inforworld, etc.).

Technology Providers

The main suppliers of technology to ASPs include:

- Computer and network hardware makers (Sun, IBM, Compaq, Cisco, Lucent, etc.).

- Designers of network and computer operating systems as well as infrastructure software vendors. Their offerings range from multiprocessor operating systems like Sun's Solaris to platform-independent technology platforms (e.g., Sun's Java-based J2EE[2]) to distributed systems middleware (e.g., IBM's MQ-Series) to application development servers (ATG Dynamo, BEA Weblogic, iPlanet Application Server), directory/messaging/certificate products and services (iPlanet Directory Server, iPlanet Messaging Server, SiteMinder), as well as products specifically focused on conducting electronic business such as billing, buying, and selling (iPlanet Buyer Xpert, Biller Xpert, etc.).

- Network services companies, such as ATT, Qwest, MCI/Worldcom, Verizon, Cingular, and others, as well as numerous ISPs who provide access and networks connecting businesses to their suppliers and customers and for connecting companies' to own internal organizations.

While many of the companies supplying technology also play other industry roles—for instance, Sun's and others vendors' professional services organizations acting as "implementers"—most companies' business models are driven by technology and products. To be successful, these companies must focus on a certain set of products, and subsequently, very few can compete effectively in more than one area

---

2. Java 2 Enterprise Edition platform.

of technology. The terms of competition tend to center on price/performance, standards, and economies of scale. With such models in hand, it therefore falls to downstream players to integrate hardware, software, and network technologies in order to create e-business solutions. Competition for the attention of the implementation community represented by Enablers/Implementers, as well as Business Users who possess implementation capabilities, becomes a necessary strategic focus for most technology providers.

Enablers/Implementers

Services to combine hardware, software, and network technologies into e-business solutions are provided by Enablers or Implementers. Following are working definitions of the key types of enablers:

SIs

SIs are businesses that provide technology integration services and develop solutions for their customers by adding intellectual capital to technologies developed, manufactured, and sold by others. SIs are sometimes considered "implementers," as opposed to "developers," of applications in that the SI's role often involves final customization and implementation of packaged applications software as opposed to the development of the software package (see ISV). Examples of well-known SIs are: EDS, IBM Global Services, Computer Sciences Corporation (CSC), Big-5 Firms, and so forth.

VARs

VARs are businesses that add their own intellectual capital or other sources of economic value to the goods and services procured from others for resale to the marketplace. Examples are MicroAge and Ingram Micro. The category of VARS also includes classic Internet access providers such as traditional ISPs, as well as firms who grew up providing Web site design and hosting. Many of these players have moved beyond these basic services and actively integrate hardware and software to deliver e-commerce solutions for their customers.

Vendor Integrators

With technology complexity increasing and integration disciplines becoming more and more technology dependent, technology vendors are frequently called upon by their customers to assist them in integrating and combining technologies to create their operational e-business solutions. For this reason, many technology vendors have captive organizations that fulfill the role of system integrators.

Since technology vendors usually have their own, well-trained and distributed sales organizations, they use this market presence to cross-sell technologies and integration services. A good example is Sun Microsystems, which occasionally competes with, but more frequently complements, the services of independent SIs for the customization and installation of Sun and compatible products into customers' e-business infrastructures.

Global Technology Trends—Shifting Paradigms

The "historical inevitability" of the ASP emergence, discussed in Chapter 1, is required but not sufficient to explain the major shift in the way IT is conducted and how its services are delivered to its users. The necessary condition for such a shift is the availability of enabling technologies. This book dedicates a significant amount of space to the discussion of enabling technologies. Some technology enablers for the new ways of IT service delivery are briefly reviewed in sections following. A more specific discussion of the ASP enabling technologies is provided in Chapter 10.

In the meantime, the material in the following section addresses two powerful and nascent technology trends impacting the fundamental business IT and the Internet. These two trends are the famed shift from a Microcosm to Telecosm, ardently advocated by George Gilder, and another critical shift from scarcity of storage to its abundance with its concomitant consequences for the ASP.

From Microcosm to Telecosm

A majority of contemporary computing and communications architectures are still built around the premise of abundant processing power and scarce bandwidth. However, most recent technology developments have begun to reverse this rule. The roots of this changeover are firmly grounded in the interplay of scarcity and abundance. A historical parallel can help. In the old industrial society, power was scarce and space (e.g., land) abundant. With the advent of electricity spurring a precipitous business and community development, power became abundant and space scarce. A similar transposition is happening now in IT at the junction of two dominant computing and communications paradigms, Microcosm and Telecosm, so dubbed by George Gilder[3] in his numerous writings on the subject.

3. George Gilder, Special Report, "Grow Rich on the Coming Technology Revolution," 1999.

According to Gilder, "the last 15 years of computer technology were determined by the laws of the Microcosm and the next 15 years will be determined by the laws of the Telecosm." To understand Microcosm, Gilder says, "take any 'n' transistors and put them on a single sliver of silicon and you will get 'n' squared performance and value." Telecosm, in Gilder's words, implies the reliance not on chips but on bandwidth, which is growing much faster than the computer chips' power. Telecosm is represented by "the domains of technology unleashed by the discovery of the *electromagnetic spectrum* and the photon. *Fiber optics, cellular telephony*, and satellite communications are examples" and is further characterized by the "wired and wireless bandwidth growing at least ten (10) times faster than computer power."

Underlining further this "scarcity and abundance" basis to explain the Microcosm to Telecosm transition, Gilder adds, "if the law of thrift in the old paradigm (e.g., Microcosm) was *waste watts and save transistors,* the law of thrift in the new paradigm (e.g., Telecosm) will be *waste bandwidth and save watts.* In the new era, engineers will exploit the power of bandwidth and push the frontiers of lower power technology to compensate for the limitations of existing computing and network architectures." In speaking of *watts* here, Gilder was referring to computing power.

This Microcosm to Telecosm transition has been caused by powerful market, business, and technology forces, and also by the Internet whose runaway success and awe-inspiring growth stimulated new research, investment, and innovation leading to bandwidth abundance. But when bandwidth becomes (virtually) unlimited, or essentially free (or at least highly commoditized), most future computing architectures should be built around, and optimized for, the network. Thus, the new Telecosm paradigm has pushed the CPU aside and confirmed once again Sun Microsystem's famous and long-promoted thesis and slogan, "the network is the computer."

"A Colossal Upset"

The same George Gilder repeatedly mentioned also points to another paradigm shift that, while lacking the panache of bandwidth, is also becoming a major (colossal) upset of common beliefs and conventional wisdoms. Gilder[4] says, "The Familiar Sun epigram, 'the network is the computer' will not suffice unless the network morphs into a colossal storage system. Today [1999–2000] the Internet contains a

---

4. George Gilder, "Gilder Technology Report," Volume IV, Number II, November 1999.

trove of 340 million web pages growing at a pace of a million pages a day... Total storage attached to the net already sums up to the hundreds of petabytes; exabytes (10 to the 18th) are coming soon." And further, "Making all this possible so far is one of the most unexpected and least understood technological feats of our age. For the last decade, in a colossal upset, hard drive technology has improved at least 50% faster than computing power. As Intel engineers increasingly confess, this differential may grow while wafer fabrication processes flounder with feature sizes below 0.13 microns."

In one word Gilder is adding storage to bandwidth in his Telecosm paradigm. Hence, his adage *"waste bandwidth and save watts"* transforms into *"waste bandwidth and storage and save watts."* Or, in Gilder's words again, "The simultaneous explosion of bandwidth and storage dictate a similarly massive growth in web caching, a solution that pragmatically "wastes" the two crucial abundance(s), while conserving the two great scarcities of the Telecosm, the speed of light (read, processing speed) and the span of life, *aka* the customer's time."

Nobody can say this better than George Gilder. The relevance and accuracy of Gilder's auspicious words has been undeniably proven by the emergence of a whole new breed of companies in late 1999 and in 2000 offering compelling and capable Internet cache solutions. It suffices just to name Akamai and Digital Island to prove this point.

An abundance of bandwidth and storage, the ever-precious commodities in outsourcing, are thus becoming the major driving forces behind ASP.

ASP's Business Drivers and Enablers

ASP Drivers

The Webster's Collegiate Dictionary defines the word *driver* as the "one who drives." While it may not explain the emergence of ASP, a derivative *driving* may. *Driving* means "exerting pressure ..." or "having a great force ..." or "acting with vigor ..." Thus, certain developments are "exerting pressure" with "great force" and "... vigor" on the business environment, driving the creation of a new IT service provisioning, applications outsourcing paradigm, the ASP.

Mostly Business Drivers

Drivers of any business paradigm are usually related to business, culture, politics, and technology. Technology is certainly a major driver of the ASP. Like other drivers, it "exerts pressure" and with a "great force" and "...vigor" on the business environment. However, technology is like a self-fulfilling prophecy. It both drives the need for and enables the new business paradigm of the ASP. For this reason, technology is assumed as a driver in this section, but discussed in detail in the following section on the ASP Enablers. Table 3.2 lists the ASP's major drivers, categorized by three types: Business (B), Political (P), and Cultural (C).

Table 3.2 *ASP Drivers*

Driver	*Type*	*Description*
External/Global Pressure	B, P	Falling telecommunications costs, pervasiveness of the Internet, easy spread of new technologies throughout the world, and falling trade barriers—all have created an equalizing effect for all types of businesses all over the world. No matter how big or small, local or remote, whatever country or industry, any business can partake in the world economy and trade and compete with others.
Focus on Core Competencies	B	IT has become too complex. Developing in-house expertise requires major financial outlays, longer learning cycles, and continuous management attention. To stay competitive, companies need to stay focused on their core competencies instead of dealing with expensive, internal IT.
Coming of Age of Small and Medium Businesses	B	Small and medium businesses (SMBs) recognize the need for the same application functionality the big companies have. Yet, these businesses cannot afford the high price of complex applications and prolonged deployment cycles. Besides, with SMBs' IT budgets being disproportionately smaller than those of their big competitors, SMBs find themselves further disadvantaged. From the outside, the large corporations that represent the most valuable customers for SMBs are also demanding that SMBs tie into their supply and distribution chains and provide compatibility with their ERP and supply-chain management systems. Thus, the trend for big corporations to become internally wired puts additional pressures on SMBs, particularly those that wish to serve customers in disparate industries or markets.

Table 3.2   *ASP Drivers (Continued)*

ISVs Going Down-Market	B	ISVs have heard the cry of small and medium companies for application functionality on a smaller scale. They are either rewriting applications for a reduced scale or Internet-enabling them for ASPs.
		The last, but not least, reason is that major ISVs have simply run out of their large customers and are thus compelled to move down-market. Even though smaller and medium markets could not generate the same revenue as the large ones, they are ISV's new targets.
TCO/Cost Pressures	B	Companies seek lower total costs of ownership for IT to reduce expense and help improve financial planning and predictability.
Shortage of Computer Science and Networking Talent	C	Increasing technological complexity, drying educational pipelines of computer science (CS) professional cadre, and low production of educational institutions,[a] as well as IT departments' losing competition for talent to the ISVs, SIs, and VARs—all make this driver viable.
Favorable Tax Laws Related to Technology	P, B	Shortened depreciation cycle for technology investments, while also attractive to business themselves, create financial incentives for the ASPs to innovate.

a. See the section "Dearth of Talent" for historical rates of computer science matriculation from U.S. colleges and universities.

"Shortage of Computer Science and Networking Talent," mentioned in Table 3.2 is a huge driver. The problem is so big that it deserves a special subsection on the situation, the "Dearth of Talent."

Dearth of Talent

The whole matter of a computer talent shortage in North America (United States and Canada) is mired in controversy. It is a vortex of issues ranging from immigration policies, protectionism, equal opportunity laws, and prevailing hiring practices to business economics, rapidly shifting job markets, and an ever-changing nature of computer and communications technologies.

To analyze this matter properly, the analysis following takes a look first at the demand for skilled computer workers in the United States, then at the supply and its dynamics, and finally summarizes the implications of the job market on the main subject of this book, the ASP.

Demand. It is not a secret that U.S. companies are faced with major problems in finding and retaining skilled technology personnel. Eschewing the temporary reprieve due to the dot.com debacle in 2000 and a recessive U.S. economy in 2001, it is this author's strong conviction that a sound demand for skilled personnel will return soon and the industry will again face the major void. To fill this void by means other than the domestic educational pipeline, many high-tech firms have gone as far as to lobby the government to increase issuance of H-1B visas granted to foreign nationals for entry to the United States. The effectiveness of this effort is not assured. Only time will tell whether the high tech industry's needs prevail over labor protectionism.

On a more empirical note, according to the U.S. Department of Labor, the demand for skilled computer labor between 1998 and 2007 has been estimated to be growing at a compounded annual rate of 7.5%, or between 1.1 and 1.3 million. This is a staggering number, but there is more. In early 1998, the Information Technology Association of America (ITAA), jointly with Virginia Tech University and some other research and market watch groups, identified a total of 346,000 vacant information technology jobs in U.S. companies of more than 100 employees. Substantial additional research revised this number in 1999 to about 750,000. The numbers predicted by other organizations in 2000 ranged from 850,000 to 1,000,000. With the pace of technological progress accelerating and technology complexity increasing—making it even more difficult to find the required skills—it is conceivable that the real demand for skilled computer workers will, by 2007, far exceed the U.S. Department of Labor statistics provided previously.

Supply. Table 3.3 provides the numbers of the Computer Science (CS) Bachelors, Masters, and Ph.D. degrees conferred by institutions of higher education in the United States from 1971 to 1997. The table and graphs are based on best information obtained from the U.S. Department of Education early in year 2001. The cumulative number of those degrees comes to about 584,000 (rounded). Figure 3.2 graphs these numbers from Table 3.3.

Table 3.3 *Matriculations in Computer Science between 1970 and 1996*

	1975-76	*1980-81*	*1983-84*	*1984-85*	*1985-86*	*1986-87*	*1987-88*	*1988-89*
Bachelors	5,652	15,121	32,172	38,878	41,889	39,589	34,523	30,454
Masters	2,603	4,218	6,190	7,101	8,070	8,481	9,197	9,414
Doctorates	244	252	251	248	344	374	428	551
Total	8,499	19,591	38,613	46,227	50,303	48,444	44,148	40,419
Cumulative	12,603	32,194	70,807	117,034	167,337	215,781	259,929	300,348

Table 3.3   *Matriculations in Computer Science between 1970 and 1996 (Continued)*

	1989-90	*1990-91*	*1991-92*	*1992-93*	*1993-94*	*1994-95*	*1995-96*	*1996-97*
Bachelors	27,257	25,083	24,557	24,200	24,200	24,404	24,098	24,678
Masters	9,677	9,324	9,530	10,163	10,416	10,326	10,151	10,098
Doctorates	627	676	772	805	810	884	867	857
Total	37,561	35,083	34,859	35,168	35,426	35,614	35,116	35,723
Cumulative	337,909	372,992	407,851	443,019	478,445	514,059	549,175	583,641

Figure 3.2   *U.S. matriculations in CS between 1970 and 1996.*

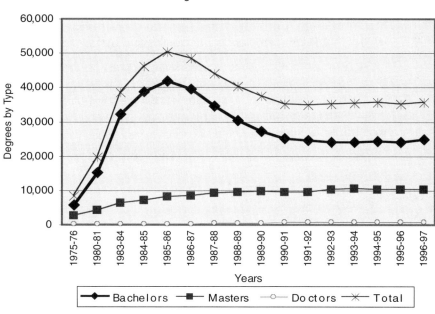

CS Degrees Conferred in the U.S

There is new evidence that the CS enrollment in U.S. universities has been on the increase over the last few years: a 5% increase in 1995, a whopping 40% increase in 1996, and a 39% increase in 1997.[5] While this confirms that the supply of CS students is adjusting itself elastically to demand, and that the market forces are at work, the truth remains that the number of future CS graduates may be severely limited by the U.S. schools' ability to train them. It takes time to build faculties, develop curricula, and promote schools'

5. Per Computer Research Association, a national consortium of cs departments.

reputations. Furthermore, just because enrollment increases, the number of degrees is not guaranteed to increase at a required rate.

A Counterpoint. Dr. Norman Matloff[6] of the University of California at Davis has made a strong counterpoint to the common notion of the shortage of CS professionals in North America. The major premise of his work concerns age discrimination allegedly found, in particular, in the U.S. industry's hiring practices.

While the legality, morality, and economic imperatives behind U.S. hiring practices—per Dr. Matloff, as well as the validity of his analyses and conclusions—are open for debate, the fact remains that meeting the hiring objectives in North America is hampered by a widening gap between the growing demand for qualified CS professionals and businesses' abilities to find them to hire.

Conclusion. The demand for CS professionals is on a sharp increase. CS college enrollment is on an increase too, but not at a rate sufficient to meet demand. Age discrimination, if proven, may result in the government's fiat to change hiring laws and practices.

Still, even if CS college enrollment trends continue to grow and if the government moves to change the hiring laws and practices and increases the H-1B visa limits, considerable time will pass before any semblance of market equilibrium for CS professionals will be achieved.

The perception of a labor shortage will remain and most probably persist for a while. Hence, the companies' motivation to find alternative means of handling IT will remain a strong driving force behind the growth of the ASP.

ASP Enablers

Enablers are forces that make it possible for the new paradigm to be implemented and take root. Like the drivers above, Table 3.4 lists ASP's major enablers categorized by their affinity to Business (B), Technology (T), and Culture (C).

---

6. Dr. Normal Matloff, Presentation to the U.S. House Judiciary Committee Subcommittee on Immigration, "Debunking the Myth of a Desperate Software Labor Shortage," Department of Computer Science, University of California at Davis, December 16, 1999.

Table 3.4   *ASP Enablers*

Enabler	Type	Description
Improved Internet's systemic qualities	T	Systemic qualities are those over-franchised, yet nonetheless extremely important, considerations of reliability, availability, scalability, security, manageability, performance, and others. To be brief, numerous technologies have lately been invented and deployed addressing Internet reliability, availability, and scalability, e.g., content caching, management and delivery; network redundancies due to thicker IP pipes and excess capacities, and intelligent peering; faster routing and switching; etc. More on this subject can be found in Chapters 5,6,7,8,9, and 10.
Strengthening of Internet security and its growing acceptance	T, C	The broad adoption of encrypted data transfer protocols and PKI[a] addressed many Internet data integrity and confidentiality problems (e.g., security). These innovations prompted credit card companies and their insurers to endorse and promote the Internet as a consumer medium. As a result, the public's fears of security breaches and privacy violations have subsided and the Internet has become an acceptable, conventional medium for conducting business. At the same time, some forms of Internet exploitation have created new threats—viruses, worms, and other types of malicious code—propagated over the Internet by unscrupulous people with a wicked or deliberately destructive intent. Fortunately, potent detection measures against this electronic scourge do exist; unfortunately, most of these measures are only reactive, because it is impossible to create ironclad protection against Internet infections, which consistently exploit all possible openings and flexibilities of existing and new technologies (just as it is impossible to create ironclad physical protection against attacks that exploit all possible physical openings and flexibilities). More on the subject of Internet security and its specific applications to the ASP can be found in Chapter 8, on ASP security.

Table 3.4 *ASP Enablers (Continued)*

Browser as the viable application user interface	T	A formerly popular client-server computing model running business logic on a "fat" software application installed and maintained on the client hardware has swung toward an "open," "flexible," and a nonproprietary GUI[b] standardized around IP networking and a browser paradigm.
Increased adoption of Thin-Client/ Server-Centric Network Computing	B, T	Having failed the scalability and interoperability tests, traditional client-server approaches gave way to replacement by an enhanced service delivery model scaled horizontally. The new model moved business logic to the network consisting of interconnected data centers running distributed applications.
Spread of e-commerce applications and their market adoption.	B	In the late 1990s many companies that had automated, integrated, and squeezed inefficiencies from back-office functions by implementing ERP turned to the front office to improve interfaces with customers (CRM) and business partners (supply chain management) via networked applications.
Emergence of ASP-enabling products to support hosting and management of multiuser, multiapplication, multiplatform environments with built-in economies of scale and scope.	T, B	The ASP infrastructure is different from an enterprise's IT. One of its challenges is to provide virtual environments for its customers. This is crucial for proper allocation of resources, assurances of security, availability, scalability, and flexible management of each customer's environment. It is also important to impart each customer with a sense of uniqueness reflected in the ability to provide reliable Service Levels and Service Level Agreements.

a. PKI—Public Key (Encryption) Infrastructure.
b. GUI—Graphical User Interface.

ASP's Barriers to Success

Barriers: Sources and Reasons

Persuasive drivers and powerful enablers notwithstanding, no major transformation involving business, people, systems, and money occurs without a fight or struggle. The ASP may be a questionable option for some for subjective reasons, or even objectively inappropriate for others. What are these subjective and objective reasons? What are the forces behind them?

Subjective Reasons

The ASPs must work hard to help their customers overcome some of the following subjective reasons against outsourcing:

- **Defensive IT.** Enterprise IT departments' resistance to outsourcing is one of the most potent forces threatening the ASP success from within a customer environment. Lack of trust in management and job security concerns—the key components of this resistance—are not unfounded. Considerations of "payroll savings" overwhelm the logic for outsourcing within many an enterprise, leading to unfortunate results for all the involved parties. Usually, this happens when an enterprise's business goals are misinterpreted by, or not coordinated with, IT planning. Frequently, enterprises cut personnel and then suffer the consequences of losing talent still required for internal support, development, knowledge transfer, and interaction with outsourcers. The remaining personnel's morale falls. Then, the outsourcers (e.g., ASPs) get the blame for the moral fallout of "payroll savings" and must deal with the frequently difficult-to-achieve service expectations in a hostile environment. While ASPs don't have control over these effects on customer personnel due to outsourcing, properly presenting their cases to customers and outlining the elements of required internal policies and programs is an advisable practice.

- **General Resistance-to-Change**. The uncertainty of the future due to outsourcing (e.g., the ASP), is a common reason for Resistance-to-Change within many enterprises despite the best efforts exerted by their managements to elaborate on, and convey to all the parties involved, the benefits of outsourcing.

- **ASP Novelty.** Suspicion of the ASP novelty and their bases of experience and lacking faith in the ASP's abilities to deliver (e.g., time-to-market, expertise, SLAs).

- **Sunk Costs.** Accounting issues may also become barriers to adopting outsourcing. Sunk costs at the enterprise, for example, are frequently viewed as a problem. However, sunk costs must be viewed as exactly that, sunk. Whatever they represent always has salvage value and may be creatively included in every business case computing the final benefits from outsourcing.

Objective Reasons

There are many objective reasons for concern about the ASP:

- **Self-Doubt.** The ASP's own ability to deliver on time, service their customers, integrate with other applications and customer's legacy systems, and so forth. This is an implicit reference to the aforementioned four C's, especially that of complexity, related to building the ASP's own business models, service definitions, performance metrics, costing models and pricing schemes, internal organizations, and business practices, and so forth.

- **A Show-Me Syndrome.** Related to the aforementioned, this is about the novelty of the ASPs, their bases of expertise and experience, and customer faith in their ability to deliver (e.g., time-to-market, expertise, SLAs). Effectively, there is a chicken-and-egg problem: potential customers want to see references first.

- **Security.** Concerns about trusting ASPs with customers' systems and information and their giving up control over sensitive information.

- **Legal Issues.** Some corporations believe their ability to protect sensitive data on their own premises from subpoena or other legal threats is superior to an ASP's ability to offer such protection.

- **State of Enabling Technologies**. Availability of the new ASP enabling technologies and methodologies whose use would lead to improved integration abilities, higher quality services, and leverage of the ASP economies.

- **Integration Issues.** The challenges of and the probability of success of integrating ASP applications with customers' legacy systems, other vendors' applications, new ASP management tools, and others.

- **Technology Maturity.** Continuous availability of scalable hardware and software, and so forth.

Many ASP suppliers understand these barriers to their success and have begun addressing the issues within their control such as product features, new product design for ASPs' use, e.g., multicustomer applications, ASP-specific enabling and management tools, etc. More details about how vendors perceive these barriers and how they are addressing them will be discussed in Chapters 6, 7, 8, and 10.

Conversion and Complexity

The last 20 years of IT evolution have been characterized by two seemingly independent, yet intimately related, developments: a conversion of IT platforms and an explosion of IT complexities. These two phenomena exhibited almost biological properties. The conversion of platforms looked like a Darwinian struggle of the species leading to the survival of the fittest. And the explosion of complexities resembled a species development in a favorable and propitious environment.

Not surprisingly, one of the drivers behind platform conversion was the networking that was required as a means of connecting applications and users. First developed for homogeneous platforms—such as IBM's SNA, Digital's DDCMP, and others—it vigorously cried out for standardization leading to an Open Systems Interconnection (OSI) stack of protocols, a parallel effort with X.25, and finally TCP/IP. The nascent demand to connect applications and users put further pressure on all types of IT suppliers—ISVs, computer hardware and OS vendors, SIs and consultants, and so forth—to create more compatible technologies and easily-connectable applications. As a result, whole computing empires stuck with proprietary designs, some of them simply ignoring market signals, began to crumble and a more pliable world of network computing began to emerge. It is hard to remember anything but the names of some systems providers such as Prime Computers, Apollo, Data Point, Data General, Burroughs, Perkin-Elmer, Sperry, Four Phase, Tandem, Stratus, and many others, along with numerous small and not so small ISVs such as Cullinet, MSA, and Cincom. A few names survived though, either those who foresaw network computing and heeded it (e.g., HP), or those who woke up to reality in time and, having enough resources to reinvent itself, did so, albeit not without major pains (e.g., IBM). Finally, numerous and successful new entrants emerged, many of them taking the lead in the new network computing world of IT (e.g., Sun Microsystems). So, by the middle 1990s and the early 2000s the number of computing platforms has dwindled to just a few: several flavors of UNIX on different hardware, Microsoft's NT for Intel chips and compatibles, and IBM legacy carry-overs such as the OS/390 mainframes and AS/400. Add to these a few specialized platforms and OSs and the list can be closed.

But has it become easier to do IT with the platform converged? The answer, unfortunately, is a resounding "No." Due to their convergence, platforms have almost become irrelevant. However, this "accidental" platform standardization fueled an explosion of technological developments with considerable complexities, stemming from extensive technology and methodology research and rapid cycles of technology transfer from inventions into tangible products.

Despite dramatic developments in thought and technology, like the rise of a client-server model capable of hiding complexity, inherent complexity didn't go away. Just to get a sense of it, Table 3.5 provides a nonexhaustive list of the requirements for implementing a common browser. The glossary at the end of the book provides definitions of numerous terms and abbreviations.

Table 3.5 *Browser Features*

Functional Area	Required Features
Software	Tools (Edit, Print, Open, Save, Help, etc.), Statistics, Security (Encryption, Access Control, etc.), Plug-ins, Cookies, Navigation, history lists, page and graphics caching, JVM, DHTML, HTML, VRML, XML, CSS, Data Bases (Addresses, Bookmarks, etc.), Java, JavaScript, etc.
Multimedia	Colors, Sounds, Images, Icons, Guides, Graphics, Background, Animation, etc.
Communications	HTTP, SSL, Email (POP, IMAP, SMTP), News (NNTP), Chat (IRC, ICQ, AIM), proxy services, Collaboration protocols, etc.
Authoring	DHTML, HTML, VRML, XML, CSS, Java, JavaScript, ActiveX, etc.

By no means is this table complete. A simple browser, yet so much "stuff!" If this "stuff" is not sufficient to prove technological complexity, the list below provides yet another insight into the phenomena of exploding complexity:

- *Chips*—from general purpose Intel Pentiums and Sun's SPARC to specialized ASICs and DSPs (e.g., from TI, National Semiconductor)

- *Hardware*—from familiar PCs to multiprocessor architectures (e.g., like symmetric multiprocessor systems from IBM, HP, and Sun)

- *Software*—like transaction management middleware (e.g., from Tibco, BEAs), network and systems management (e.g., from IBM/Tivoli, BMC, Sun, HP), or whole application development and run-time platforms like Sun's Java 2 Enterprise Edition (J2EE)

- Endless lists of *Applications* covering every conceivable human activity and business function (see Pure-Play ASPs in Chapter 6)

- *Networking and Communications* products—such as routers/ switches/hubs/accelerators, modems, load directors, etc.; as well as diverse protocols such as BGP, EBGP, IBGP, shortest-path first, IP over ATM, SONET, fast Ethernet, Gigabit Ethernet, and so forth

- *Storage Devices*—from simple disks to RAID (0+1, 1+0, 5), server-attached storage, network-attached storage, storage area networks, RAM-cache, tape, CD, CD-R (W), DVD, DVD-RAM, and others (e.g., from such vendors as EMC, IBM, Sun, Compaq)

It is almost impossible to speak of IT technologies without getting dizzy. Technologies' mere variety, let alone the number of vendors and brands, can be overwhelming.

Earlier, complexity was identified as one of the most salient characteristics of the ASP. Overcoming complexity and/or turning the abilities to manage it into a competitive advantage are major challenges facing ASPs that require visionary management, astute planning, and skillful execution to create lasting business success and concomitantly drive the entire ASP industry forward.

Summary

This chapter offers foundational ideas for understanding the ASP. It addresses the ASP's key business characteristics, its ecosystem, the global trends that influence ASP development, plus ASP drivers, enablers, and barriers to success.

- **Business Characteristics.** It is important to understand the ASP's key characteristics distinguishing it from traditional outsourcing. They are the four C's: application-centricity, technology convergence, complexity, and control.

- **ASP Ecosystem.** ASPs essentially become surrogates (a clearinghouse or proxy) of all traditional vendors and suppliers of IT technologies and services to their customers.

- **Global Technological Trends.** In a nutshell, Gilder's Microcosm-to-Telecosm metamorphosis reassigns scarcity and abundance from computing to networking and storage, ultimately directing market forces toward the latter two. Abundant networking and storage bode well for the ASP.

- **ASP Drivers.** Mostly business, culture, and even politics-related drivers of the ASP boil down to a few very important ones: globalization of markets, equalization of businesses in terms of their "rights" to technology and access to markets, and financial pressures—all mostly due to the developments of the Internet and increased companies' cost consciousness. Another big driver is the dearth of CS talent which, while possibly controversial in nature, is nonetheless a real problem facing the U.S. corporate world and varied vendors alike. The silver lining of this problem is the renewed interest in application outsourcing benefiting the ASP.

- **ASP Enablers.** The ASP enablers are mostly technology-related, such as "better" Internet qualities, stronger Internet security, more flexible new network computing paradigms, and new, capable ASP enabling tools.

- **ASP's Barrier to Success.** The subjective reasons against outsourcing and ASPs can be summarized by: IT's general defensiveness and resistance to change, problems with sunk costs, and mistrust of novelty. The objective reasons are mostly related to ASPs' lack of expertise and experience, as well as missing tools and disciplines to run ASPs efficiently. Both types of reasons provide sufficient food for thought for real ASPs regarding the need to work closely with their customers, perfect ASP offerings, and continue general market and public education about the ultimate benefits of outsourcing. Complexity, as noted, can be viewed as a barrier to success and an opportunity for differentiation. It is obviously advisable to treat it more as the latter rather than as the former.

Chapter 4

Taxonomy for ASP Economies

Chapter 3 only alluded to the economic drivers behind ASP. This chapter, however, analyzes them in more detail. The drivers arise from the economics of using information technologies effectively, and especially when the ASP applies them to more than one system, or one application, or one customer.

The material in this chapter doesn't analyze the theoretical causes of the ASP economies. Nor does it attempt to explain how such economies are achieved in real life ASPs. This is left to the other chapters of this book, which enlist and describe specific technologies and processes used for planning, designing, implementing, and managing ASPs. What this chapter does, though, is to develop taxonomy of ASP economies. This taxonomy is based on standard practices and principles of achieving savings, efficiencies, and other cost-related improvements in business, in general. For an ASP, these cost-related improvements can help reduce its operational costs, subsequently pass the savings to customers, and thus realize the sustainable cost-based competitive advantages.

Technology Progress and Economic Benefits

New technologies don't often bring immediate economic benefits. They must be understood and applied first, and only then can the economic benefits be recognized and measured. This transition from a technical invention to economic progress has been studied extensively both by academia and business in a quest to extract verifiable data of IT's economic contributions. Two academic researchers, T.F. Breshahan and S. Greenstein[1] write as follows:

> Economic gains don't come from solely the act of invention, but also from the adoption and adaptation of technology by users.[2] This is a well-understood point, as it has arisen in historical episodes of technical change (some researchers compare IT revolution to the development of electricity in factories). The force of the point is not to debunk the gains from technical progress. Instead, it places emphasis on understanding the factors that influence the flow of services from technology...

The term "co-invention" crystallizes the concept of what users do with technology, but it takes time, as T.F. Breshahan and S. Greenstein state in the same article quoted previously:

> It takes time to translate an invention into a viable commercial product. It takes time to develop business models for the delivery of the invention in the commercial form. New distribution channels must be developed to make possible for inventions to spread geographically, from the region to region. It takes time for one set of users to learn from another distinct group of users; and so on.

Echoing many other researchers, T.F. Breshahan and S. Greenstein add, "research is just starting to understand coinvention activity in the US." They further acknowledge that, internationally, understanding co-invention looms to be an even more challenging problem.

The gap between technology progress and economic benefits is intimately related to the ASP model. Indeed, ASPs adopt and adapt technologies for meeting specific customer needs, like the needs for information technology, in the case of ASPs. ASPs also promise economic benefits from leveraging these technologies, thus further making it important to learn how to measure the benefits.

---

1. T. F. Breshahan and S. Greenstein, "The Economic Contribution of Information Technology: Value Indicators in International Perspective," Working Papers, 1999, Stanford University.
2. The authors call it "co-invention."

This chapter develops a framework for addressing ASP's economic benefits, both qualitatively and quantitatively (as much as possible). The framework is also applied throughout the book for analyzing the diverse ASP-related business and technical phenomena, trends, and developments.

Necessary Conditions for ASP Success

The previous chapters defined the ASP and justified rationale for its emergence. The ASP is widely and strongly believed to promise increases in a customer company's operational efficiencies and improvements in strategic advantages. But what really enables the ASP to be so effective? For instance, if there are N customers building separate computing and communications infrastructures, how can an ASP build one large infrastructure supporting these N customers for less? How can an ASP develop, customize, and deploy applications faster than customers? What enables an ASP to manage applications and infrastructure better than customers could? How can an ASP offer high levels of services exceeding customer expectations? These questions seem to never end.

And there are no straight answers to these questions. Since the real-life ASPs are so young, no empirical data to analyze ASP efficiencies are known to exist. Moreover, even traditional IT outsourcing, an acknowledged forerunner of today's ASPs, mostly lacks data to support its own claims of economic efficiency after so many years in business, as was shown in previous chapters. The lack of such a strong empirical base for IT outsourcing may be a serious barrier for the ASP to overcome.

But there is light at the end of the tunnel. The same researcher, Paul Strassmann,[3] having provided substantiated arguments about delusions of large scale IT outsourcing, also assembled the following "good reasons for outsourcing:"

1. The organization is incapable of attracting or retaining talent for specialized technologies, especially for innovative use.

2. The budgeting and capital investment process is spasmodic, short-term oriented, and subject to reversals in the goals, objectives, and preferences of top management.

---

3. Paul A. Strassmann, "The Squandered Computer," New Canaan, CT: *The Information Economics Press*, 1997, p. 197.

3. The learning curve for a new or risky technology is especially steep. Therefore it pays to have an experienced firm to introduce the technology at a much lower cost.

4. The organization is internally in turmoil and cannot manage IT because its managerial energies are concentrated on survival of the firm.

5. The organization is very profitable but doesn't wish to devote scarce managerial resources to managing IT.

These "good reasons" are amazingly consistent with the ASP's value propositions that are provided in the later chapters. It is also easy to give them an early "sneak preview." The first reason alludes to the dearth of technical talent already described in Chapter 3. The second reason implies that any cost-effective alternatives to purchasing hardware, software, applications, and hiring personnel are welcome as long as they help reduce costs. And they do, because using services and not building one's own technology infrastructure and hiring and training staffs results in direct savings of a company's capital and operational costs (see substitution effect in Chapter 2). Reason three is about time-to-market, that is, about how to quickly and effeciently assess, select, and deploy complex technologies, achieve less downtime, and improve customer service. There is a lot of goodness in that short sentence. Finally, reasons four and five suggest that companies' managements had better focus on their core competencies rather than on running IT. Though intuitive, all these "good reasons" are hard to argue with, much less to dimiss.

With the convergence of empirical analyses (Strassmann, et al.), and the aforementioned intuitive analysis, the stage is set to address the major question of what really makes the ASP a success. The answer lies in the ASP's Business Models and especially Economics.

Cost Economies and ASP

The tested and proven conventional wisdom, also written extensively about by numerous scholars and authors, states that there are two types of competitive advantages to ensure a business's success in a highly competitive environment: those that produce lower costs of products and services, and those that produce a superior product and service offering. For the former, an ASP offering an equal-quality service at lower cost would capture more sales through clever pricing, promotion, product packaging, and delivery strategies. For the latter, an ASP offering a superior service can immensely profit from premium pricing without jeopardizing its market share. For example, if it offers faster time to market for application development, or efficient customization and deployment, or superior customer care, or a proven record of reliability, availability, or security, higher prices could be justified.

Cost control is a major activity in every business. In and of itself, it is operational. If viewed as a belt-tightening measure only, it can provide for temporary improvements. However, when cost control is focused on the efficient use of resources and is based on well-defined and articulated strategies, sustainable competitive advantages could be achieved.

To exercise cost control within the ASP, both internal and external sources of economies must be addressed and exploited. Figure 4.1 depicts a high level taxonomy of diverse cost economies applicable to the ASP. The design of this taxonomy owes much to the work of Richard Langlois of the University of Connecticut.[4]

Figure 4.1   *Cost economies—high level taxonomy.*

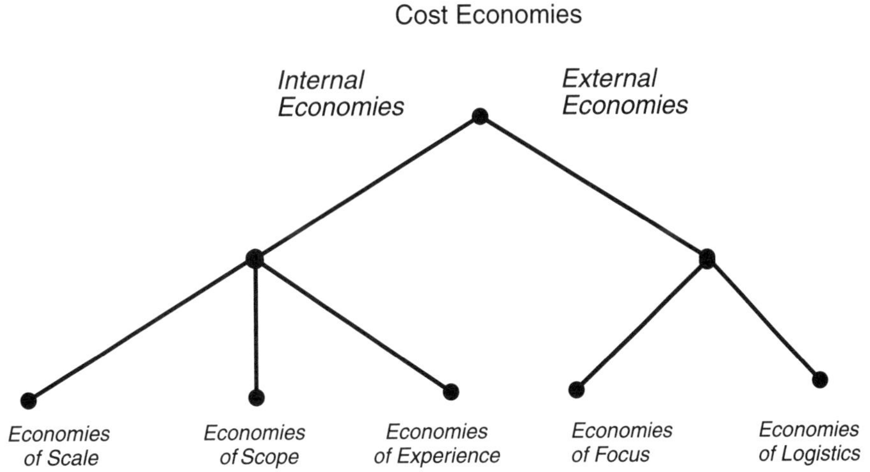

---

4. Richard N. Langlois, "Scale, Scope, and the Reuse of Knowledge." Paper presented at a conference in honor of Brian J. Loasby, Stirling, Scotland, August 26–28, 1997.

Internal Economies

ASP, as a business, can and should devise strategies for cost reductions by organizing itself to skillfully exploit the diverse economies of scale, scope, and experience. Most of such internal economies have been referred to and written about extensively, but informally, in numerous research papers on IT in general, and outsourcing and even the ASP in particular. This section attempts to create a formal taxonomy of internal economies for application later on in this book.

Economies of Scale

Whatever a company does, there is always a tendency for costs to decline as the scale of operations increases. Hence, there exists a simple rule: If costs increase slower than output (of products or services), ascribe the effects to economies of scale. For the ASP, economies of scale apply equally to applications, support services, infrastructure, application development, provisioning and configuration, operational systems and network management, security, and so forth.

There are four major sources of economies of scale, the so-called subtypes:

1. As an operational scale increases, personnel start specializing, which leads to higher work efficiencies. These division-of-labor, or *specialization*, benefits have been known since the times of Adam Smith, who wrote about them in the 18th century. They fit well as a justification for the ASP.

2. When an operational environment, like the ASP's infrastructure, grows in size, multiple economies can accrue. Indeed, *substitution* of larger systems for smaller ones effectively results in a substitution of machinery for labor, since fewer systems typically require less support personnel.

3. Fixed factors, or *overhead*, are also related to scale because of higher savings when these fixed costs are spread over an arbitrary larger scale of operations. For the ASP, examples of this could be the costs of application development or volume discounts in purchasing tools, hardware, systems software, hosted applications themselves, and so forth.

4. The final effect of economies of scale is *geometry*. A simple parable can explain it quite handily: If one data center has twice the dimensions of another, it offers four times bigger footage and eight times bigger volume that can be used for equipment deployment, storage, and so forth. Applied to systems, increased size lowers unit costs for CPUs and storage, and increases different resource pools for sharing.

The four items above are elements of the taxonomy of the economy of scale: Specialization, Substitution, Overhead, and Geometry. To use them in analyses later in the book, the following questions should be asked:

1. *Specialization*. Is technology handled by personnel with roles and responsibilities refined enough to result in specialization? While the question itself may beg other, mostly definitional, questions (e.g., what is refined enough?), it alludes to time spent observing changes in personnel performance and possibly even tracking these changes quantitatively.

2. *Substitution*. Can any consolidations be done to reduce a larger number of smaller technology units to a smaller number of larger units?

3. *Overhead*. Are there any fixed costs that can be applied to more units of the same kind? For example, if a particular software service runs on a computer, can it also be used by other computers in the network in lieu of buying more copies of this service software for those machines?

4. *Geometry*. What has geometric properties (physical or logical) that can leverage the effect of geometry? Physical geometry examples are data center space and systems enclosures (cabinets). A good, yet powerful, example of logical geometry is the vast expansion of addressable Internet space resulting from the adoption of a new IPv6 addressing standard, versus a current IPv4. By doubling IP address fields the address space increases from around four billion to around 16 quintillion (over nine orders of magnitude). This geometry effect is very impressive!

Here is an example of the application of economies of scale for two ASP customers, similar in size and requirements, and wanting the same application. Due to economies of scale, the second customer's deployment would cost less:

*   The second instance of an application may run on the same server, if it is large enough, of course (Substitution)

*   Development personnel have experience and should use less time deploying the second customer (Specialization)

*   Some code developed the first time can be used again (Fixed Factors or Overhead).

It should be noted that all subtypes of economies of scale are strongly dependent on time. Certain developments must take place before such economies commence. Specialization is more time dependent because it requires learning. Substitution and geometry can be achieved early, however, yet with an increased level of initial investment.

Thus, there are numerous interpretations of economies of scale. Different economic research uses different formulas and proformas to account for them. This book applies the aforementioned frameworks (or taxonomy) of economies of scale to the ASP extensively in later chapters, and especially, Chapter 9.

Economies of Scope

"Economies of scope" is a greatly overfranchised term that is also poorly understood. Consultants allude to scope in client proposals to delineate the boundaries of their future work, in order not to overcommit. They also talk about scope in engagement management. Marketing uses scope to define addressable markets. Management uses scope to delineate the realms of control. Finally, economists define scope as the shared overhead (i.e., shared costs) that produces cost economies in varied business functions, e.g., production, logistics, marketing and sales, distribution, customer care, and training.

This book uses scope in the latter, economic sense, and will apply these definitions to derive economies of scope later in the analysis of ASP designs and processes. For a more formal definition of economies of scope, the following formulas could be used. If an ASP offers customers two applications, X and Y, *scope economies* will be present when an average cost $C_A = C_A (X, Y)$ of providing these applications jointly (or, concurrently) is less than the cost of providing these applications separately:

$$C_A (X, Y) < C(X) + C(Y)$$

Scope *dis-economies* will be present if the sign is reversed:

$$C_A (X, Y) > C(X) + C(Y)$$

For the ASP, scope refers to the range of service offered by providers to their customers. Then, an ASP's goal should be to design a synergistic portfolio of offerings sharing common costs. By carefully planning such portfolios, it is possible to concurrently maximize shared costs and minimize going-to-market prices. The latter, in turn, provides a sustainable competitive advantage.

Common costs[5] can be found in virtually every element of ASP design, either tangible, like a technical architecture, or intangible, like knowledge. Reuse is applicable across multiple applications, projects, and customers, and can also provide for add-on synergies of applications and user communities.

Two forms of reuse are technology and knowledge reuse. Technology reuse implies using the same components of technology throughout the entire ASP without additional fixed costs of acquiring and deploying new components. An application utility like Currency Conversion is a good example of technology reuse. Fed by an outside source (e.g., Reuters), this utility—a Java servlet—can be found on local proxy servers or a central location and run by multiple applications locally and/or across the network on an as-needed basis.

Economists frequently refer to technology reuse as Fixed Factors in the economies of scope. But there should be no confusion between economies of scale and scope regarding technology reuse. In economies of scale, technology reuse applies to multiple units of the *same products or services*, while in economies of scope, technology reuse applies to *different products or services*. To further explain it, if "Credit Card Payment" at an ASP's multiple locations uses a version of "Currency Conversion," this is an economy of scale. If "Credit Card Payment," "Product Pricing," as well as other applications use it, this is an economy of scope. Standardization is another potent means of fostering technology reuse contributing to economies of scope.

Knowledge reuse occurs when knowledge accrued within an organization or possessed by its members can be shared among, or applied to, several *different* applications, projects, or customers. For example, managerial ability and capacity can be applied to new and/or related areas of the ASP. This may include project management, application development, customer expectations management, personnel supervision, and training.

Both technology and knowledge reuse are adopted as criteria and used extensively later in this book for insightful analyses of economies and efficiencies intrinsic to the ASP strategy, design, architectures, and ecosystems.

In summary, the overall purpose of economies of scope is to identify major areas of common costs (or, major areas of commonality) and exploit them across the ASP's multiple functional and physical domains, especially expensive ones.

---

5. Thomas T. Nagle, *The Strategies and Tactics of Pricing*, Englewood Cliffs, NJ: Prentice-Hall, 1987.

Economies of Experience

The phenomenon of the experience curve (for labor, it is called a learning curve) has been recognized since the late 1940s when it was discovered by the U.S. military and The Rand Corporation for studying the large production volumes of airplane frames.[6] But it had not hit the mainstream of business strategy until Boston Consulting Group (BCG) popularized its use as the basis for its experience-cost-economies strategic consulting.

By definition, experience economics refers to reductions in cost of production (or service offerings) in direct relationship to accumulated production volume. A simple rule of thumb, which has been confirmed time and time again by decades of observing manufacturing experience economics effects, is as follows:[7] "Experience economics generate an equal percentage reduction in unit cost for each doubling of accumulated volume." A sample experience curve is shown in Figure 4.2. Now, how can it apply to the ASP? For the ASP, volume could be the number of customers and users (a customer usually has multiple users). Other effects of experience economics for the ASP can be derived from learning how applications are run, from deployment of systems, from personnel training, and from many other information sources.

Figure 4.2 *Experience (learning) curve.*

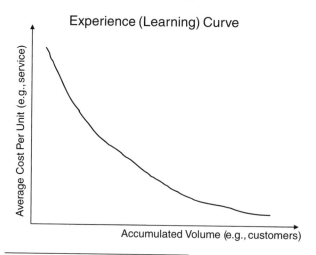

6. Armen A. Alchian, *Economic Forces at Work*, Ch. 13, Indianapolis: Liberty Press, 1977.

7. Thomas T. Nagle, *The Strategies and Tactics of Pricing*, Englewood Cliffs, NJ: Prentice-Hall, 1987, p. 224.

In summary, the purpose of economies of experience is to identify the effects of time and learning on ASP operational costs. However, the scarcity of accumulated data about ASPs and their performance may initially limit the practical application of experience to the tuning of ASPs.

External Economies

External economies flow from an ASP's interactions with the outside world, that is, the ASP's own ecosystem. External economies also allow ASPs to achieve cost advantages. They result from carefully selecting and defining external relationships between an ASP and its suppliers, partners, and customers and designing either unilateral or mutually agreed upon strategies.

The ASP industry has already begun to exploit these economies through creative partnerships and vertical integration of supplier and partners. A recently announced alliance between a leading ASP, USi, and AT&T is a good example of the former; USi's own acquisition of systems integrators specializing in particular applications (e.g., Siebel) evidences the latter point.

From the classification point of view, there are two well-defined types of external economies: economies of focus and logistics integration.

Economies of Focus

Focus implies consciously concentrating resources on a few business decisions versus spreading them broadly. The company may decide to focus on some of its products, markets, preferred customer types or sizes, certain technologies, or combinations thereof. Focus holds a promise of lower production costs, stronger product differentiation, and lower overhead (e.g., in marketing and sales). Small companies, and especially start-ups, are particular beneficiaries of focus strategies. Start-ups have few, if any, internal economies to leverage and hence opt for external economies. Concentrating their limited resources on certain endeavors and behaviors enables small businesses (and start-ups) to compete with their larger rivals who, due to their size and experience, can enjoy the benefits of internal economies such as scale, scope, and efficiencies.

Yet contrary to common opinion, a company must not necessarily be small to find it attractive to focus. A company's growth is only limited by the growth potential of its markets and its ability to compete. If the market grows quickly, the company may enjoy the advantages of growing with it. A good example is America Online (AOL). It had the right vision and followed it by focusing on providing on-line access to information to the early-adopter user community. As the numbers of these users grew, so did AOL. It has eventually made AOL the Number-One value-added ISP in the world.

One common practice among young ASPs is to focus on niche application markets. Cost benefits also can accrue quite quickly from focusing on vertical industries (e.g., claims processing in health care, specialized oil-gas applications, consulting companies' accounting support), functional markets (e.g., such as HR, Finance represented by Oracle Online, Corio hosting PeopleSoft), or analytical applications such as marketing campaign analysis and planning systems (e.g., Macromedia, E*Piphany), or product configurators like Fire-Pond, and so forth. Knowing customer needs in niche application markets—vertical, functional, or analytical—may lead to the following competitive advantages:

- Building close working relationships with a limited number of ISVs—application "suppliers" (e.g., Corio and PeopleSoft)—resulting in improved knowledge transfer and faster time-to-market.

- Focusing R&D work on enhancements to features and functions of fewer applications.

- Concentrating on better integration with the ASP environment and leveraging the inherent economies of scope in the ASP infrastructure.

Economies of Logistics Integration

Some ASPs have already started comprehending the large savings potential from better coordination of their current and future operations with their own software vendors, direct customers, and marketing channels. The advantages ASPs can achieve from pursuing economies of logistics are as follows:

- Enhanced application specifications to minimize product modifications for meeting ever-evolving customer needs.

- Coordinated pricing decisions by both ASPs and application vendor to be more price-competitive and profitable.

- Closer location of data centers to the niche application's users (e.g., the oil industry in Houston or small-scale ERP in Silicon Valley to support start-ups).

Taxonomy of ASP Economics

Figure 4.3 depicts an itemized taxonomy of internal and external economies with subtypes (e.g., substitution, overhead, geometry), in addition to major types (e.g., scale, scope, and experience).

Figure 4.3 *Taxonomy of ASP economics.*

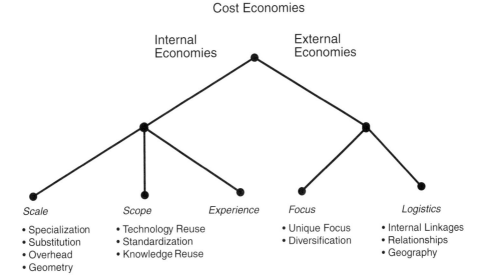

A Counterpoint

In his book *New Rules for the New Economy*,[8] Kevin Kelly suggests that we shall view opportunities before efficiencies. According to Kelly, "Productivity is exactly the wrong thing to worry about in the new economy" and "To measure efficiency you need a uniform output. But uniform output is becoming increasingly rare in an economy that emphasizes smaller production runs, total customization, personalized 'feelgoods' and creative innovation. Less and less is uniform."

Kelly's postulates apply perfectly to the domains of innovation and progress. They also hold true for most pre-IPO start-ups. However, in the real world and for post-IPO start-ups, when a scrutinizing public starts looking for revenue now and/or a promise thereof in the future, a sound philosophy for economic efficiency and a rigorous implementation program become critical competitive advantages and key for a company's survival. The dot.com calamity of 2000 offers ample proof for this point.

---

8. Kevin Kelly, <u>New Rules for the New Economy</u>, New York: Viking, 1998.

Summary

Cost reductions from cost economies are extremely attractive to ASPs for several reasons:

- Cost savings from economies and efficiencies are more sustainable than circumstantial, one-off cost benefits that may arise from lucky deals, occasional bargains, economic cycles, and other random happenings.

- Cost savings from economies can frequently be achieved without major adverse impact on the relationships within the company, for example, with its workforce, or with outsiders like suppliers, customers, investment community, and others. On the contrary, ASPs vigorously pursuing cost reductions stand to earn a strong reputation of astute businesses leading to tighter relationships with their ecosystem, that is, infrastructure vendors, network providers, systems integrators, and, of course, customers.

- Strategies to achieve economies may lead to additional differentiation, hence, increased attractiveness of each ASP's services to its customers.

The ASP is a complex business. Yet, complexity begets opportunities for the ASP's economies and efficiencies. While more formal analyses are provided throughout the book, here is a casual look at potential areas of savings for the ASP—by the types of economies.

- Scale in software license acquisition and purchasing hardware in volume.

- Scale due to the centralized application version control and code distribution.

- Scale and Scope economies due to focus on smaller sets of applications, further reducing licensing costs and support, development, implementation, and operations personnel (fewer support groups for fewer application systems).

- Scale and Scope economies due to the reuse of hardware/OS/ middleware.

- Scale and Scope economies from using easily customizable applications.

- Scale and Scope economies due to using the best-of-breed products for Network and Systems Management (NSM) products.

- Scale and Scope economies due to specialization and expertise (e.g., NSM).

- Scope economies due to the reuse of application utilities, reuse of common services, and emergence of new software targeting the ASP.

- Use of application development and runtime management platforms designed specifically for the ASP. An example may be a platform that helps manage application portfolios run in a mixed technology, shared-server environment, with additional functionality to support provisioning (e.g., user and subscriber management).

Finally, as promised in Chapter 1, frameworks are introduced wherever possible in this book. This chapter is not an exception. This chapter introduced the ASP Economics Analysis Framework (Figures 4.1 and 4.3), which is used throughout this book and applied to all components of the ASP. A main theme for the book, this framework is also a major source of economies and efficiencies for ASPs of the future.

Chapter 5

Network Computing and ASP Architectures

This chapter introduces the approach to designing architectures for large-scale networked systems, their frameworks, architectures, and design methodologies.

Introduction

ASP has been defined in the preceding chapters as a business that provides access to applications to multiple customers over the network. This definition is quite broad and high-level and doesn't state what technologies and methods are used to design, build, and manage such ASPs—their architectures, infrastructures, and processes.

There are two ways to look at the ASP today: as a legacy business emanating from the traditional outsourcing or as the new, Internet-era business endeavor, completely changing the technical and business landscape of how the diverse application services are positioned, designed, and provisioned for the delivery to their users over the network. At the time of this writing, traditional outsourcing companies still dominated the scene of application service provisioning. For economic reasons (e.g., sunk costs), customer preferences, or other motives, many of them still remain in the fold of legacy methods and technologies such as the older traditional "waterfall" software development models, mainframe computers, and dedicated networks, to name just a few. Conversely, the new outsourcing companies, ASPs, all gravitate towards the portfolio of new technologies and techniques such as the open standards, object-oriented designs, distributed systems, and the Internet, thus representing a new and promising embodiment of outsourcing of the future.

But these ASPs are only one type of many new, promising, and nascent Internet-based businesses that have lately been emerging and finding the Internet and its attendant technologies alluring, promising, and profitable. To generalize the definitions and simplify terminology used to describe all such businesses, the term Network Computing (NC) will be used throughout this chapter and the book. While the NC model applies to all new Internet-based businesses, it also applies to the ASP, the main subject of this book.

Having made this leap of faith, it is easy to go one more step forward and assume that whatever frameworks and methodologies are used to design the NC will also apply to the ASP. The validity of this assumption and possible deviations from it will be examined later. For now, the material in this chapter introduces the definition of the NC, its Architecture Framework, Sun's Three-Dimensional Framework (3DF), and the NC Design Methodology.

What Is Network Computing?

It was only about 10 years ago when client-server was labeled a "wave of the future—the computing paradigm of the 90s." Client-server was a special form of distributed computing and it became attractive due to the availability of inexpensive computers (both for the clients and servers) and high-speed networking. This model became an IT design archetype in the era of emerging networked computing and was adopted by many companies as a strategy in their quest to minimize IT costs while improving IT service.

Client-server computing (Figure 5.1) implied three elements: a client, a server, and a network connection. Under the client-server model, application processing was distributed between the client and the server. The client generally executed business logic, the server handled data input, output, and storage. The network was viewed as a communications channel between the client and the server.

Figure 5.1   *Client-server and network computing models.*

A. INCUMBENT CLIENT-SERVER MODEL

B. NETWORK-COMPUTING MODEL—"THE NETWORK IS THE COMPUTER"

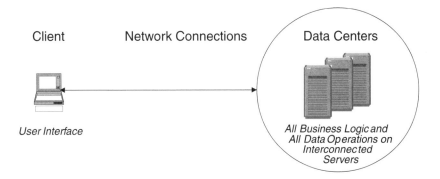

Servers were used for different functions: database, communications, print, fax, mail, and so forth. Clients varied too: engineering workstations, PCs, dumb terminals, printers, telemetry devices, and so forth. Finally, client-server networks were combinations of Local Area Networks (LAN) running Ethernet, Token Rings, FDDI and others, while Wide Area Networks (WAN) would run vendor-specific protocols such as IBMs SNA, DECs DDCMP, some TCP/IP, as well as Telco's protocols like X.25, frame-relay, and so forth.

The client-server model was a step up from the previous, centralized (so-called glasshouse) model of computing and promised several major advantages. First and foremost, it held the potential for more reliable processing by distributing applications across multiple computers configured for automatic failover or a standby takeover in the case of failures. Also, by design, client-server was supposed to be scalable and platform-independent, the latter achieved through the deployment of different computers and operating systems both on the server and the client.

However, migrating from the old centralized application systems to client-server was not easy. The client-server folklore is littered with both success and horror stories. As time has shown, though, client-server was merely a transitional, and a generally positive, development at that. It raised and brought to the attention of business, academia, and technical communities a number of important issues currently considered mainstream: open systems and heterogeneity; distributed processing and remote access; systems and network scalability; and reliability, availability, security, and manageability, just to name a few. It built a foundation for a momentous transition into the world of network-based computing, the Internet technologies, the world in which "the network is the computer."

The Internet and its technologies (largely the Web) completely altered the understanding of network-based computing in the 1990s and subsequently morphed the client-server into what is now commonly called "network computing." It did so by mitigating a client's application functionality and expanding and further distributing the processing roles of networked servers (Figure 5.1). This *new* network quickly demonstrated its ability to perform many processing tasks for "anyone, anywhere, anytime" and with access from "any device."

As time goes on, numerous ISPs, Portals, vendors, TelCo, B2C and B2B E-Commerce sites, and finally, the ASPs are continuing to provide strong evidence to support the claim for success of network computing. Here is what ASPnews.Com published recently:[1]

> Important though they are, ASPs are just one element of a much broader trend taking shape in computing today. The trend runs through many other emerging sectors, such as NC, dot-coms and B2B marketplaces. All these sectors have one characteristic in common: they use network-based computing as a platform for delivering business services.
>
> What is the trend driving every one of these new sectors? Very simply, computing is moving onto the Internet. Whether you call it application services, Internet portals or digital trading, the same dynamic applies. Computing is escaping the confines of individual enterprise data centers and migrating to the open spaces of the shared, global network.
>
> … When computing moves onto the Internet, the end result is that the Internet itself becomes the computer.

Network computing applies to every networked computing sector. Does it also offer a uniform architectural framework for these sectors? And if it does, what is this framework? What does it look like and how can it be used? How will the different network-computing sectors map into it? How will the ASP map into it? The list of questions can go on

---

1. Phil Wainewright, "When the Internet Becomes the Computer...," The ASPnews.Com, October 5, 2000.

and on. Some answers can be found on the following pages. And the rest of the discussion in this book is based on the premise that the ASP is just another materialization and embodiment of NC.

NC Architectural Framework

The three-dimensional Architecture Framework (3DF) described on the following pages has been developed and put into practice by the Professional Services organization of Sun Microsystems, Inc. The description provided here is abridged, simplified, and slightly modified from that used by Sun, albeit without altering the major tenets and principles captured in 3DF (see Figure 5.2).

An Architectural Framework is a reference model that directs and organizes the analysis, design, and development of architectural components and services. Using functional segregation, the Framework defines these components and the interfaces between them. The Framework is assumed to be comprehensive as it strives for the completeness of inclusion of all the different components of the NC architecture. It is also assumed to be invariant towards the functional, quantitative, and qualitative requirements of any specific, that is, real-world NC implementations.

Figure 5.2   *The cube of 3DF.*

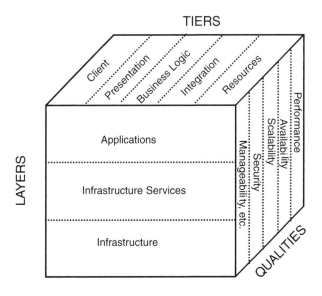

Additionally, the Framework provides for an evolutionary design approach with bi-directional traceability, helps select and enforce standards, offers a planning roadmap, ensures consistent documentation, and improves overall understanding of the NC development challenges. In a word, the Architectural Framework provides a complete and comprehensive environment from which the different NC architectures can be derived.

The Framework that Sun has developed is defined as a three-dimensional space (the Cube) consisting of Tiers, Layers, and Qualities.

- **Tiers:** Tiers segregate application functionality into a well-ordered set of logical or physical components across the network (e.g., the Internet). The relationship between Tiers can be viewed as that occurring between service requesters and servers. Tiers on the right provide services to Tiers on the left. That is, services are flowing right to left in response to requests flowing left to right. More discussion about Tiers is provided later. But then, the roles and direction of service provisioning might as well be reversed, further proving the value of tiers for this analysis. Indeed, the Client provides interface services to the Presentation. Presentation, in turn, provides interface abstraction services to the Business, and so on.

- **Layers**: Layers are a well-ordered (vertical) set of software and hardware components within a Tier. Like Tiers, they provide services to one another. The layer above requests services from the layer below and so on. Services requests flow downward, services—upward. More discussion about Layers is also provided later.

- **Qualities**: Derived from the Requirements specifications of a target NC, these properties (features, characteristics, etc.) comprise the requirements for Performance and Quality of Services (QoS). More detailed definitions of Qualities can be found later in this chapter.

Application Tiers

In the past, when the mainframe ruled the world, nobody talked about Tiers. The mainframe was monolithic; its components came assembled in one box and were placed inside a big glass-house computer room. The mainframe-based applications were mostly batch, with scheduled downtime, and the use of resources was programmed and strictly controlled.

Client-server computing, and later its bright younger sibling the NC, presented a different set of requirements: real-time and interactive applications, continuous systems availability, heightened security, improved usability and accessibility, and dynamic management of resources—all combined with the scalable and flexible designs to accommodate future loads and ever-changing application functionality. To accommodate this new set of requirements, a radically new approach to building scalable flexibility into the NC architectures was needed. The solution came in the form of logical decomposition of applications into their discrete components identified by their services distributed across the network. Breaking an application into discreet processing components greatly increased the independence of component evolution, the adoption of new technologies, scalability, security, and manageability.

The new approach also further expanded the familiar client-server terminology: of "two-tier" and "three-tier" into an "N-tier" model. Incidentally, the five-tier architecture depicted in Figure 5.3 is but one instantiation of the N-tier approach written about so much lately, both in computer, professional, and business literature. The five tiers are: Clients, Presentation, Business, Integration, and Resources.

Figure 5.3   *ASP architectural tiers.*

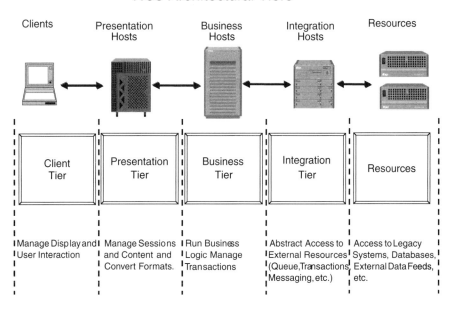

NCs Architectural Tiers

A *Client* Tier implies the end-user entity. As shown in Figure 5.3, the client's major functions are to manage display, process user interface, and network with the presentation tier. Clients can be different types of entities, at times not even known or controlled by the enterprise whose services they use. These different entities may include, but are not limited to, the stationary and mobile (e.g., laptop) personal computers, engineering workstations, PDAs,[2] Web-enabled phones (e.g., those using WAP[3]), embedded intelligent devices, pagers, smart-card readers, or even an application exchanging messages with another application (at the enterprise or the ASP).

FLASHBACK

It may be enlightening to draw parallels between the tiers in Figure 5.3 and a classical model of a digital computer. The five tiers, along with their potential physical equivalents, can be easily matched against its components with similar functionality. A common IBM mainframe is a good example of such a model. Indeed, a venerable IBM 3270 terminal would correspond to the client tier; an IBM terminal controller could correspond to the presentation tier; IBM CPU to business logic; the famous IBM Channels to integration, and finally, the IBM DASD to resources.

A *Presentation* Tier manages sessions between clients and business tier(s), formats and packages information exchanges, aggregates content, and converts data formats, as needed. Presentation services can be located wherever the business tier services are hosted or may be distributed around the network acting in a proxy or cache capacity for data exchanged between clients and business tier hosts. Effectively, the presentation tier provides an abstraction between the user and the business services being requested.

A *Business* Tier is where business logic services reside and execute. Business services run applications, process user requests, access resources via gateways, and submit processed business appli-

---

2. PDA is a Personal Digital Assistant, such as 3COM's Palm Pilot.

3. WAP stands for Wireless Application Protocol. It is an open, global specification that provides mobile users with easy access to information and services. WAP protocols are based on Internet standards such as HTTP, XML, IP, and others, and are all optimized for a wireless environment.

cation data to presentation for delivery to clients. The business tier defines the computational "product" being offered.

An *Integration* Tier refers mostly to the gateways between applications implemented by business tier and legacy resources. Additionally, gateways may link to external data sources or destinations, such as financial data and news sources for the former, and remote reporting locations for the latter. Effectively, the integration tier is an abstraction between the business logic and the resources it requires.

A *Resources* Tier is where applications store and maintain their data. These frequently are data storage farms that keep user data or even users' own IT systems linked to the architecture via the integration tier or external links.

Tier-to-Tier communications can be interprocess or across the network. Tiers that communicate over the network can be viewed, for all practical purposes, as physical entities. Clients are almost always located remotely from other tiers (e.g., Data Centers) and are connected to them via a network. Resources may be remote customer facilities too or stand-alone network-connected "storage farms." Presentation may also be deliberately located closer to the client, albeit still in the network, as cache and/or proxy facilities.

Infrastructure Layers

Another dimension of architectural decomposition is that of Infrastructure Layers. Layers should be familiar to many readers from other computing and networking disciplines. For example, the eminent reference model for Open Systems Interconnection (OSI[4]) has seven protocol layers stacked so that the lower layer provides services to the layer above, and so forth. Figure 5.4 offers a simple view of this OSI reference model for OSI with brief explanations of its layers.

The 3DF, described earlier in this chapter, assumes that multiple infrastructure layers are required for implementing each tier. The high-level definitions of layers are the infrastructure (hardware, OS, network support, and real estate), infrastructure services (e.g., middleware, and reusable components), and finally, applications. The horizontal layers are stacked in a similar manner to the aforemen-

---

4. In 1978, the International Standards Organization (ISO) released a draft of its specifications for the reference model of Open Systems Interconnection with the intent to create a set of international data communications standards.

Figure 5.4 *Reference model of OSI.*

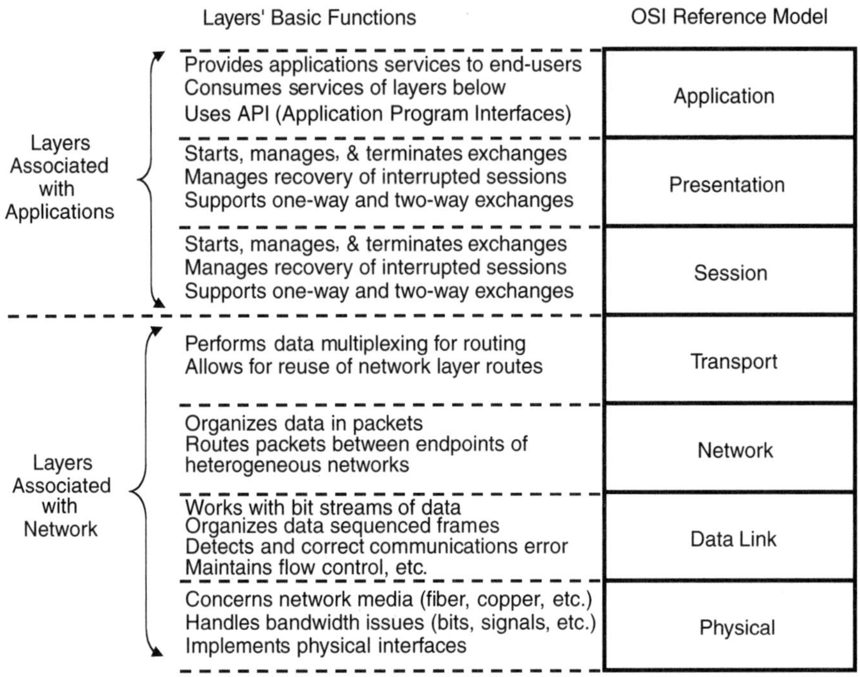

Layers' Basic Functions	OSI Reference Model
Provides applications services to end-users Consumes services of layers below Uses API (Application Program Interfaces)	Application
Starts, manages, & terminates exchanges Manages recovery of interrupted sessions Supports one-way and two-way exchanges	Presentation
Starts, manages, & terminates exchanges Manages recovery of interrupted sessions Supports one-way and two-way exchanges	Session
Performs data multiplexing for routing Allows for reuse of network layer routes	Transport
Organizes data in packets Routes packets between endpoints of heterogeneous networks	Network
Works with bit streams of data Organizes data sequenced frames Detects and correct communications error Maintains flow control, etc.	Data Link
Concerns network media (fiber, copper, etc.) Handles bandwidth issues (bits, signals, etc.) Implements physical interfaces	Physical

Layers Associated with Applications brace encompasses Application, Presentation, Session.

Layers Associated with Network brace encompasses Transport, Network, Data Link, Physical.

tioned reference model for OSI. Each layer receives requests for service from the layer above and consumes the services of the layer below. Note that in the OSI model, layers are standardized, meaning a concentration of pertinent functionality exists at each layer (e.g., routing and addressing for the OSI Network Layer) with a minimization of interface complexity. In the framework in Figure 5.5, however, the ordering of layers is intuitive and historical in its genesis. It addresses the network computing model's functional domains rather than the requirements for, and priorities of, the generic Internet architecture.

The three high-level layers of a network computing architecture shown in Figure 5.5 can be subdivided into sublayers. There are two sublayers to the Application Layer: Applications and Application Utilities. Infrastructure Services also has two sublayers: Component-Ware and Integration-Ware. And finally, the Infrastructure Layer consists of three sublayers: Platform, Network, and Space. These layers are briefly discussed in the following sections.

Figure 5.5   *Infrastructure layers itemized.*

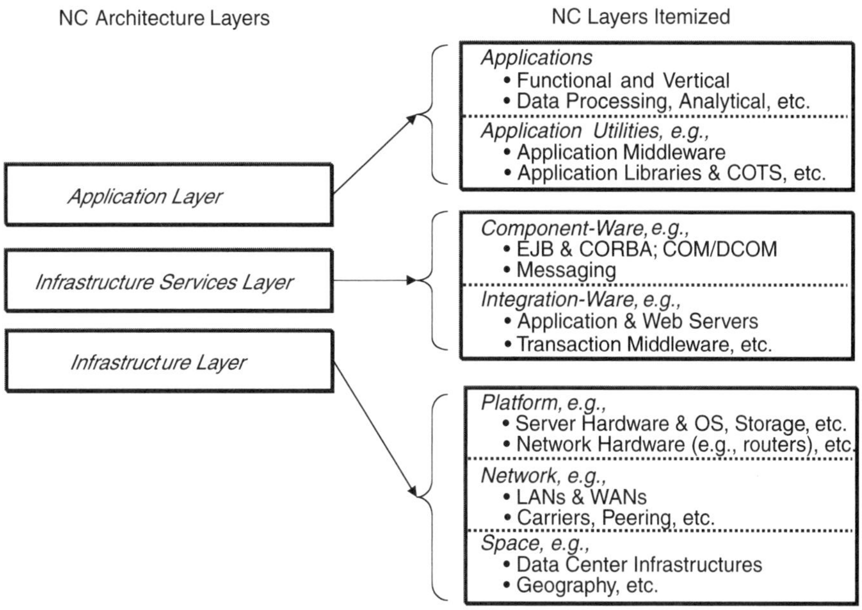

NC Architecture Layers   NC Layers Itemized

Applications and Application Utilities

The NC Architecture's applications can be anything: portals, B2B and B2C e-commerce sites, market exchanges, specific consumer applications (e.g., auction sites), ISPs, and, of course, ASPs.

Application utilities are a new rendition of the old concept of reusable components. In a nutshell these are libraries of applications and application components as well as COTS.[5] Application utilities are programs that provide application-level services, enacted by other applications or utilities, and shared by different applications, possibly even across different platforms and networks. Sometimes these libraries and COTS are called application middleware, examples of which may be language translators, data format converters, and so forth. For example, when Sun's StarOffice personal productivity software converts Microsoft Office files, the conversion routines are true representatives of application middleware.

5. COTS is a de-facto standard term standing for Commercial Off-the-Shelf Software. These are typical software products purchased to execute specific functionality.

Good examples of COTS are plug-and-play applications like the event collection agents for remote network management, bill preparation programs, address verification, credit card verification and authorization, fraud screening services, auction, catalog, publishing, and advertising modules; shipping and fulfillment programs, payment authorization service, order taking and tracking, and many others.

Many application modules and COTS perform functions based on the de-jure or de-facto industry standards. This helps to ensure application adaptability to different infrastructures and allows application modifications to be made without changing underlying infrastructures. Additionally, using these modules and COTS promotes reuse as a powerful means of achieving economies of scope, especially when applied across heterogeneous platforms. As will be shown later, economies are a key factor for success for ASPs.

In summary, Application utilities enable the network computing architecture to standardize on application integration, service management, and support.

Component-Ware and Integration-Ware Layers

Component-Ware offers services that support interactions at the application layer between applications. These services implement the abstractions that come in the form of APIs like those based on de-facto industry standard specifications such as Sun Microsystems Inc.'s J2EE or Microsoft's COM/DCOM, OMG,[6] CORBA, and so forth.

Integration-Ware is another term for "middleware." Like most middleware, Integration-Ware helps hide the complexities of underlying service layers such as those provided by the computing platforms' operating systems and hardware from the applications. The features that middleware masks may include load balancing and replication, DBMS access, hierarchical storage management, directory service access, security systems access (e.g., Kerberos); process thread, connection, and session pool management; transaction and message management; and many, many others. Integration-Ware frequently resorts to the use of complete integration environments like Application Servers, Web Servers, Transaction Monitors, Transaction Managers, and so forth.

---

6. OMG is an Object Management Group

Platform, Network and Space Layers

The collections of server technologies (e.g., processing, data storage) are commonly called "server farms." They are interconnected by LANs at each location and WANs over longer distances, and are managed by NOCs.

Server farms are usually located at the Data Centers, which, in turn, are more than just space. Data Centers require specialized facilities and designs including raised floors, adequate load bearing capabilities, local points of presence (POP) for communications carriers, access to power, and specialized HVAC (Heating, Ventilation and Cooling) systems.

Qualities Belong in Requirements Specifications

Without an overly ambitious claim to be comprehensive, Figure 5.6 attempts to provide a view of four sets of typical requirements specifications for building an NC for a particular application. The Functional specifications define the type of application to be designed and implemented—its functionality, specific activities, and interfaces. It is like answering the question about what type of application it will be and what it will do.

The Quantities requirements define the scale of the would-be application environment, addressing the implied questions about who will use these applications, how frequently and when they will use them, and how much information will be exchanged, processed, and stored. The Implementation requirements put certain design constraints on and around the NC design and implementation effort. They inform the NC designers about the incumbent components, preferred technologies and products, methods and modes of systems, and the application development within the enterprise. The Qualities aggregate the requirements for *how* the NC must operate as designed and how it should respond to changes (expected or not) in its environment. Examples of such changes are provided here:

- Many new users are being added to the system (Scalability) and are expected to personalize the Graphic User Interface (GUI) to their tastes and requirements (Usability);

- New users with physical limitations—deaf or blind or using the system in noisy environments or bright sunlight—are being introduced to the NC, requiring new modes of information delivery to them (Accessibility);

- Server or network components fail (Availability);
- The NC is penetrated or thwarted by unauthorized parties, such as hackers (Security, Manageability);
- Modifications to applications or NC architecture are needed in response to planned or unplanned events (Flexibility);
- Performance requirements change (Performance);
- The NC system's components must be serviced, and so on (Serviceability).

Since the world is not perfect, NC's operational conditions will always change, frequently and without warning. Performance planning would continue to baffle designers, frequently remaining underestimated or underinvested in. Hackers would forever remain the instigators of continuous innovation in, and major stimuli for, investments in security. And customers would be seeing more and more NCs supporting their mission-critical business applications, therefore requiring exceptional availability, scalability, and performance.

The degree to which each specific Quality affects the NCs architecture and constituencies—enterprises owning the applications, users, designers, ASPs, and others—vary significantly. Knowing the specific domains impacted by each Quality, or a group thereof, helps the NC architecture design and implementation, as well as operational monitoring, measurement, management, and planning.

Figure 5.6 *NC's requirements specifications.*

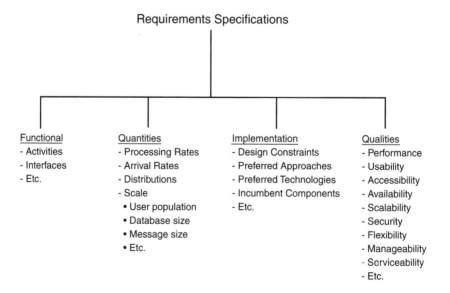

Major Qualities

Usability

Definition. Usability is a common Quality impacting the users and user interface. The terms describing the user interface include different measures of its "goodness" such as intuitiveness, look-and-feel, eye appeal, ease of navigation, layout, number of clicks, nesting, short-term memory, reversible actions, etc. Apple Macintosh in the 1980s was the first to introduce an appealing, easy-to-use, communicative, and functional GUI[7] for a mass-market user. Microsoft Windows, Sun's CDR, and GUIs from many other vendors have very successfully imitated many of Macintosh's GUI features. The key design tenets of Macintosh's GUI still remain intact.

Another aspect of usability addresses the users' ability to easily perform an authorized function such as changing their personal preferences.

Strategy. Usability is extensively studied both by academia and industry. Many books have been written on the subject and many useful improvements have been implemented. Usability also has a cultural connotation. The most common strategy for most contemporary GUIs is to allow for GUI personalization to help users address their cultural (and personal) preferences, especially in the context of internationalization.

Accessibility

Definition. Accessibility refers to the users' abilities to get and comprehend information provided by the NC. Accessibility has many dimensions, including language translation with cultural sensitivities, color-coding for dealing with the color-blind, access by the blind and deaf, and so forth.

The now-popular information search engines on the Web represent another Accessibility issue. Selecting and packaging the right responses to a user's request fed into the search engine is not an easy task. Many ideas, developed by academia and business, have resulted in a large number of different, interesting, and, to varying degrees, successful commercial implementations. Nonetheless, the search for a "perfect" search goes on.

Strategy. While the technical means to meet the varied requirements of Accessibility exist, the key challenge to NC designers (as well as the ASPs) is to know whether and when to provide for access diversity.

---

7. Incidentally, Macintosh itself borrowed the ideas of the 1970s GUI development from Xerox's Star project.

Reliability and Availability

Definition. Reliability and Availability impact the Quality of service provided by the architecture to its users. Reliability is a common concept in engineering defined through a statistic called the Mean Time Between Failures (MTBF). The MTBF doesn't address the time required to bring the failed component back to operation. Another measure, the Mean Time To Recovery (MTTR) is used for that purpose. In its turn, MTTR combines two other measures, the Mean Time To Isolate (MTTI)—the time required to isolate the real fault that caused the failure from its external manifestations—and the Mean Time To Restore (MTTE). Reliability of systems with multiple components is a complex statistical function of the reliabilities of underlying components.

Availability is a Quality that combines MTBF and MTTR and provides an easier-to-understand number—a probability of a system's uptime. Availability is frequently measured in the so-called 9s. For example, a 99.9% availability is referred to as a three 9s availability, a 99.999% is referred to as five 9s, and so forth. Raising availability, by adding another 9 at the right, is very expensive. Evan Marcus and Hal Stern wrote in their book, *Blueprints for High Availability*, that when adding one 9 "costs increase from 5 to 10 times."[8]

$$\text{AVAILABILITY} = \frac{\text{MTBF}}{\text{MTBF} + \text{MTTR}}$$

Strategy. In a classical sense, Availability is a function of the reliabilities of systems and their components. However, it can also be achieved through other means: special design techniques, experiential heuristics, metrics, and other approaches. The designs of software and hardware architectures and business processes have a major effect on Availability.

In response to the requirements of continuous uptime of the NC, systems Availability can be achieved through architectural solutions involving redundancies (for server, routers, networks, etc.), replication, and intelligent failover mechanisms. Application Availability can be realized by designing applications capable of self-healing and recovery as well as via remote management (e.g., from the monitoring and operating centers). Data availability may be accomplished, among other means, through the use of transaction-based middle-

---

8. Evan Marcus and Hal Stern, *Blueprints for High Availability*, New York: John Wiley & Sons, Inc., 2000.

ware with flow control, databases' two-phase commits, replication, and on-line access to archives.

Properly established processes also play an important role in ensuring availability including backup and restore, monitoring and management, operations management, disaster recovery, and others.

Scalability

Definition. Scalability as a Quality describes the ability of NC to add capacity for providing services on a larger scale, as required. "Larger scale" means that when needed, and without changing its architecture, the NC would be able to support more users and/or more transactions, or higher frequencies (e.g., arrival rates), or any combination thereof. Scalability analysis and planning is usually based on the assumption that systems architectures and functionality remain the same. When the architectures or functionality do change, different calculations for scalability are required.

Scalability is a very common term used in many different contexts describing business domains and applications. For example, Scalability of the IP (Internet Protocol), due to its large address space, is one frequently quoted reason for the success of the Internet. In another example, the Web-based customer support systems would always be infinitely more scalable than any conventional call centers and help desks.

So, what do people mean when they call something scalable? After all, additional capacities (bandwidth, servers, storage, etc.) can always be procured and deployed, and operational personnel can be added to meet increased business demand. The answer is that when speaking of scalability, people mean costs and time. This leads to new questions. What additional capital will be needed to get the incremental capacity? How long will it take to deploy it, how much more will it cost to operate it? When will the additional investment pay for itself? Thus, Scalability is an economic concept. If it takes a 100% (or more) increase in capacity to satisfy a 100% increase in demand (volume, users, etc.), the architecture in question is not scalable. Yet, if it takes a 50% capacity to satisfy a 100% increase in volume, after the initial investment has been made, the architecture is scalable.

Figure 5.7 offers a graphical view of this logic and introduces the concept of the Scalability Cost Curve. If the angle of the curve of a particular architecture is consistently less than 45°, then the architecture is said to be scalable. If it is more than, or equal to 45°, the architecture is not scalable. The Scalability Cost Curve is actually a step-wise function. This is due to an incremental nature of all acquisitions and expenses associated with the architecture's major costs elements: space, hardware, software, labor, and so forth. The curve in Figure 5.7 is smoothed out to provide easier observation.

Strategy. Formulas and cost models can be designed to track costs and, hence, analyze architecture's scalability. These models would in themselves incorporate all the cost elements of building and operating an NC architecture by capturing capital costs, operational expenses, time to market opportunity costs, training costs, and the like.

Further, by performing a what-if analysis with these models, one could pick and choose the right technologies to build the architecture to lower its cost scalability curves or just smooth them out. For example, adding extra processor boards to the same server usually costs less and takes less time compared to buying and deploying new servers. Using processor boards provides for lower and smoother scalability curves. Consolidating multiple smaller servers into one large one may also have a similar effect.

Figure 5.7 *Scalability cost curve.*

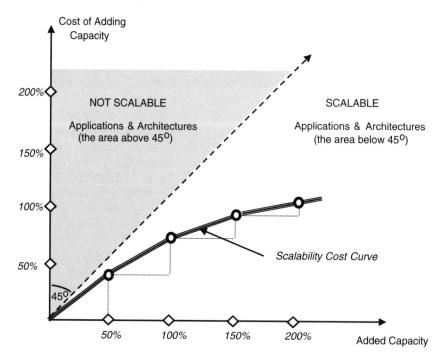

Scalability can be achieved in many different ways. For the NC architectures, most common approaches are vertical and horizontal scalability. Vertical scalability is achieved by increasing individual unit capacities, for example, by raising bandwidth on existing networks, adding processor boards to multiprocessor systems, or installing additional disk drives on a storage chassis, and so forth. This approach helps achieve higher capacities without architectural changes, extra real estate, and duplicated operations. The bottom line is lower incremental costs. However, larger systems without redundancies spell lower reliability and higher business risks.

On the other hand, horizontal scalability implies adding complete units to the architecture, for example, new networks and network connections, new servers, new storage systems. This approach builds groups of loosely coupled entities that can be (and almost always are) configured for redundancy and failover, portending higher service reliability and availability. Yet, the bottom line is higher cost, both in capital (e.g., server purchases) and in expenses—for real estate, operations, and so on. Another lesson from this simple analysis is that Scalability is very closely related to many other Qualities.

Which scalability approach is better and when to use it is almost impossible to answer in the abstract. Opinions vary, but the final scalability plan must ultimately depend on the combination of the factors and other qualities that play key roles in Scalability planning. In practice, the nature of the underlying application being scaled often determines the choice of horizontal or vertical scalability. Some transactions, such as Web page requests, inherently scale horizontally; others, such as database queries, inherently scale vertically. Still, some common Scalability heuristics have been developed. For example, it is frequently recommended to first scale horizontally until availability through redundancy is achieved, then scale vertically as far as the application can scale, then scale horizontally again, as much as needed.

Scalability is defined and planned by the pragmatic discipline of NC's Capacity Planning, always performed against the goal of achieving a particular scale objective sometime in the future. By doing a right-to-left planning exercise—from the goal backwards to the present—one can design a capacity plan for achieving the goal at the least cost, e.g., by varying the horizontal and vertical scalability options. Conversely, it may be possible to accurately estimate the cost of buying into Reliability/Availability to achieve Scalability.

Capacity Planning also has a strong relationship with timing. For example, it is possible to plan for a minimal interval within which server capacity upgrades will be needed while still maintaining a manageable server environment (constant change is inherently difficult to manage, though). In another case, it may be possible to match a server's life span (three to five years) and/or accounting depreciation schedules to the server's upgrade schedules, and so on. And finally, Capacity Planning must make sound economic sense that is usually expressed in the form of mandatory fiscal constraints.

Flexibility

Definition. At least three distinct levels of flexibility can be recognized: component, architectural, and managerial.

- Component Level. For components, flexibility is achieved when it is possible to add, remove, or replace components without adversely impacting the delivery of NC services.

- Architecture Level. The architecture is flexible when it is possible to assign or reassign services, at any layer, from one component to another or even across tiers. Some other qualities may, however, be impacted as the result of these reassignments, such as performance, availability, scalability, or security.

- Management Level. Management flexibility is the ability to effect component or architectural changes from an NC management console.

Flexibility is tightly coupled to other Qualities. A simple example can prove this point. Say a particular NC runs multiple applications. Application 1 is business-logic-intensive. Application 2 is presentation-intensive. Architectural flexibility is exercised when the Business Tier has a backup server that can be reassigned and reloaded with executable code to bolster the capacity of the Presentation Tier during the time when Application 2 has higher usage. What happens here is a play on availabilities. The Presentation Tier's availability is temporarily increased while the overall Business-Logic Tier's is decreased. If this reassignment could be done from an NC management console rather than through programmers and installers, this represents a case of management flexibility. Since, in all probability, this management capability occurs faster than using programmers and installers, a longer interruption that might have adversely affected the overall NC services has been prevented.

Another NC architecture's flexibility is realized through component reuse, that is, the ability by multiple NC services to use the same underlying components.

Strategy. The use of open standards such as protocols, interfaces, objects, data formats, and cross-platform technologies such as Java are major factors for improving and increasing flexibility. Flexibility can also be built into the architecture itself by building with reusable or substitutable components.

Security

Definition. Preventing unauthorized access to, tampering with, and incapacitation of the NC resources, as well as providing its users with secure virtual executing environments, presents the NCs with continuous challenges. Security always requires a variety of responsibilities, processes, and products for all types of NC activities. Security is a very complex architectural element, both technically and in a business sense. It is a discipline pervading every NC element: facilities, people, hardware, software, networks, applications, and processes. The purpose of this brief subsection is to offer high-level security taxonomy helpful for designing the NC security architectures in the future.

The four key functions of network-computing security are Prevention (or Deterrence), Protection (or Defense), Detection, and Response. The logic of applying these functions is as follows. When a threat is recognized, first consider prevention. If prevention is not possible, build defenses. If defenses can be circumvented, prepare to respond in order to minimize damage. Finally, use detection to identify what happened and leverage the newly acquired knowledge of how and why it happened to build new preventive and defensive measures, as well as better detection and response in the future.

There are five basic facets (dimensions) of NC Security that provide an umbrella for, and abstract from, the many specific means of prevention, protection, and detection. These facets are Authentication, Access Control, Confidentiality, Data Integrity, and Non-Repudiation. The definitions of these security facets are as follows:[9]

- "*Authentication* means establishing proof of identity"

- "...*Access Control* relates to who (or what) may have access to some object"

- Data "*Integrity* refers to the current condition of some data as compared to its 'pure' and original state"

- *Confidentiality* is a provision for privacy of information processed by systems and exchanged over the networks

- *Non-Repudiation* is a proof against fraud attempted or committed by the end user

---

9. The first three are borrowed from the book by Larry J. Hughes, Jr., *Actually Useful Internet Security Techniques*, Indianapolis, IN: New Riders Publishing, 1995.

A number of commonly known security technologies and techniques—userids and passwords, encryption algorithms, digital signatures and certificates, scanning and systems verification tools, firewalls, intrusion detection tools, and others—are all the security measures and tools underlying one or several of the security facets defined above. Chapter 8, dedicated to ASP security, provides a more insightful analysis of security requirements and measures.

Security impacts the NC architecture by pressing conditions on processes and constraints on design. It is common knowledge that increasing security may adversely impact other qualities such as maintainability, manageability, and flexibility. Simply stated, Security may make it more difficult, if not impossible, to perform certain functions associated with these other qualities.

Strategy. Designing Security for an NC starts with the identification of security policies derived from the analysis of security threats to, and risks and acceptable losses of, the NC in question. Security policies are used to build the so-called security architectures consisting of different security measures permeating all aspects of the NC's architecture and processes.

While the primary security implementations are mostly software-based (e.g., username/password, firewall rules, encryption, intrusion detection, log analyses), NCs must also support certain physical security through a compartmentalization of facilities, systems, and networks. This can be done both for NC production activities (development, testing, staging, training, etc.), as well as operations (monitoring and management, change and problem management, help desk, backups/restores, etc.) The planning and implementation techniques as well as mechanisms for doing both are similar. By establishing the security implementation practices early, NC management can ensure faster time to market, higher value to its customers, higher quality, and reliable and trusted security for its customer implementations.

Manageability

Definition. Manageability impacts the entire NC architecture: the hardware, software, networks systems, and the facilities. It has two functional dimensions: reactive and pro-active. Reactive manageability is exercised via three distinct activities: monitoring, analysis, and control. Monitoring polls the architectural components for status information and/or gets this information sent by these components either according to a predefined schedule or as problems or failures occur. Once received, this information is analyzed to determine if corrective actions (controls) are needed to bring the components (or whole systems) back to their original state. An example of reactive manageability with manual control is provided in the description of Flexibility earlier.

Proactive manageability is the ability to modify (change, replace, remove) the NC architecture components as desired. It is usually planned and uses the same controls as the reactive manageability. Proactive manageability depends on the ability to monitor, log, analyze, and model operational parameters of NC.

Manageability has strong relationships with other Qualities. It generally has an inverse relationship with Security, as was discussed previously: increasing security usually tightens Manageability and vice versa. Improved Manageability helps improve overall Availability, enhance Flexibility, and may impact Usability if, for example, the GUI can be configured remotely.

Strategy. The quality of Manageability of an NC's architecture depends on two facets: (1) the sophistication of monitoring, analysis, modeling, and control tools and (2) the ability of the NC architecture to work with these tools. Both can be planned.

Recapping Qualities

The Qualities described so far are not the only ones used for designing NCs. Many more Qualities exist such as Serviceability, Portability, Interoperability, and others. The list of Qualities can potentially be endless. A few points on how to use Qualities for designing the NCs are as follows:

- Weight. Different qualities have different degrees of importance or weight in architecture design. A medical portal NC may emphasize Security (perhaps, at the expense of Availability); industry portal NCs may be more concerned about Scalability; ASPs about Availability, and so forth. Technologies, business type, and perceptions about risks and allowable loss are but a few important criteria that determine the implicit weight of Qualities in the design decisions of NC architecture.

- Complex Relationships. All Qualities are interrelated. Changing one may impact another. Examples abound: higher component Reliability increases overall Availability, stronger Security may adversely affect Flexibility and Manageability, horizontal Scalability increases the costs of Manageability and Serviceability, and so on. Yet, clever architecture design may at times make up for the deficiencies of certain Qualities, for example, while component reliability is key to increasing service availability, server redundancy can also contribute to increased availability.

- Integrated View. Since the relationships among Qualities are complex and always shifting, an integrated view on how they impact design decisions is preferable and strongly recommended.

Architectural Methodology

A simplified high-level view of the steps of Methodology for designing NC architectures using 3DF is shown in Figure 5.8.

The very first, and very important, step is to select a proper Framework. This may appear somewhat surprising since 3DF has already been introduced earlier. However, there are many tacit assumptions incorporated in 3DF to support the design of NC. They are:

- 3DF's transaction orientation;

- Assumption about a large number of users expected to be talking to the NC;

- Strong functional cohesion existing among certain components and services within an NC architecture empowering the segregation into tiers;

- Directional constancy of information flows in the stack of layers and between the tiers, and so forth.

There could be many other classes of applications that use the Internet technology, yet operate under a different set of implicit or express assumptions. Or, there could be applications using a completely different technology. Then, the Architectural Framework appropriate for that scenario may be different from 3DF.

Figure 5.8 *A three-dimensional NC development methodology.*

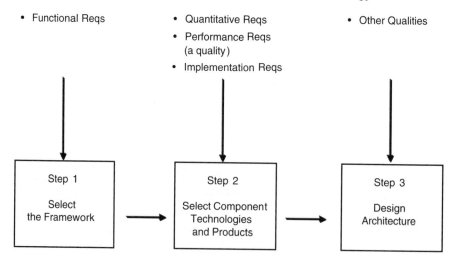

So, the first step of Methodology is to select the Framework. The inputs into this step are the Functional Requirements, depicted in Figure 5.8, which help understand the nature of applications to be implemented. With this information in hand, the selection of the Framework can be done in a number of ways:

- By using prior experience (that's when an experienced architect is indispensable)

- Through a deep understanding of the needs of applications and their environment

- Having familiarity with other frameworks and/or access to a "framework library" if one exists

- Attempting to see through the nature of applications, their environments, and applicable/available technologies in the manner similar to the brief discussion above about functional cohesion, relationships, information flows, and so forth.

The second step of 3DF Methodology is to assemble and organize information about how to populate the tiers and layers with technology solutions, products, and services. The inputs into this step are the Quantitative, Performance, and Implementation Requirements. Quantitative and Performance Requirements are needed for selecting the right technologies and products to meet the scale (not scaling, yet) and scope requirements of the NC system and its performance characteristics. The Implementation Requirements help define the constraints on this implementation in terms of preferred technologies, incumbent components and services, as well as preferred design and development methods.

The last step of Methodology introduces Qualities. It is here that the NC architecture designers would start bringing in different solution sets to address the diverse quality requirements to design the final NC architecture. For example, if Scalability is a critical issue, architects would decide on the use of horizontal or vertical scalability designs and bring in proper solutions; if Security is very important, security specialists may decide to implement multiple firewalls between the tiers, harden the operating systems, build directories for authorization data with secure internal access, and deploy reverse proxy mechanisms for authentication. If Availability is important, architects may choose to use multiple servers with a backup and dynamic load balancing.

Implications of 3DF and Methodology to ASP

Equating the ASP with the NC at the beginning of this chapter was a necessary condition for casting the ASP into the NC model in order to analyze its architecture, design characteristics, and methodologies. Useful as it was, this equating was a necessary but not sufficient condition to complete the ASP analysis. The NC is only the ASP's architectural foundation. A real ASP is expected to act as if it were multiple NCs, one per customer. Yet, this ASP may not be a simple sum of multiple NCs. It must be a smart assembly of tiers and layers with the capabilities that collectively meet the service requirements of multiple customers. This implies an overarching spirit of commonality for certain architectural and management elements, for example, the sharing of components within tiers and layers, scalable designs of software and hardware to decrease future incremental costs, common management tools and processes, and many other synergistic features and functions applicable across a wide range of customer applications and service requirements. What these synergies promise to gain is wide-ranging cost economies of scale, scope, learning, focus, and logistics, just as defined in Chapter 4. Without these synergies, the ASP's business potential could be compromised and its value propositions to its customers greatly diminished.

Leveraging NC's Framework

Here is a simple example showing how such synergies are possible. The example is made to look realistic by the use in the illustration of real products from real companies.

Suppose (as shown in Figure 5.9) there is one ASP providing access to *different* applications over the Internet to N customers whose *many* users access ASP via *three kinds* of client devices: browsers on PCs, WAP-based wireless devices, and XML-based automation clients for Business-to-Business (B2B) exchanges. Suppose there are *two* types of application platforms, one based on Sun's EJB and one based on Microsoft's COM/DCOM. Suppose there are *four* types of Integration layer implementations: IBM's MQ/Series, BEA's Tuxedo, as well as asynchronous Java messaging services (JMS), and synchronous Java transaction-based services (e.g., JTS), to Resources that understand JMS and/or JTS. Suppose also that all users' transactions flow back and forth through all tiers of this ASP. And finally, assume that the ASP's external network can easily handle all transaction volumes without experiencing any performance problems. How does this ASP work?

Figure 5.9   *ASP and its synergies.*

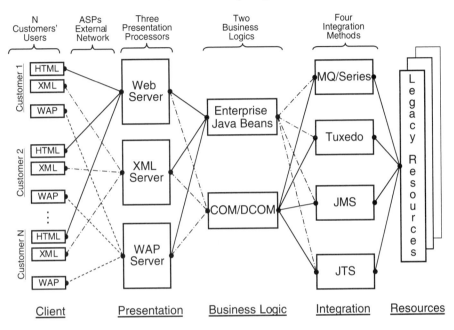

ASP and Its Synergies

The users of HTML browsers would send their transactions to one set of Presentation processors and the users of WAP would send their transactions to another set of Presentation processors supporting WAP, and finally, the users of XML (i.e., B2B users) would send their transactions to yet another set of processors. Note, though, that the notion of a processor doesn't necessarily imply a separate instance of hardware platform and its operating system. From this point on such instances will be called servers or server sets.

In the next step, user transactions processed by Presentation servers would be dispatched to their Business Logic's designated applications running in one of the two application environments: EJB or COM/DCOM. Finally, these multiple applications would deal with Integration using one of four methods: MQ/Series, Tuxedo, JMS, or JTS.

ASP's Generic Cost Economies

If customers needed a separate NC each, there would be N separate NC environments. However, in an ASP, these N different NC environments are collapsed into one ASP environment with a synergistic collection of shared components within its tiers and layers. Proper routing on behalf of all such components helps resolve the resultant communications mesh.

Thus, in this example, there are N customers, three user access technologies, two application environments, and four methods of integrating with Resources. However, there is only one ASP that supports all these N customers by substituting its own architecture for those of their multiple NCs.

Summarily, here is a brief analysis of the varied economies achievable by the ASP by leveraging the NC architecture. Chapter 9 offers a deeper analysis of these economies.

- In the Presentation Tier, the number of server sets depends on the number of protocols used (WAP, HTTP/HTML, XML), but not on the number of customers. This spells economies of scale.

- In the Business Logic Tier, the number of server sets is determined by the number of application environments (EJB, COM/DCOM, etc.), not the number of customers or applications. The result is economies of scope and scale.

- Since all server sets must support multiple customers, larger and more scalable servers could be used, in every tier. This leads to economies of scale.

- Similar economies of scope and scale could be achieved within the Integration Tier and even Resources (e.g., multiple database instances running on a single machine).

- If an ASP should narrow down the variety of environments it supports (e.g., only HTTP/HTML in Presentation and EJB in Business Logic tiers), and perhaps, convert applications to using these technologies only, it can achieve the economies of focus.

- Economies of learning and experience are achieved when an ASP selects the tools and products more appropriate for its business purposes.

Incidentally, as is frequently true for many new businesses, learning is one of ASP's most critical factors to success. Here are a few examples of what ASPs can learn and subsequently leverage.

- How to select tools, materials, products to improve Qualities and services, in the context of the NC-based ASP architecture;

- How to staff organizations and how to recognize, accumulate, and propagate knowledge inside these organizations;

- How to recognize effective business and ASP operational processes and institutionalize them.

Managing NCs and ASPs

Figure 5.10 uses two blocks of stacks to represent the NC and ASP Architectural Layers and their corresponding management disciplines, respectively. The left block shows the NC Management Services (assumed implemented in the NOC) and the stack of the NC's Architectural Layers to which these services apply. The right block shows the ASP Management and ASP Consulting Services, both applied to the ASP's Architectural Layers.

An ASP delivers to its customers the management services similar to those of the NC's, except that the ASP delivers them to multiple customers. For that reason, the ASP's management tools (software and hardware) and services must be able to isolate, track, measure, and report on each customer's systems separately, without commingling information, and in compliance with that customer's SLAs.

Figure 5.10   *ASP's management functions.*

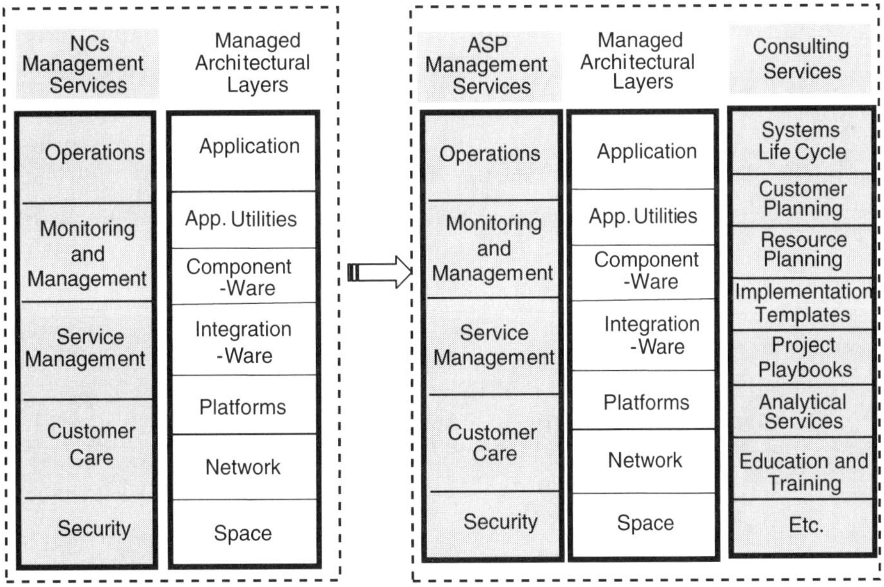

ASPs may also offer a broad range of professional services including:

- Systems Life Cycle services delivered either by the ASP's own professional services or by contracted-out systems integrators, consultants, and contractors;
- Design and implementation of Analytical Services such as trend analyses;
- Continuous education and training, and so forth.

To be efficient, ASPs may also have developed other customer service and support disciplines such as resource planning, implementation templates, and project playbooks. The ASP management services—traditionally and professional—are discussed in more detail in Chapters 6 and 7.

Costs Saved or Costs Spent

As was shown previously, ASPs can leverage the component-based NC architecture to create cost economies. The next step is to add Qualities to the architecture and observe how Qualities affect these economies. While in general, Qualities are known to increase costs, certain synergies between them also hold the promise for cost economies. For example,

- Redundant facilities required by multiple customers to increase availability can be shared;
- Fixed costs of scalable products can be shared;
- A powerful firewall can protect multiple customers without much commingling, if any; therefore allaying customer concerns;
- A comprehensive (and scalable) suite of network and systems management tools and processes can apply to multiple customers and even used throughout the entire ASP.

These are obvious synergies. However, the real potential for cost economies would very much depend on an ASP's ability to manage all the complexity of delivering Qualities. Or, speaking in the service provider's language, the cost economies potential would ultimately depend on the types of Service Level Objectives (SLOs) and SLAs between an ASP and its customers. Chapter 7 addresses the ASP's SLAs in more detail.

To recap, while in the absence of Qualities the real cost economies of ASP are easy to identify (costs saved!), adding Qualities introduces higher costs (costs spent!), but value added. Since the ASP

markets are so young and little heuristic data is available, only analytical and theoretical insights into the ASP cost economies (this
book being one of them) are possible.

Summary

This chapter offers foundation ideas for developing ASPs. Some of
them are summarized here.

- Designing ASPs requires a solid understanding of client-server
  and network computing (NC) paradigms, their characteristics,
  legacies, costs, benefits, and potential.

- The recommended approach to visualize an ASP is via an NC's
  Architectural Framework—a three-dimensional space of
  Application Tiers, Systems Layers, and Services Qualities
  dubbed as 3DF. In 3DF:

  - Tiers are a logical or physical arrangement of application
    functions that request services from, and provide them to,
    each other. NC's Tiers are ordered according to the logical
    (or physical) flows of application information.

  - Layers are represented by a stack of well-ordered service
    components each receiving requests for services from the
    layer above and consuming the services of the layer below.
    Layers are designed to aggregate as much pertinent func-
    tionality at the individual layer as possible and minimize
    inter-Layer interface complexity.

  - Qualities are descriptive architectural characteristics
    requiring specific strategies for their implementation. Qual-
    ities differ by tiers and layers.

- The ASP architecture is initially based on the designs of the
  NC, yet accrues new and powerful synergies due to its multiple
  customers using similar components. These synergies can be
  translated into cost economies. Striving for and achieving such
  synergies helps create ASP business strategies.

- The complex management requirement for ASPs are key to
  their ability to deliver value to customers and achieve their
  profitability margins. They are described in detail in Chapters
  6, 7, and 10.

Chapter 6

ASP Types and Services

This chapter consists of three discernible parts. Part One includes two sections, ASP Topology and ASP Data Centers, focused on the structure of a typical ASP and its components. The first section, ASP Topology, provides visual examples of a hypothetical ASP and its NOC connected by the ASP network across the United States and globally. It also shows how the ASP architecture is distributed across multiple locations. The second section, ASP Data Centers, offers brief insights into the structure and components of an ASP Data Center itself.

Part Two consists of one section only, Taxonomy of ASP Types and Services, describing an approach to categorizing the ASPs and their services into four distinct types. These ASP types flow from the reviews of existing ASP business models (co-location, Web hosting, storage services, etc.), from mapping these models against the layers of ASP architecture described in Chapter 5, and the general understanding of traditional Data Center functions and ASP management expectations. Part Three details the services of all three ASP types: Co-Location and Managed Infrastructure Provider (MIP), Application Infrastructure Provider (AIP), and a Pure-Play ASP.

ASP's Topology

Geography and Data Centers

Figure 6.1 depicts the topology of a hypothetical ASP with its Data Centers situated at multiple key locations in the United States and possibly in foreign countries (see Link to Other Countries from New York). The ASP network links all data centers together. Some ASPs are network providers themselves, while others lease or outsource their network to other carriers. Whatever the arrangement, the network is a critical component of practically every ASP's services portfolio. Since it impacts the performance of distributed applications and customer access to them, an ASP must be in control of its network.

Figure 6.1 also shows the NOC located near Dallas's data center. The best NOC implementations use their own management network (not shown in Figure 6.1.), which may or may not have the same topology as the one an ASP uses for customer traffic. This network is frequently called a management network and typically uses network facilities other than those the ASP uses to carry customer traffic.

The question of how many data centers to build and where to build them is mired in controversy. First, it very much depends on the types of services offered. For now, it suffices to say that some ASPs expect customer personnel to be present at, or visit, the hosting facilities, while others are accessed via the network only and hence neither they nor their users should worry about where the data centers are located.

Next, many existing ASPs' topologies differ widely and, whether for objective or subjective reasons, many ASPs pursue aggressive expansion plans no matter what services they intend to offer. Subjective reasons for this vary: some ASPs want to offer broad-range services including customer visits (e.g., co-location), others intend to become wholesale providers, leasing their facilities out to other "retail" ASPs, whose requirements are not known as yet. One objective reason for ASPs building multiple data centers is to address network performance problems. Customers and their users accessing hosted applications may be using different network providers resulting in less predictable performance. So, if an ASP has a local data center, local network access can be better controlled.

Another quite powerful reason is human psychology. Many customers still prefer having their data centers within a reasonable drive's range. This reason may go away in the future, yet old habits die slow. Finally, there are other, subtler reasons for distributing data centers geographically:

- When data centers are large and have already maximized or exceeded their intrinsic economies of scale, expanding existing centers or building new ones at other locations may become economically identical propositions.

- Different locations may have different regulatory requirements, especially in foreign countries. This may necessitate the use of different technologies, processes, and staffing.

- Some regulations, and hence some customers, may require using local data centers for security reasons.

- Finding or attracting qualified staff may compel ASPs to locate data centers at or near centers with attractive cultural or recreational amenities.

- Access to network facilities (e.g., the Internet NAPs[1]) may stipulate the data center location decisions.

To sum up, the geographical distribution of Data Centers is a fact of life attributed to diverse technical, marketing, and psychological reasons.

Figure 6.1 *Topology of a typical ASP.*

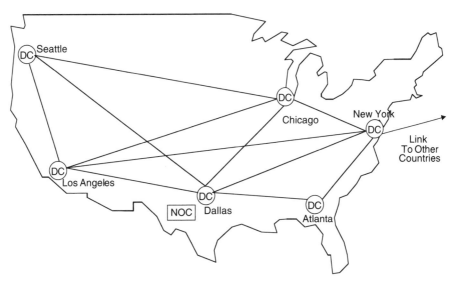

---

1. NAP—network access points, for example, MAE West, the major Internet junction near San Jose, CA.

Example of ASP Architecture

As was mentioned in the discussion of Application Tiers in Chapter 5, clients are almost always located far from the ASP Data Centers. These Data Centers don't cover a client's functionality, but do host the other four tiers: Presentation, Business Logic, Integration, and (possibly) Resources. Also, as was mentioned before, tiers may be distributed geographically and networked. The reasons for distributing ASP tiers vary for different customers or applications, including:

- Locating the Presentation Tier closer to users to improve network performance;

- Using the Presentation Tier as a content proxy located closer to users to minimize the bandwidth consumption in the network and improve user access to content;

- Situating Resources at a secure site where Business Logic and Integration Tiers cannot be placed;

- Using alternate locations for certain tiers when the original Data Center is full;

- Business Logic Tier needing to access customer legacy systems (most common example), but not locating where the Resources Tier is;

- Business Logic needing access to multiple Resources scattered geographically.

Figure 6.2 depicts a hypothetical implementation by a wholesale ASP of a hosting customer's application distributed across the ASP's multiple facilities: Client and Presentation Tiers in New York, Resources in Seattle, and Business Logic and Integration Tiers in Chicago. The hosting customer may be an ASP customer or a retail ASP itself offering unique application services to its own customers (or users) in the New York City metropolitan area. The retail ASP has a deep understanding in the particular application provided to its own users or its own customers on a subscription basis. But it doesn't have the expertise or experience in building and running the Data Centers, or in hosting and managing the hardware and software systems, or in networking. That's why it contracted with the wholesale ASP. Yet, it is not concerned about where the facilities of its wholesale ASP are physically located as long as it can reliably obtain satisfactory service guarantees from the wholesaler.

Figure 6.2   *Distributed ASP tiers.*

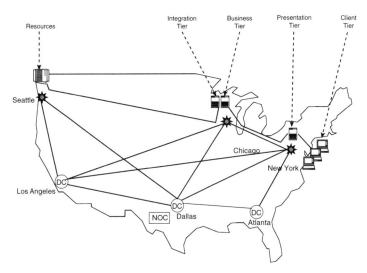

Over time, this retail ASP's user base or population of its own customers may expand beyond New York. If needed, it may then approach the wholesale ASP for locating Presentation proxies in other geographical locations and/or even contract with another wholesale ASP to support quality network services to access a Presentation Tier in New York. The topological flexibilities due to tiers and service diversity offered by numerous providers offers a great many possible options and solutions.

ASP Data Centers

Each Data Center is a physical environment—usually a separate building, but could be a set of floors in a shared building—used to house and host customer's servers and other architectural components. Data Centers offer a comprehensive set of architectural and environmental services such as raised floors, HVAC temperature control systems, and seismic bracing (to name a few).

Figure 6.3 depicts a schematic representation of a hypothetical Data Center along with the major components considered to be must-haves for all Data Centers. Additionally, Data Centers offer a wide range of physical security measures such as fire prevention (e.g., smoke detection and fire suppression systems), physical access control with guards on duty 24x7x365, security alarms, and video surveillance.

A key word for Data Centers is *redundancy*. This implies redundant fiber trunks (or other media) linked to multiple network carriers, redundant power supported by duplicated stand-alone power generators (e.g., gas or diesel), redundant HVAC systems, and others.

Figure 6.3 *ASP Data Center and essential components.*

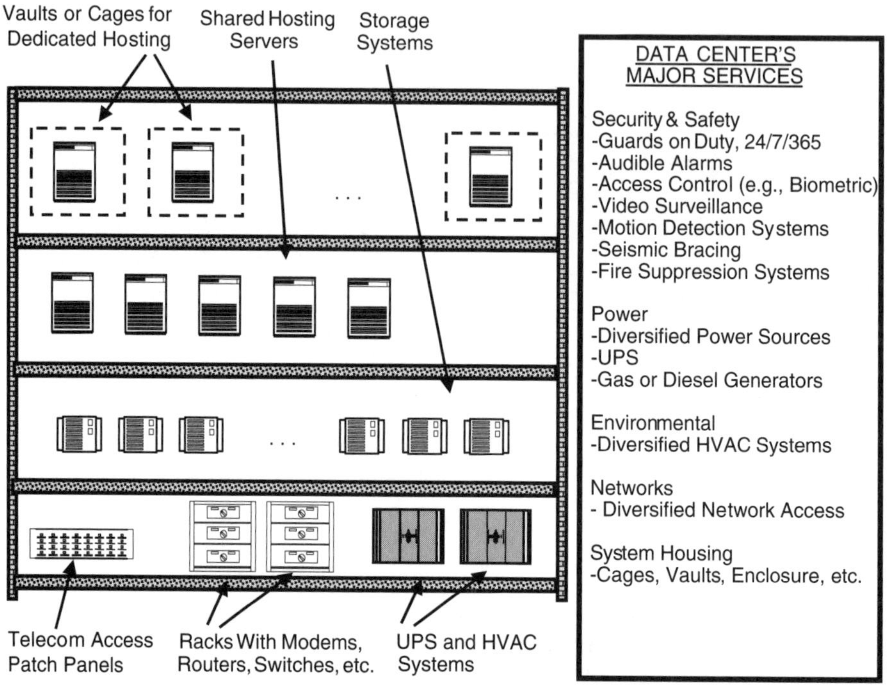

Vaults or Cages for Dedicated Hosting

Shared Hosting Servers

Storage Systems

DATA CENTER'S MAJOR SERVICES

Security & Safety
-Guards on Duty, 24/7/365
-Audible Alarms
-Access Control (e.g., Biometric)
-Video Surveillance
-Motion Detection Systems
-Seismic Bracing
-Fire Suppression Systems

Power
-Diversified Power Sources
-UPS
-Gas or Diesel Generators

Environmental
-Diversified HVAC Systems

Networks
- Diversified Network Access

System Housing
-Cages, Vaults, Enclosure, etc.

Telecom Access Patch Panels

Racks With Modems, Routers, Switches, etc.

UPS and HVAC Systems

REALITY CHECK

NEWS BYTES ABOUT ASPS AND THEIR DATA CENTERS

"AT&T operates a large number of Data Centers around the world, and has dedicated 6 (six) Data Centers in the U.S and one in Europe for Internet Hosting. Additionally, AT&T has announced plans to build seven Data Centers this year. AT&T also plans to have a total of 26 Data Centers by year-end 2002, including centers in Asia, with the availability of these centers to be announced shortly. In addition, AT&T has the flexibility to provide facilities through Concert, its Joint Venture with British Telecom." (From ATT Standard Proposal for Managed Services, Q3/2000)

"IBM and Qwest Communications yesterday announced a long-term alliance in which IBM will build 28 new Internet data centers over the next three years . . . . The new relationship will give Qwest a total of 42 data centers in the USA and Canada; 14 are expected to be operational by the end of this year." (March 28, 2000 InternetNews – ASP News Archives)

Taxonomy of ASP Types and Services

ASP Service Components

Figure 6.4 borrows from the right part of Figure 5.10, yet gives it a different interpretation. In Figure 6.4, every stack represents a dimension of the ASP services.

Figure 6.4 *ASP service components.*

ASP Service Components

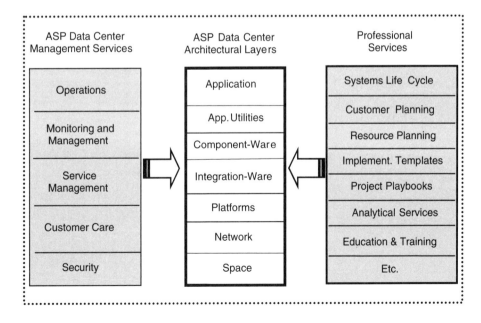

- The central stack describes the layers of 3DF architectural framework. These layers are reasonably stable and agree, in general, with how the network computing architectures are described and built today.

- The left stack describes the five ASP Management disciplines. Reducing ASP Management to a mere five disciplines may appear incomplete. A more comprehensive description of the ASP Management is found in Chapter 7.

- Finally, the right stack is the most arbitrary. It flows—as did some other lists of ideas and features earlier—from a generalization of experiences and published features of "soft" services provided by existing ASPs. This stack's components are the most flexible and subject to change.

Using these three stacks is a convenient way to explore the ASP services. Before this exploration begins, however, here are some disclaiming words on the material relevance and time scope:

- The ASP industry is evolving rapidly. It is almost certain that by the time this book is published, most services defined will change and require updates to their functions and descriptions.

- However comprehensive the descriptions of the ASP services may be, no ASP should be expected to implement them all.

- All services are defined within the technological capabilities of the time frame in which this book was written.

Taxonomy of Service Providers

Chapter 1 listed a few types of service providers. This section tries to do the same but more accurately and in greater detail. It assembles the common service provider acronyms used in the industry (as of the time of this writing) and maps them against the NC/ASP architecture layers defined in Chapter 5 and earlier in this chapter.

At the end of the year 2000, Sun Microsystems published the White Paper entitled "The Elements of The ASP Market."[2] Using the content from that White Paper (page 6), albeit with some modifications, Table 6.1 offers the common service provider acronyms and their simple definitions.

---

2. This White Paper can be found on Sun's Web site: www.sun.com.

Table 6.1   *A Smorgasbord of Service Provider (SP) Acronyms*

ACRONYM	*STANDS FOR...*	*PROVIDES*	*EXAMPLES*
ISP	Internet Service Provider	Network access and application services	AOL, Earthlink, Mindspring, ATT Worldnet, etc.
ISV/ASP	Independent Software Vendors going ASP	Hosting of their own established software applications	Oracle Business Online, Peoplesoft's eService, JD Edwards' Jde.sourcing, etc.
NSP	Network Service Provider	Network Backbone Infrastructure and services such as voice-over-IP, VPN, bandwidth management, etc.	Quest, Uunet, Concentric, BT, Enron, BellSouth, etc.
FSP	Full Service Provider	Turnkey Enterprise Services, IT Services (including Application Lifecycle)	EDS, CSC, ATT Worldnet, etc.
CSP	Capacity Service Provider	Hosting of commercial Web sites (essentially, co-location—Co-Lo—business)	ATT, AboveNet Communications, IBM, etc.
MHP or MIP	Managed Hosting Provider or Managed Infrastructure Provider	Servers and Net Equipment; Net, System and Service Management, Operations, and Customer Care, provided to either in- or out-sourced customer installations.	Exodus, ATT, Conxion, etc. (MHP may have own data centers)
AIP	Application Infrastructure Provider	The entire application hosting infrastructure (all but servers and OS)	LoudCloud, Breakaway, etc.
IPP	Internet Presence Provider	Hosting of commercial Web sites	Exodus, UUnet, etc.
PSP	Portal Service Provider	Aggregator of network services and content	Yahoo!, AOL, Netscape, MSN, Excite@Home, etc.
SSP	Storage Service Provider	Outsourcing of data storage and backup services	GTE Data Services, Storage Networks, Qwest, etc.

Table 6.1 *A Smorgasbord of Service Provider (SP) Acronyms (Continued)*

ASC/ASD	Application Service Creator and Developer	Create application code and license it as an aggregator or ASP itself	Biztone.com, Niku, Weborder.com, Portera, etc.
ASP	Application Service Provider	ISVs and custom application hosting and management over a WAN	USinternetworking Corio, Applicast, etc.
Pure-Play ASP	Application Service Provider	Hosting ISV applications over other's infrastructures. Usually, functionally or vertical industry focused	eAlity applications support business management processes for small and medium clients.

Figure 6.5 correlates the Service Provider acronyms from Table 6.1 to the layers of the ASP stack presented in Figure 6.4.

Figure 6.5 *ASP layers and service provider acronyms.*

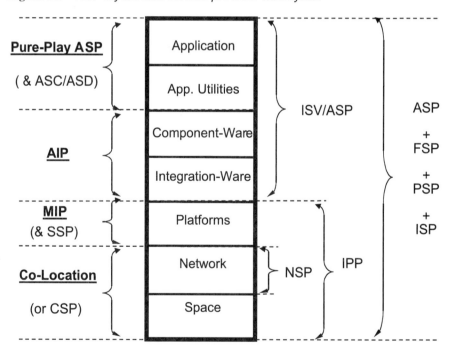

Essentially, there are four basic provider types: Co-Location, MIP, AIP, and Pure-Play ASP. They are all shown in bold on the left side in Figure 6.5. Why are they called *basic* types? Well, there are three reasons for that. First, their corresponding layers are all adjacent, making up an entire ASP stack. Next, every other provider is made up of these basic types (except NSP). Finally, the basic types are totally invariant to:

- Business strategy (whereby SSP and IPP are not invariant to strategy);
- Markets served (PSP);
- Application types (ASC/ASD);
- Application life cycle (FSP);
- Legacy and incumbencies (NSP, ISV/ASP).

Figure 6.6 provides another view of how the service provider's basic types map into the ASP architectural layers.

Basic Service Provider Types

Figure 6.6 is key to defining the ASP service types. Its left side uses the layers of the 3DF architectural framework borrowed from Figure 6.4.

Figure 6.6   *ASP types.*

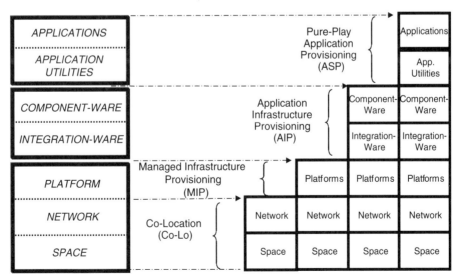

Service Provider Taxonomy

The right side of Figure 6.6 shows how these layers stack up to define the ASP types. Dashed lines with arrows delineate the layers comprised by each ASP. However, it should be noted that the boundaries between the ASP types are flexible. Each ASP may "push" these boundaries up and down by adopting functionality from either the layer above or below. This flexibility helps the real-life ASPs to achieve unique competitive advantages.

All ASP types are interdependent. Co-Location Providers deliver real estate to Managed Infrastructure Providers; Managed Infrastructure Providers host servers and software for Application Infrastructure Hosting; and Hosting, in turn, runs Pure-Play Application ASPs. Pure-Play Application ASPs don't own an infrastructure and, hence, contract infrastructure services out. However, when they provide service guarantees to their customers they act as general (prime) contractors for all other services underlying and supporting their applications. The four major types of ASPs are defined in the following section.

Co-Location Providers

A co-location ASP's key offerings are systems and network-ready data center space and network access. Customers must bring, install, and run their own equipment and applications. Co-location providers may assist customers at some of these tasks for a fee charged by their professional services.

Co-Location Services—Space

Geographical Proximity

To be exact, co-location is more than just real estate for housing hardware and connecting to telephone companies' networks. Its key criterion for success is geographical proximity to its customers. That's why, and this is also true anecdotally, a Service Provider with data centers in many cities, or a potential provider planning to build data centers in many cities, is most probably a co-location ASP. However, moving up the stack of the ASP Model, starting with Managed Services, geographical proximity to the end-user is becoming less important and, most likely, will eventually be irrelevant. Indeed, Managed Infrastructure or Application Infrastructure Providers' customers don't need to visit data centers where their servers and applications are run. Hence, for Managed Infrastructure and Application Infrastructure ASPs, fewer remote data centers are sufficient.

Real Estate/Facilities

The co-location facility must have raised floors for wiring, powering, conditioning, and maintenance. Also, the floor space must allow,[3] and provide for, installation space in the form of vaults, cabinets, enclosures, and so forth. Finally, the co-location service provider should offer storage space to its customers and, if necessary, temporary or permanent office space to house customers' personnel for installation, support, management, and maintenance.

Environmental Provisions

Historically, hardware has always been sensitive to environmental conditions. While engineers continue to develop denser processor and memory chips and infinitely smaller mechanical devices—such as microscopic optical routers with mirrors, or miniature disk drives—environmental requirements still remain very tight. Dust particles, fluctuating temperature and humidity, altitude, seismic characteristics, vibrations, EMI,[4] and even acoustics must be carefully considered when building data centers, as even minor changes to these parameters have been known to render data centers unreliable.

Proper environmental conditions must be provided through the use of state-of-the-art climate control systems, redundancies, fire protection measures, and other pertinent measures to ensure 24x7x365 data center availability and sufficient operations and customer support.

A co-location ASP that addresses all these issues early on stands to benefit long term from improved customer satisfaction and retention as a result of higher operational reliability of hosted systems.

Power and Light

Providing ample conditioned AC power reliably and consistently is a major challenge for most co-location (and other) ASPs. For that, there are qualitative and quantitative reasons. The qualitative reasons flow from the need for "clean" power, a major requirement for running contemporary mission-critical business applications. "Clean," in this context, implies a very high reliability of power delivery (many nines after the period, see Chapter 5), which can be provided both by buying power from the utilities (with historically low nines) and sup-

---

3. This brief description of IT co-location is sufficient to distinguish it from the telephone company's co-location. Despite a common name, these businesses are very different.

4. As alternating electric current creates electromagnetic waves, electromagnetic interference relates to the undesired, so-called dirty emissions, from all types of electric and electronic equipment causing interference with other equipment.

plementing it with the standby power-generating and power-switching facilities to increase the nines, yet at a very high cost.

Quantitative reasons are based on the need to deliver large amounts of this clean power in a concentrated fashion to large data centers. And finally, another quantitative reason arises from the market and regulation-related quandaries that were impacting the power industry in the United States at the time of this writing (2000 to 2001).

Co-Location Services—Networks

Access to Bandwidth

Most customers want data centers to provide PoPs[5] from different NSPs and the ability to quickly switch providers without impacting their business. Five issues are behind this requirement: network service *Access Diversity, Availability, Scalability, Manageability,* and *Security.* The first three services are described here. A discussion of Manageability and Security is deferred to the next sections.

- A co-location ASP must be able to connect to its customers in a variety of different ways. Thus, for *Access Diversity,* co-location ASPs must offer, at their data centers, dedicated link services at different rates over different types of carrier networks, for example, ATM, Frame Relay, dial up, leased line services, and so forth. It is also frequently assumed that these carrier networks are IP-enabled.

- For *Availability,* co-location ASPs must provide for private and public peering. The former assumes the presence of PoPs from different multiple NSPs, both regional and global. The latter implies access to major public Internet peering points such as MAE-East (Virginia), MAE-West (California), and others like Sprint NAP (New York). Peering is a style of communications (between computers or networks) without the help of a central dispatcher (server, backbone network, etc.) Thus, the Internet idiom for peering underscores direct connections between different Internet traffic carriers. The aforementioned MAE-West, MAE-East, and others points are big Internet exchange points where traffic flows from major Internet carriers converge.

- *Scalability* implies that these networks have access to spare capacity to be utilized as customers' demands increase. Sometimes it implies an instant capacity, or in common parlance,

---

5. A PoP is a Point of Presence, a term used by network careers to designate the location where they bring their lines.

capacity on demand. With the emergence of media-intensive applications, bandwidth access and "instant" scalability have become ever more critical.

Content Services

As discussed previously in "Access to Bandwidth," the advent of bandwidth-intensive applications—such as streaming media—brought about a new set of requirements for how to network content and content-intensive applications. Very quickly, a young industry[6] for content distribution, delivery, and management emerged and became an important purveyor to service providers. A co-location ASP can offer Content Services in several ways: first, through partnerships with the Content Delivery Service Providers (CDSP) who already offer Content Services, or by deploying its own content distribution servers in its data centers and over partner NSP's networks. This enables these co-location ASPs (as well as other ASPs hosting on this ASP's infrastructure) to distribute and deliver content quicker by serving it from caching servers at the edges of the network—e.g., closer to the subscriber—to improve performance, scalability, availability, customer satisfaction, and retention. Content Services deployed by co-location providers may include, but are not limited to, these varied capabilities:

- Caching frequently accessed content closer to end user on the network's edges;
- Implementing streaming media caches;
- Smoothing out traffic spikes for servicing customer requests;
- Minimizing "upstream" traffic of service requests for already cached content;
- Replication, synchronization, distribution, delivery, and management of all types of content used by customers' end users and/or a particular customer within its virtual network;
- Management and monitoring of content delivery to ensure performance and data collection for reporting and billing;
- Load balancing the available network capacities.

Most content technology is installed on NSPs and, since access to the NSPs belongs in the co-location layer of the ASP Model, the ASP's Content Services belong in the co-location ASP's portfolio of services too. Content Services are a major source of co-location ASP's differentiation.

---

6. Well-known brand names in Content Services products are Inktomi, Akamai, and Mirror-Image.

VPN Services

Besides providing access to bandwidth, co-location ASPs are well positioned to offer Virtual Private Networking (VPN). VPN is implemented as a corporate Intranet replacing a private WAN. It connects a company's multiple offices over the Internet yet still ensures manageability and robust communications security (e.g., using tunneling protocols) typical of private networks.

Ultimately, the combination of the Internet, content services, and VPN creates a powerful competitive advantage for Co-Location.

Elements of Co-Location's Management Services

While Chapter 7 will offer a detailed description of the ASP management, this section provides a "sneak preview" of management services uniquely belonging to co-location ASPs.

Based on the definitions of services in Figure 6.4, co-location ASP's Management Services fall into five categories: Operations, Monitoring and Management (M&M), Service Management, and Customer Care, and Security.

Operations Management

Facilities, environment, and power management are bona-fide co-location ASP services. They fall under a formal charter of providing space for physical computer "gear." By ensuring smooth operations, they are the functions of Operations Management. Disaster recovery policies and procedures also fall into the category of Operations Management, as well as all other activities, the ASPs perform on behalf of their customers in emergency situations.

M&M

Co-location's M&M consists mostly of network management services, including, but not limited to the following: configuring, connecting, monitoring, switching, and swapping; preventive, protective, and detective means for combating network service denials; and, finally, management functions for the co-location ASPs' own networks (if any). The latter function addresses traffic distribution, congestion avoidance, and other issues of network optimization. Often, co-location ASPs will outsource this function to the NSPs.

Service Management

Service Management is the largest category of the co-location ASP's services. While Chapter 7 dedicates considerable space to the discussion of Service Management, this section focuses mostly on the unique aspects of co-location ASP's Service Management functions: provisioning, configuration, and SLAs.

Provisioning. With a co-location ASP providing mostly physical capacities to its customers, provisioning concerns all things physical required within the data centers. This includes raised floors, wires and cables, racks, cabinets, enclosures, vaults, physical security devices, power and HVAC equipment, NSP connection distribution and patch panels, network management probes, content distribution servers, network (and systems, if needed) management servers and consoles, and others. Other key functions of provisioning include diverse management applications like Asset Management (see later) and their business related processes; facilities planning activities based on the assessments of business growth, market trends, and customer preferences; and so forth. These latter functions are closely related to the challenge of growth accommodation (see Change Management later), and many other business planning and operational issues. Depending on the point of view, not all aforementioned services may be expected by customers and/or required for a co-location ASP's operations. It is critical, though, that co-location ASPs have a comprehensive portfolio of services to meet varied customer requirements in a timely fashion and remain flexible and attentive to their dynamic and changing nature.

Configuration Management. Configuring a customer's space (racks, vaults, enclosures, power, HVAC, etc.) and network connections must combine the experiences of historical Telco co-location enhanced with the requirements for dynamic management, SLA Management (see following), and most importantly, Change Management, to accommodate growth (see following).

SLA Management. While Chapter 7 offers a detailed description of ASP's SLAs, several of them are unique to co-location ASPs. These SLAs are focused on the availability of the network, power, HVAC, security systems, content distribution, and so forth. Another category of SLAs focuses on time to respond to change and problem requests, escalation procedures, and status updates, to name just a few. Co-location ASPs must specify who is involved in escalation procedures and financial liabilities for failure to deliver on these SLAs. Co-location ASPs must be able to measure these SLAs, conduct statistical performance analyses in order to correct and improve their future operations, and then report these SLAs to their customers.

Customer Care

Customer Care is another co-location ASP's category of services with unique characteristics and requirements. Key requirements for Customer Care are reliability, availability, and responsiveness. Customers need around-the-clock access to experienced personnel who understand customer needs and are capable of answering service-related questions. Help must always be a phone call away and provided with a reasonable response time. While qualified personnel are critical at data centers and support help desks, tested processes and well-defined roles and responsibilities are required to ensure timely problem resolution and proper communication with customers. Customer Care's major functions of a co-location's ASP are as follows:

Change Management. A key challenge is accommodating customer's growing needs. The problem is akin to that of allocation and fragmentation of a computer hard disk. When customers want to expand and install new systems physically close to their old ones, it may not be possible to do, as most adjacent space may be occupied by other customers' installations. Accommodating customer growth is not as easy as disk defragmentation and requires sophisticated planning.

Problem Management. Problem Management records and tracks problems from initiation to an ultimate closure using a system of trouble tickets. Both Problem Management and Change Management work closely with Asset Management, which is the ASP's internal system of accounting for all the ASP's assets. Asset Management may not be a customer's concern. However, the co-location ASPs may offer their Asset Management services to help track customer assets too, for a fee.

Help Desk/Call Center. Traditional help desk/call center services may address both the internal and customer requests (see also Customer Care).

Security

Traditionally, Telco's co-location data centers offered mostly physical security, and it was limited at that. Today, ASP's data centers can be turned into truly secure world-class facilities with ID key cards, biometric scanners (for finger prints, eye retina reading, etc.), and closed circuit television systems. Today, it is possible to literally enclose IT environments in bulletproof structures virtually impermeable by fire, flood, and even terrorist attacks, all while maintaining their services. There are companies[7] that produce such enclosures adaptable to different size, space, form, or shape.

Privacy between hosting customers is another important requirement. Privacy, however, goes beyond physical security provided by vaults, cabinets, and enclosures. It relates to a more complicated issue of sharing CPU cycles, bandwidth, and applications. These and other issues are addressed in subsequent chapters of this book.

While more sophisticated network security capabilities belong to the next type of ASP service, MIP (Figure 6.6), co-location ASPs offer

---

7. Otto Lamperz, GmbH, of Germany, is a well-known manufacturer of solutions for the physical protection of IT.

physical segregation of network access for different customers, provide certain types of firewalls, and firewall management. Co-location ASPs can also offer certain prevention of denial of service. By collaborating with the NSPs, running their own network management, and pursuing policies for network availability (e.g., through facility switching, on behalf of their customers), co-location ASPs may prevent malicious sabotage, spamming, or some forms of eavesdropping.

Managed Infrastructure Providers

There is nothing new about providing NSM services on a contractual basis. Most Telcos have been doing so, though mostly for telephony applications, for decades. And in the mid-1980s, the non-Telcos— EDS, IBM, Andersen, and CSC, to name a few—also started offering remote NSM to their systems integration and outsourcing clients. The emergence of the Internet as a viable means of business communications stoked anew the interest in remote management. As of this writing, there are literally hundreds of providers offering remote management services ranging from the diagnostics of customer-premises Windows PCs, to monitoring and management of powerful UNIX servers, to management of complex applications. It is important to emphasize that all such services are provided *remotely* and delivered from a provider's NOCs to the customer-premises systems. These providers are exactly what the market calls the Managed Hosting Providers (MHP; see Table 6.1).

This book, however, uses the term MIP to describe a slightly different type of provider. Applied to the ASP, the term MIP refers to those who *host* customer systems and applications over their computing and networking infrastructure and *then* provide management services. These are hosting MIPs and their spectrum of services is much broader than that of the remote management ones.

A hosting MIP is the next immediate ASP layer above co-location (Figure 6.6) and below AIP. It offers customers computing, storage, and networking platforms, both hardware and software, on which to host and run customer applications. MIPs procure these platforms, install them in their data centers, and provide customers access to them on a rental basis. Customers install their applications on MIP platforms and run them remotely. MIPs also offer network and systems management services to help ensure continuous operations of customer systems according to customer requirements and service guarantees written into the SLAs. Some MIPs don't require that *they* procure the equipment. These MIPs accept customer-purchased systems. Platform ownership is only an accounting issue and doesn't conceptually change the MIP services.

MIP's management services apply to all hosted systems (hardware and software) including the Web, messaging and application servers, data storage systems, diverse security devices (firewalls, intrusion detection systems, encryption accelerator boards, log servers, etc.), load balancers, routers, and switches; operating systems, and so forth. MIP may also provide such ancillary services as software distribution and deployment, customer/user provisioning, support of multichannel clients (e.g., wire-line browsers, wireless devices, PDAs), integration with different types of telecom networks and their OSS,[8] billing, and some other functions.

MIP's Professional Services offer systems life cycle services such as platform installation, personalization, testing, tuning, configuration, and customization; analytical services such as configuration and capacity planning, modeling and testing; as well as certain marketing support services. Because of the nascent commoditization trends—due to platform convergence and other reasons discussed in Chapter 3—these auxiliary services are becoming the MIP's key marketing differentiators and frequently its major sources of revenue. Many MIPs also offer customers access to basic Internet applications such as those typically offered by traditional ISPs including email, chat, Web access, news, and others.

Since MIPs are built on top of co-location ASPs, their characteristics are additive to those of co-location. Thus, MIPs inherit most co-location ASPs requirements and services,[9] competitive advantages, value propositions, and economies. Still, MIPs offer more. These unique characteristics of MIPs are addressed later.

Notwithstanding this author's ambition, the following material cannot claim to cover all the bases of the MIP services. It tries to frame their scope and show only those services that belong to MIPs and not to the co-location and AIP Providers (i.e., those below and following the stack of ASP types, respectively; see Figure 5.10). Therefore, the material offers only brief definitions of the MIP services. Chapter 7 provides more comprehensive descriptions of the ASP management services, including those of MIP. And Chapter 8 offers a detailed description of security concepts and practical security measures.

---

8. OSS—Operational Support Systems (common term in the telecom industry).
9. Geographical Coverage is an exception.

How an MIP Serves its Customers

There are six basic activities describing how an MIP services its customers:

- Study the customer architecture and its requirements and procure all the system and network components needed for building it, including hardware and software.
- Deliver and deploy all these components in its data center(s), and build the customer architecture.
- Hook all these systems to the MIP's own or NSP's networks, as needed.
- Build a management network over the customer's architecture. To do this an MIP installs the network and systems management agents and probes on all architectural compnents—for example, servers, routers, load director, firewalls, OS, switches, and so forth—which, for the purposes of NSM, are frequently called *managed elements*. Finally, it links all these agents and probes, over the MIP management network, to the MIP's Network Operating Center(s) (NOCs).
- Install the runtime environments of systems and applications, jointly with the customer.
- Engage the customers to conduct integrated systems tests. These tests draw on the MIP's knowledge of customer architecture and its implementation and on the customer's knowledge of its applications. The tests could focus on different things such as functionality, performance, availability, security, and so forth.

The scope of the tests in the last step is quite broad and may include the following activities:

- Certify customer architecture
  - Validate all systems configurations against customer architectures;
  - Confirm that all systems are properly installed and connected;
  - Ensure that systems are provided with management probes and agents;
  - Check for necessary operations support software (e.g., for backup).
- Verify that the MIP's management system's connections are established to all the architecture's managed elements
- Conduct the stress test of the entire architecture and all its components (managed elements) to determine their initial performance levels

MIP Platforms

Servers, Routers, Switches, and so forth

It may seem, at first sight, that an MIP should support all types of platforms (computer servers, routers, switches, etc.), in all conceivable configurations, all the time. As logic goes, this will enable an MIP to accommodate all kinds of customers and hence capture larger market share. That would be great, of course, except that the price of such universality may be too high. It simply is not advisable to be a "jack of all trades" in the MIP business. It would be expensive and impractical as it would require supporting multiple sets of skills, developing multiple vendor relationships, marketing and sales strategies, and business models. In one word, it would dilute the business focus. Hence, most MIPs use a more pragmatic, targeted approach: they limit the number of supported platforms. Normally, their decisions are driven by their preferred vendor relationships or marketing strategies and visions or by a combination thereof.

Another strong reason for this pragmatism is the phenomenon of platform convergence discussed in Chapter 3. With the advent of new technologies, such as Java, that promote and enable platform independence, third-party developers, ISVs, and many endusers are becoming more focused on how good their solution would be rather than what platform it would run on. This "solution-oriented reality"[10] presents MIPs with the generic requirements of the platform's reliability, scalability, price-performance, security, and manageability. It doesn't point MIP to a particular platform but provides a set of parameters, based on the generic requirements, to help MIP select a preferred platform. Similar considerations should guide platform vendors in designing their products.

Content Services

Based on the definitions of ASP types (see Figure 6.6), co-location ASPs offers hosting facilities (e.g., real estate) and MIPs offer hosting platforms and their management. Content services are add-on services both for co-location and MIP ASPs and either one may vary the degree of sophistication of their content services offerings to meet their customers' changing needs and achieve desired marketing differentiation. Still, if it reasonable to assume that MIPs are better positioned to understand (and care) about a customer's applications and hence help them design and effectively use content services. The types of applications standing to benefit the most from content services are software distribution, database replication,

---

10. Aaron Goldberg, "The End of the Alpha Vendor," *Upside Magazine*, September 2000, p. 32.

streaming audio/video, web-based publications, email broadcasts, and computer graphics (like medical records, e.g., MRI, X-Rays), to name just a few, all allowing ASP customers to better service their own and their end users' needs and quality expectations. While the earlier section on co-location ASPs provided a list of content services capabilities, two key concepts—caching and mirroring—are critical to MIP's portfolio of content services offerings.

Caching notably enhances end-user experiences while simplifying network performance management. Web caching improves quality of services (e.g., response time), reduces network traffic by delivering content from local caches, and protects both the content network and user experiences from overloads due to demand surges. Caching uses sophisticated algorithms to identify frequently used content and to either retain it at, or bring it across the network to the servers located closer to its consumers.

Mirroring is a data replication process used to bring static, non-cacheable content—in large volumes—to network locations closer to customers. Examples are authenticated FTP and Web sites, data-bases, and bundles of software to be distributed across the network. To enable mirroring for customer access, MIP must build IP redirection capabilities that will transparently point customer requests to the mirrored, local sites. Mirroring can dramatically increase customer performance and reduce network traffic.

MIP Space

The MIP's data centers differ from those of co-location services. In the co-location model, customer personnel come to data centers frequently to manage their installations and applications, the MIP's customers are expected to deal with their systems remotely. With a few exceptions, this is a common practice and it simplifies the MIP data center's requirements, vis-à-vis co-locations. Here are a few points on the subject:

- When a customer expands, co-location providers frequently face the challenge of situating new systems next to the old ones already surrounded by other customer systems. In the MIP data centers, where most customer systems are unattended, physical togetherness is not necessary. Instead of rearranging adjacent systems to accommodate growth, customer expansion systems can be located anywhere on the MIP floor, or even remotely.

- An MIP can focus mostly on a data center's peripheral physical security versus providing for secure isolation of customer systems from each other through vaults, enclosures, and specialty security devices.

- The MIP's own management network may service multiple customers, provided all security and privacy measures are addressed. In a co-location ASP, multiple customers always have separate management networks.

MIP Networks

The MIP network services and requirements are additive to, and built upon, co-location's network services—Access Diversity, Availability, Scalability, Manageability, and Security. The discussion that follows is, therefore, based on the premise that while co-location does provide bandwidth access, the more advanced services, such as a sophisticated network and systems management, fall mostly to MIPs. For the sake of avoiding controversy, it should be added that many co-location companies are gradually but steadily moving up the ASP stack (Figure 6.6), and are beginning to offer network and systems services similar to those of MIPs.

MIP's Private Networks

Most MIPs (and even some co-location ASPs) build private networks linking up their data centers together in order to compensate for the performance uncertainties of the overloaded and undependable Internet. To design these networks, many MIPs borrow from the book of traditional network designs. One key network design recommendation calls for a reduction in the number of network hops. These hops are the network intersections where traffic tends to be delayed, routed, and even lost. The more hops, the slower the traffic, the higher the uncertainty of message delivery, and the lower the quality of service. By minimizing the number of hops, MIP can build a network with the right balance of quality, reliability, and control in order to meet the most stringent requirements of modern business applications.

There are many different network topology designs possible to reduce the number of hops. Of them all, star-shaped networks are best. Thus, many MIPs strive to build their private networks as stars, as much as possible.

To summarize, an ideal MIP's private network should have the following capabilities:

- Data centers connected by a dedicated high-speed network infrastructure;
- System redundancy ensuring the availability of customer applications;

- Robust facilities with back-up and disaster recovery programs;

- Ability to handle contingencies, automatically and manually, via continuous monitoring, communications, automatic event processing tools, and on-site staff.

Another critical characteristic is network redundancy that contributes soundly to the overall network reliability and availability. For most MIP's private networks, redundancy can be achieved by the design when every network circuit serves as a backup for every other one and the redundant network topology that complements the aforementioned star-shape designs.

Connectivity to the Internet

A well-designed and managed MIP's private network is a major asset and a powerful value proposition to its customers. If it is large and ubiquitous enough geographically, or at least has data centers in major strategic geographic locations, the MIP network could support large-scale distributed business applications with their many dedicated connections to their many different customers (especially, the B2B links, which tend to be dedicated). However, if the MIP customer, or its customers (businesses and consumers), or its partners or endusers are widely scattered, the MIP's private network may not be enough. To improve on connectivity, the MIP network must have direct connections to the major Internet NSP's at virtually all of its own locations. The common term used for this is "direct peering" and it implies direct links into each geographical area's Internet backbones.

Network Bandwidth Management

An MIP must be able to provide scalable and reliable bandwidth to its customers. Effective bandwidth management and bandwidth availability are key to ensuring the MIP's support for ever-changing customer bandwidth needs. This translates into more specific requirements of constantly managing network utilization, providing bandwidth buffers to handle abnormal peaks, load balancing between data centers by dynamically directing traffic to the closest available servers via a single URL, allowing bandwidth reservation, and assuring access to the permanent reserves of bandwidth capacities.

Network bandwidth management also depends on the MIP's business models in relation to bandwidth pricing. Some MIPs employ usage-based charges (and billing), or flat fees, or combinations thereof.

IP Services

For Internet access and management, MIPs are expected to help their customers with some unique functions like IP address assignments, primary and secondary domain name service (DNS) services, access control support, and DNS and access control change management capabilities. These are very valuable services and, since they are the legacy of ISPs, MIP customers would always expect them.

MIP Management Services

The portfolio of management services offered by remote and hosting MIPs differ substantially. The hosting MIP, by definition, hosts customer systems. It is therefore responsible for provisioning and management of space, network, and systems (the former two possibly contracted out to a co-location provider), while a remote MIP is only responsible for remote management. The subsets of their management services are similar but are not the same. Here again, the hosting MIP may offer more because of its direct access to systems and networks used by the customer.

The following material explains briefly which unique management services MIP offers its customers. These services are broken down by ASP management categories, such as Monitoring and Management, Operations Management, Customer Care, Security, and Service Management. The purpose of this discussion is largely to differentiate the MIP management services from other ASP types. Later, Chapter 7 returns to these ASP management categories and describes them and their constituent functions at a much more detailed level.

Monitoring and Management

MIPs must offer a comprehensive gamut of monitoring and management services covering most of the network, server, Web, and storage systems (notice, no applications!). Some of the key requirements for the MIP Management and Monitoring are:

- Monitor system's health using standard protocols and interfaces;

- Implement secure management controls for remote dynamic reconfiguration;

- Employ comprehensive event management (perhaps, with other vendor tools);

- Collect data for predictive dynamic failure analyses to warn of problems before they occur (see also Problem Management);
- Conduct real-time performance monitoring and store results for review and analysis.

These hosting MIP management services must also include Event Management, Correlation, and Action Automation for analyzing the real causes of alarms and attempting to remedy these causes without involving, but reporting to, the ASP personnel. When automatic problem resolution is not possible, Monitoring and Management systems must escalate problems to Customer Care and Service Management. Monitoring and Management functions for remote and hosting MIPs are essentially identical, except where they are interfaced to security.

Many MIP Monitoring and Management tools come from the hardware/OS vendors themselves. MIPs use them to ensure the ease of systems management, optimal performance, systems scalability, application availability, and to manage multiple systems from a single management console while using simple, easy-to-implement interfaces (e.g., Java-based). Most of these tools are standards-based, allowing extensibility and easy integration with Simple Network Management Protocol (SNMP)—or even CMIP—platforms (e.g., Tivoli TMS, Computer Associates Unicenter TNG, BMC Patrol, and HP Open View), and offering secure active configuration management controls for remote, dynamic reconfiguration.

Operations Management

The spectrum of hosting MIP's operations management is similar to what any organization's internal IT performs and includes the following major functions:

- OS administration (patches, versions, systems software distribution, etc.);
- Comprehensive backup/restore and archival;
- Load management and batch jobs;
- Hardware and OS related contingency management processes, and so forth.

MIPs have full control of their hosting environment allowing for higher and more reliable service guarantees (captured in the SLAs) and potentially lower costs from diverse economies. However, this is just a logical deduction. While the possibility to prove this point always exists, no formal comparison of such services, to this author's knowledge, has been conducted yet.

Operations Management capabilities for remote and hosting MIPs are similar, except that hosting MIPs have better access to, and control over, their own facilities.

Security

While remote MIP's major security concern is network security, hosting MIP's security scope is much broader. If a hosting MIP is also a co-locator, it must offer all co-location security measures. If it rents space from others, it must bind them contractually for security. Additionally, hosting MIPs must provide many other security measures to hosted hardware and OSs, all ensuring separation of customer domains for access control purposes using firewalls, and other measures, such as:

- Intrusion detection systems;
- Defenses against denial of service attacks;
- Host level access control (for all hosts: servers, routers, storage systems);
- Systems and network logs;
- Secure OS builds;
- Specific systems and network architectures designs.

Customer Care

Key Customer Care functions that a hosting MIP is expected to offer are Help Desk, Call Center, Change/Request, and Problem Management. The first two are standard offerings, with tools and practices already well developed and used extensively for managing multiple remote customers. The latter two are defined in a little more detail here:

Change/Request Management. MIPs implement Change/Request Management processes to affect changes to hardware (servers, network equipment, and storage systems) and various OSs, and adding new customer users. Changes to the hosting MIP and its customer environments may arise from the operations management decisions for hardware upgrades, removal/replacement of faulty equipment, and OS version update and patch installations. While the latter may not necessarily result from customer requests, it is critical that customers be advised when changes to the OSs are made to ensure compatibility of the customer's applications with new OS versions. The MIP's customers can be end-user customers or other ASPs (e.g., AIP and Pure-Play).

Problem Management. MIP's Problem Management functions—Call Tracking, Problem Tracking, and Resolution Management—apply primarily to hardware and OSs. Problem Management is invoked by the Monitoring and Management function or via Customer Care (Help Desk and Call Center) for problem escalation. MIPs use various tools for Problem Management, many of which may be integrated with the Monitoring and Management and Customer Care applications.

Service Management

Service Management is the ASP's newest and most complex management category. While Chapter 7 introduces a formal framework for the ASP Service Management functions and offers their detailed descriptions, the material in this section focuses mainly on the service management functions specific to the MIP. They are provisioning, configuration, and SLA management.

For provisioning, MIPs must deal with a broad set of suppliers, vendors, and service providers. MIPs negotiate and sign contracts spelling out agreed-upon lead times, quantities, and other terms for all deliveries so that the MIP can rely on its provisioning cycles and reliably commit to customer projects.

Provisioning of Computing Platforms. An MIP must demonstrate superior expertise in the technology and management of its supported computer platforms and related operating systems. Most MIPs therefore choose a few dominant platforms such as Sun Microsystems servers with Solaris OS or Intel Servers running Microsoft's NT, Linux OS, and others. The major requirements and expectations of the MIP computing-platform provisioning services are as follows:

- Specialize in the chosen technology;
- Demonstrate superior expertise in this technology;
- Have active provisioning and support contracts with the chosen technology vendors to meet customers' expectations for time to market and benefit.

Provisioning of Networking Platforms. Network Platforms for LANs, WANs, and VPNs—routers, switches, load directors, firewalls, and so forth—are selected to accommodate most customers' varied requirements for bandwidth, performance, network configurations, and management. Thanks to the maturity of major communications standards, most network platform products can interoperate and successfully integrate. This affords MIPs the freedom of combining and interconnecting equipment from different vendors without major compatibility concerns. Still, there are caveats. All such equipment must be managed. Since every vendor comes with its own management package and most of its equipment has its own MIBs,[11] Network Management must accommodate and integrate these multiple packages and train operators to deal with their features, performance and operational idiosyncrasies, and error/bug reports. The major requirements and expectations of the MIP networking-platform provisioning services are then as follows:

- Specialize, yet offer a complete portfolio of LAN and WAN equipment, for example, routers, LAN switches, load directors, firewalls;

- Demonstrate superior expertise in its chosen technology;

- Have active provisioning and support contracts with all equipment vendors.

Provisioning of Storage Platforms. Chapter 2 already addressed the "colossal upset" in which the "hard drive technology has improved at least 50% faster than computing power." Concomitantly, storage is assuming a life of its own, moving farther away from its "umbilical" connection to computing systems. Nowadays, businesses buy storage independently of computers and new MIP outsourced storage offerings are emerging rapidly. These offerings serve many markets, from consumers and SOHO[12] operators to larger corporations. These offerings include, among others, Network Attached Storage (NAS) and Storage Accessed Network (SAN) technologies.

NAS is a new storage paradigm in which storage devices are directly connected to a LAN rather than being integrated into servers. NAS allows easy and fast addition, removal, and change of storage devices without bringing servers down. With the relentless growth of data volume, said to be doubling every six months in some organizations, storage control is becoming a daunting challenge for most IT organizations. For MIPs, this challenge is further multiplied by the number of its customers. NAS offers a solution to this challenge. It is fast, easy to use, and economical (e.g., lower MIP data center labor costs).

SAN is a data communications networked environment that links dispersed servers and storage. It uses Fibre Channel technology for gigabit-speed connectivity among all communicating entities. SAN allows for very flexible network topologies that can support server-to-server, server-to-client, server-to-storage, client-to-storage, and other forms of data exchanges without adversely affecting server or LAN performance.

---

11. MIB stands for Management Information Base, a generic term used to describe the network managed device's control and reporting parameters. The most common protocol to talk to MIBs is SNMP, which has over the years survived numerous attempts to "overthrow" it.

12. SOHO—small office, home office.

Both NAS and SAN technologies are perfect for MIPs, offering design flexibility which can lead to higher service availability, increased scalability for computing and storage, and more efficient operations and management—all leading to manageable economies and competitive advantages.

Configuration Management. While a more formal definition of Configuration Management will be provided in Chapter 7, MIP's Configuration Management includes all the basic functions for the identification and naming of systems and network resources, tracking configuration changes, and defining, setting up, and reconfiguring these configurations as needed to ensure required levels of operational qualities (e.g., performance, availability, scalability, security, manageability).

SLA Management. Major MIP's SLAs deal with the operational qualities of hardware, OSs, and the network. Note that if an MIP contracts a co-location provider that provider may support some key network SLAs conditions such as network availability, throughput, and performance of network equipment. The general scope of MIP-specific SLAs may be as follows:

- Hardware and OS's SLAs:
  - Availability and scalability of servers/storage-systems/routers;
  - Alarm (Event) tracking, management, and remedial actions;
  - Security of all such systems (see MIP security services);
  - Administration of all such systems: backups/restores, contingency and disaster recovery processes, data archival, and so forth;
  - Software maintenance, for example, OS patch/version installation schedules and other terms;
  - Output management.
- Network SLAs:
  - Bandwidth size provisioning;
  - Data loss;
  - Delay characteristics;
  - Network availability;
  - Network throughput;
  - Performance of network equipment;
  - Customer Care SLAs such as: availability, response, waits, and so forth.

Chapter 7 provides a more comprehensive explanation of SLAs, service guarantees and their performance and measureability, and overall concepts of a service provisioning culture.

As of this writing, different service providers offer different SLAs. The absence of SLA standards hurts the ASP industry as it makes it difficult for customers to understand and negotiate ASP contracts. For that reason, the ASP Industry Consortium has started initiatives for defining and standardizing ASP SLAs and has published its first SLA White Paper for ASPs (November 14, 2000). More details on SLAs in general and specific SLA standards suggested by the ASP Industry Consortium can be found in Chapter 7.

AIP

Application hosting has evolved from traditional Web hosting in which a Web-hosting provider offered its customers floor space, network access, server capacities, choice of OSs to run under, and rudimentary systems and network management capabilities. Customers used to bring their own applications—mostly informational Web sites with limited interactivity—and then installed, ran, and managed them on the provider's servers by themselves. Additionally, the Web-hosting providers offered off-the-shelf e-commerce packages, of varying degrees of sophistication, to move its customers into interactive B2C and eventually into B2B electronic commerce.

As Web hosting has matured to the AIP, customers still bring their e-business applications, either developed by themselves or for them. Examples are the now commonplace B2C and B2B e-business endeavors, external and internal portals, and many others. Sometimes customers collaborate with providers in the development of their applications. The following material examines both of these situations.

The AIP is positioned one level up from the MIP and one level below Pure-Play ASPs (see Figure 6.6). When the AIP doesn't own or manage the co-location and MIP infrastructures, it contracts with co-location and MIP providers and, in addition to its own services, becomes ultimately responsible for them all. The entire package of the AIP services then includes:

- The facilities, hardware, and OS from the contracted co-location and MIP providers; and
- The AIP-specific offerings combining application infrastructure hardware, software, and services.

One real benefit enjoyed by the AIP—long promised by open systems and finally beginning to materialize—is design flexibility. The AIP-specific components can be designed and organized like the parts of a Lego set and then assembled per customer requirements. Figure 6.7 illustrates such an approach.

Figure 6.7   *AIP's component based services.*

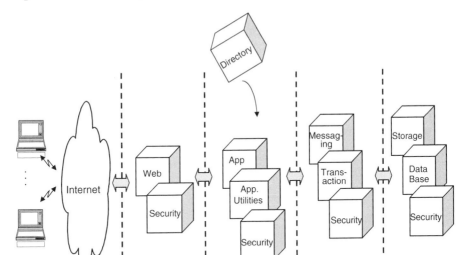

Besides providing systems components, the AIP is also expected to offer comprehensive professional services to help customers who want help in designing and implementing their applications. These services may range from a simple management-enablement of customer applications to a complete application life cycle of application design, development, deployment, and operational management. In fact, the AIP's major differentiation stems exactly from its abilities to provide such higher level services. The more capable the AIP is of providing life cycle services, the more successful it should be.

There is a caveat here, though, related to sharing. It is easy to imagine sharing floor space, networks, even servers and OS among multiple customers and still ensure the required levels of performance and security. However, the higher up the stack of services, the more difficult it becomes to find the *tangible* components to share. But the situation is not desperate. The analyses that follow help identify components that are candidates for sharing and leverage. Chapter 9 addresses the economic effects of such sharing in more detail. Chapter 10, on the ASP enabling technologies, offers some practical advice on the technologies to use to enable this sharing.

There is another form of sharing. Over time, as different business application implementations for functional or vertical markets likely become more common, complete repeatable solution sets made up of certain components will start appearing. This is already being recognized by some AIPs and Pure-Play ASPs focusing on certain functional or vertical markets (or a combination thereof).

How Applications Are Hosted

The AIP is the services domain where customer applications are hosted. Hosting a customer application at an AIP raises the following four important questions:

- What will be the application runtime environment?

- How will the application users access it?

- How will the application access legacy systems (programs and data)?

- How will this application be integrated with other applications the customer already runs or wants to run?

There should also be other questions—specifically those related to the technologies AIPs should use to enable satisfactory answers to the aforementioned questions and leverage for cost economies.

Two architectural layers defined in Chapter 5 (Figures 5.2 and 5.5), Component-Ware and Integration-Ware, represent the *anchor* architectural domains for the AIP. The word anchor is used intentionally as it addresses the layers attributed to the AIP in Figure 6.6. However, as will be shown later in the discussion of Pure-Play ASPs, the AIP services extend beyond these two layers, mostly up into Application Utilities and even Applications.

Hosting Customer Applications

Figure 6.8 shows the architectural tiers and layers based on the 3DF Architectural Framework from Chapter 5. Customer applications are placed in the Application Layer of the Business Logic Tier. They may also use Application Utilities and COTS provided by an AIP. Such Utilities and COTS may contribute handsomely to the AIP's economies of scope.

Figure 6.8   *How AIP hosts customer applications.*

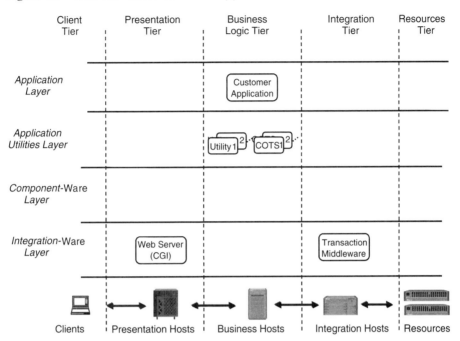

Customer applications need to talk to clients (to the left of Business Logic and Presentation Tiers) and legacy data and applications (to the right of Business Logic and Integration Tiers). When an application's business logic was implemented within the Web server itself (using CGI[13] programming) the Web server and client talked to each other directly. When this logic is moved to the Business Logic Tier, as in 3DF in Figures 6.8 and 6.9, the Tiers must talk to each other using standard protocols, such as HTTP, XML, and others.

Applications must also talk to legacy systems and databases. This is done via transaction middleware, located in the Integration-Ware Layer of Integration Tier.

Developing and Hosting Customer Applications

When a customer wants to design and develop its own e-business applications or have additional logic added to them, an AIP must offer application life cycle implementation services, usually through its professional services. Assuming that AIP consultants agree with

---

13. CGI stand for Common Gateway Interface, a mechanism for processing Web transactions within the Web server itself.

Figure 6.9 *Customer applications can fully populate 3DF.*

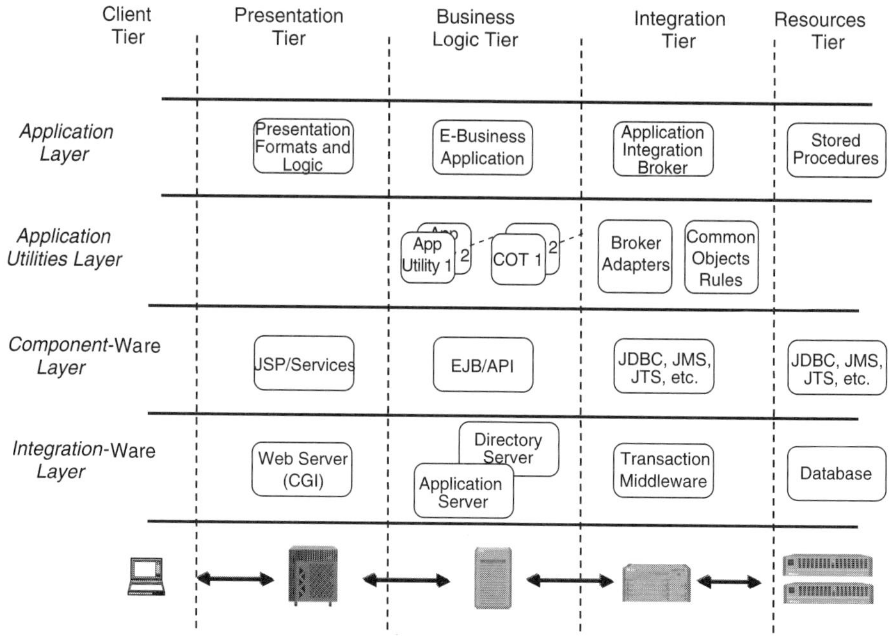

3DF, application architecture will be built within 3DF. Figure 6.9 depicts the components of this application architecture. The discussions of Middleware, Application and Web Servers, as well as Application Integration techniques provided here offer itemizations of the AIP technologies.

A Word on Middleware

Many components described here can generally be categorized as middleware. This includes Web Servers, Application Servers, and specialized transaction middleware packages for transaction monitoring and management. Middleware is the solution to the problem of heterogeneity encountered in most, if not all, distributed systems. In this role, middleware is used to hide the complex details of interfaces, protocols, and data formats used by distributed applications. "Complexity Hiding" is the key defining factor of middleware.

Unfortunately, a consistent and reliable definition of "middleware" doesn't exist. In and of itself, the term "middleware" is greatly overfranchised and means different things to different people. For some, it is the "stuff" residing between the end users and data. For others, it is whatever "lives" between the applications and systems platforms (OS and hardware). Still others believe that the entire environment of distributed applications is middleware. This brief on middleware doesn't strive to define it. It simply attempts to identify middleware the AIP can provide to its customers and possibly leverage for cost economies. The four prominent types of middleware used extensively in distributed network computing, including AIPs, are:

- Communications Middleware;
- Computing Middleware;
- Distributed File Systems;
- Database Middleware.

Communication Middleware helps to hide the complexities of communications protocols, interfaces, data formats (e.g., data objects), databases, programming languages, and execution environments—all to enable communications among heterogeneous components of a distributed environment. Specific technologies used for Communication Middleware are Transaction Monitors/Managers, Object Request Brokers or ORBs (e.g., CORBA); database stored procedures; and some simpler, older forms of middleware like RMI and RPC.[14] AIPs use all these middleware types. The ones shown explicitly in Figures 6.8 and 6.9 are Transaction Monitor/Managers.

Computing Middleware helps to hide the complexities of server hardware and OS (e.g., 3DF's Infrastructure Layer) to achieve higher systemic qualities in the application runtime environment. Computing Middleware allows application developers to focus more on application logic rather than on runtime infrastructure. Computing Middleware hides from the developers all the major computing environment management functions such as process threading, load balancing, caching, state maintenance and recovery, and so forth. Application and Web Servers shown in Figure 6.9 are distinctive examples of Computing Middleware.

Distributed File Systems represent middleware hiding the complexities of accessing data distributed among multiple heterogeneous file systems, possibly across a geographical expanse. The most characteristic example of distributed files systems is Network File System (NFS) developed by Sun Microsystems, Inc. and used for sharing files in a heterogeneous environment. Like some other distributed file systems, NFS hides the details about hardware and communication protocols behind file abstractions. NFS, however, doesn't hide the particulars of Operating Systems because file naming cannot be hidden from file access. NFS can be used across local (LAN) or wide area networks (WAN). Distributed File Systems are not shown in Figure 6.9. Yet, they are assumed to be there on server hosts, in all tiers, including legacy systems.

---

14. RMI is a remote method invocation; RPC is a remote procedure call.

Database Middleware enables access to heterogeneous databases. Different vendors implement database access protocols and stored procedures differently, even for standard "relational" database models. Database Middleware functionality is implemented within the Database Gateways that translate access methods and data formats. Applications speak SQL[15] to the Gateways. The Gateways then translate SQL requests into target database formats, route them to the database, and then translate responses back to the format of the original requesting application.

Application Servers

Application Servers are middleware platforms used to develop, deploy, and manage large-scale e-business applications while also ensuring the ability to integrate these applications with legacy systems and data. Application Servers usually come as a collection of development, runtime, and management components. As middleware, Application Servers efficiently support the major premise of complexity hiding. Thus, the developers writing applications for modern Application Servers should not be concerned about the following features:

High Performance gained from performance enhancement mechanisms such as:

- Support for multithreading capabilities of the host operating systems for a better utilization of CPU cycles;

- Diverse forms of caching, such as results caching, to avoid repeated computations or database link caching to reuse established connections.

Scalability for ultimate performance levels under heavy transaction loads via:

- Application logic partitioning, that is, a distribution of business logic among multiple servers, without violating the integrity of the overall application.

Availability achieved via auto-failover among multiple servers running applications.

Most Application Servers support applications written in Java, C, C++, and other languages. Most Application Servers' programming models extend to support newer programming technologies and paradigms such as J2EE, COM/DCOM, and others. For example, the Sun/iPlanet Application Server supports Java Servlets for presentation logic, Java Server Pages (JSP) for presentation page layouts, Enterprise Java Beans (EJB) for business logic, Java Data Base Connectivity (JDBC) for database access, Java Messaging and Java

---

15. SQL is a Structured Query Language invented by IBM and standardized by ANSI.

Transaction Services (JMS and JTS, respectively) for communications among applications and to legacy systems, and so on. All these Java-based technologies are implemented as component technologies that are inherently reusable, modifiable, scalable, and extensible. An ASP that focuses on certain functional and/or industry-specific domains of AIP is in a good position to leverage these inherent Java technology qualities to achieve significant economies of focus and scope (due to specialization and subsequent reuse), as well as scale (due to general scalability of Java technologies). These components "reside" in the 3DF's Component-Ware Layer (Figure 6.9).

Application Servers come as packages with multiple development and operations management tools. In summary, AIPs that master the Application Server technologies stand to benefit from them in many ways: better utilization of systems resources (scale economies), better reuse of technologies (scope economies), improved management of application environment (scope and scale), and faster time to market for application development and deployment and higher ROI.

Web Servers

Modern Web Servers have come a long way from simple programs supporting HTTP and exchanging static HTML with user browsers. Modern Web Servers are complex middleware platforms used to develop, deploy, and manage large-scale e-business presentation and navigation logic. Similar to Application Servers, Web Servers also come with sophisticated development, runtime, and management components. Web Servers hide the complexities of technologies ensuring all the major systemic qualities of the following:

- **Performance and Scalability** (e.g., caching, multithreaded and multiprocessor execution);

- **Reliability and Availability** (e.g., multiprocessing and automatic failover);

- **Manageability** (e.g., dynamic reconfigurations and management of access control lists);

- **Security** (e.g., support for SSL, digital certificates, integration with directory services).

Most modern Web Servers also implement Java Virtual Machines (JVM) to execute Java Servlets and Java Pages, and/or offer support for Microsoft's Active Server Pages, and can also execute JavaScript and some other scripting languages.

While most AIP's Web services are (and should be) Web Server neutral, most support popular servers such as Apache, iPlanet Web Server, and Microsoft's IIS.

Enterprise Application Integration

Application Integration Challenges

A typical ASP customer runs multiple business applications, usually from different vendors. Most such applications are exclusive vendor-specific compilations of data objects and business processes reflecting those vendors' philosophies and interpretations of application functionality. If a particular vendor publishes more than one application, those applications may be integrated in some fashion and work together in a business workflow. However, as a rule, applications cannot "talk" to other vendors' applications without major programming.

When a customer turns to an AIP, it usually already has many applications from many vendors. Yet the customer wants them to communicate to implement the business workflows. Making this happen is the major challenge facing virtually every company today and the AIPs as well.

What is the essence of this challenge? Each organization has established business workflows involving different business functions executed in a certain sequence. Each organization runs different computer applications to support and execute these business functions. The challenge is to make these applications talk to each other so that when a workflow must be executed, applications exchange data according to the workflow rules. Alas, applications cannot learn flexible workflow rules, and if they come from different vendors they would most likely use different data objects used for data exchanges.

Several approaches to solving this challenge exist. The first approach is to assume that all vendors' applications use standardized business objects—such as a purchase order, invoice, product, customer, user, and so forth—and can therefore easily exchange these objects among themselves. The assumption is useful, but unfortunately most efforts to standardize business objects for different functional domains and industries have met with limited success. While these efforts are still under way, the young ASP industry cannot afford to wait for them to succeed.

Another approach is to custom code all application interfaces. While certain economies of scale and scope can be achieved this way, especially with the use of XML and its derivative technologies, this approach can be complex, protracted, and offer low investment leverage.

Application Integration Brokers

Yet one more integration approach—that which uses Application Integration Brokers—provides for flexibility, reuse, scalability, and faster time to market. At the time of this writing, brokers are gaining popularity among systems integrators, e-business companies, and ASPs. This includes such ASPs as US internetworking, Inc., Corio, Inc., AristaSoft Corporation, just to name a few. Incidentally, all mentioned ASPs use the broker "webMethods Enterprise" published by webMethods, Inc.[16] There are other vendors of similar systems that may be dubbed as brokers, message or transaction exchanges, dispatchers, coordinators, and the like.

Application Integration Brokers manage the queuing, routing, processing, and storing of all data exchanged among applications. They support the following functions:

- Transformation of data object formats among disparate applications;
- Modeling of business processes across the enterprise in the form of implement-able workflows;
- Implementation and deployment of business processes according to recorded workflow rules.

Figure 6.10 depicts a typical Application Integration Broker and its components.

- Application Integration Broker (itself);
- Application Adapters;
- Business Logic Agents;
- Business Process Rules Database(s);
- Common Business Objects Database(s);
- Process Modeler.

The basic, conceptual design principles of the broker architecture are simple. The broker acts on business events generated by applications that require involvement of other applications and data exchanges among them. Each application has an adapter that "watches" for application events, such as receiving an order, processing an invoice, or posting to accounts receivables. When an event occurs, the adapter sends information about it to the Broker, which engages an agent who knows how to process it. The Broker agent then involves other applications by sending them messages and waiting for them to respond. It also maintains the workflow state and status needed for its recovery and recordkeeping.

---

16. See: www.wwebmethods.com

Figure 6.10 *A conceptual view of an Application Integration Broker.*

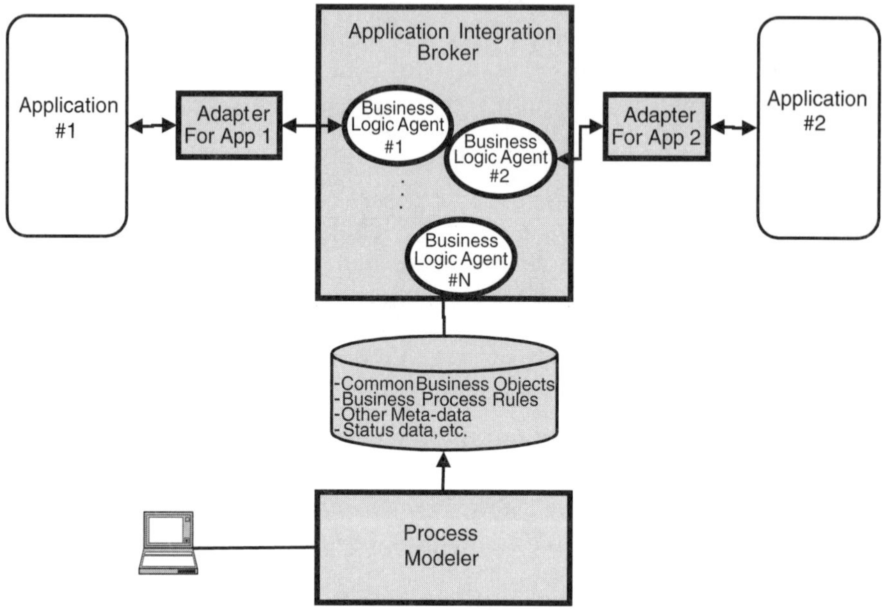

The information about process flows is stored in the Business Process Rules Database. Process Modeler is a designer-friendly (usually visual) program that allows process designers to specify the terms and actions of each process flow. The Common Business Object database contains business objects used by the broker like those already mentioned before: purchase orders, invoices, products, users, and others. Additionally, Broker packages come with monitoring tools allowing customers to observe their workflows visually on the terminal screen. Customers can watch and track the state of each workflow, the applications engaged or waited on for response, and exchanges of business objects.

Where in the five-tiered architecture depicted in Figure 6.10 should the broker be located? The first impulse is to place it in the Business Logic Tier. Indeed, it mediates application exchanges and handles workflow business rules among them. However, it doesn't execute any business logic itself. Also, there is absolutely no reason why it cannot be used to integrate business logic with legacy systems. For that, it may have to use the middleware services of transaction monitors, transaction managers, and database APIs. Thus, it is logical to place the broker in the Integration Tier (see Figure 6.9).

Summary Portfolio of AIP Services

Table 6.2 lists AIP service components. The list is long but by no means complete. Many listed components can also be found in Figure 6.9.

Table 6.2   *AIP Infrastructure's Shared Components*

Component	*Description*
Web	The Web Component implements the 3DF's Presentation Tier in support of user-interface. Assuming that the floor space, network, and hardware for servers and firewalls plus routers and LAN switches are contracted out to the co-location companies and MIPs, AIP provides Web Server software, management agents, and network. Additionally, the Web Component may offer implementation services—analysis, design, deployment, testing, and runtime management—and extra features to deliver and control the 3DF's Qualities of: • Load-balancing and redundancies (Availability); • Management agents (Manageability); • Host access control (Security); • Extra systems slots and/or other capacities (Scalability); • Booster hardware (Performance).
Application	The Application Component implements the Business Logic Tier's application software hosting environment—the deployment, operations, monitoring and management of customer applications. The Application Component may include a full-featured set of services for development of applications for deployment and management by Application Servers as defined previously. The Application Component may also include the implementation services similar to those of the Web Component.
Application Utilities	The Application Utilities deploy the reusable application components in the form of libraries and COTS. These utilities are usually implemented within the Business Logic Tier, but may also be implemented in the Presentation Tier. As was indicated earlier, the AIP's utilities and COTS may be business function or industry specific.
Database	The Database Component offers the necessary tangible elements for storing the customer's dynamic and static data. This Component may include server hardware and database, database development and system/storage management capabilities, and implementation services—all tailored for high-availability, scalability, management, and performance. The Database Component may also include the implementation services similar to those of the Web Component.

Table 6.2 *AIP Infrastructure's Shared Components (Continued)*

Directory	The Directory Component provides a (e.g., LDAP-based) directory service that aggregates information on user and group profiles, access control, administration, computing resources, hardware and software assets, and others.
	The Directory Component may also include implementation services similar to those of the Web Component.
Messaging	There are two aspects to messaging: application messaging and email. The former supports application integration; the latter offers generic email services and is used for notification purposes (e.g., alarming).
Application Integration Broker	The AIP may support Application Integration Brokering including broker implementation and operational management services similar to those described for the Web Component.
Transaction Middleware	This component implements the transaction monitoring and management services (middleware) at the Integration Tier. This component may also be a combination of server hardware and transaction management software (e.g., IBM's MQ/Series).
Security	There are many different Security Components including firewalls, intrusion detection systems, access control and authentication mechanisms, systems, host logs, and log analysis tools, and so forth. The AIP is expected to provide all ASP Security except for application security. The latter is dependent on application design. For applications supporting the application management conventions (see Chapter 7), the AIP may provide application security management as well.
	Chapter 8 provides a detailed account of ASP security.
Management	The AIP is expected to provide comprehensive ASP management services, such as M&M, Operations Management, Service Management (e.g., SLAs), and Customer Care.
	Chapter 7 provides a detailed account of ASP management services.
Content Services	The Content Services components offer solutions for managing the entire content life cycle from content creation through its distribution and deployment to its users. Content Services Component offers generic tools for handling specific content-intensive e-business applications such as product catalogs, portal sites, amassing and transforming large amounts of data, libraries of publishable materials, B2B and B2C content intensive applications (e.g., book selling), and others.
	The Content Services Component may also include the implementation services similar to the Web Component.

Table 6.2   *AIP Infrastructure's Shared Components (Continued)*

Development	An AIP may provide application and other types of development capabilities (e.g., for unique systems management) via its internal professional services organization or by contracting out development services.
	The AIP may need to have specialized development facilities.
QA Testing	Quality assurance and stress testing—unit, systems, change, and architecture feature testing (e.g., failover, clustering) are frequently conducted on a reduced-scale replica of a customer's system.
	The AIP may have to provide the services for supporting such activities.
Staging	For hosting customers with high expectations of systemic qualities, especially Availability, it is advisable to maintain an exact-replica secondary site used for application staging and real-world load and stress testing. If located remotely from the master site, the staging facility may double as a disaster recovery backup site.
	The AIP may have to provide the services for supporting such activities.
Disaster Recovery	Recovering from a disaster effectively requires special skills, processes, equipment, and facilities. The Disaster Recovery Component helps meet these requirements plus offers support for a failover to the backup site, if one is available.
Storage Management	Customers normally desire common management of their magnetic storage resources regardless of location, vendors, formats, storage organization, access protocols and security arrangements. The Storage Management component addresses these challenges using diverse management facilities—consisting of hardware, software, caches, and so forth—and comprehensive processes.

Pure-Play Application Service Providers

Market analysts created the term "pure-play" to designate those providers that focus solely on the *real application services* delivered to their customers online, and if possible, on a rental basic. Pure-play ASP's business models, marketing strategies, research, and operations focus mostly on business applications: value chain activities, data processing, or analyticals (see application taxonomy). In their purest form, they:

- Host applications whose licenses they buy from ISVs
- Don't host customers' custom applications
- Don't own the hosting infrastructure

While some *true* pure-play ASP's do exist, most *real application services* ASPs diversify beyond these restrictions. Some may host customers' homegrown systems, or help integrate them with their own standard offerings. Others may own the elements of the infra-structure, especially the management and security components. Still others may host applications they developed and possibly integrated with the ISVs' products. Thus, the term "pure-play" is simply a con-venient means for designating the ASPs residing at the very top of the ASP stack depicted in Figure 6.6.

Application Management Services

The application management services pure-plays deliver to their customers are complementary to those provided by other types of ASPs: co-location, MIPs, and AIPs. They fall into the same familiar management categories of Monitoring and Management, Opera-tions, Customer Care, Service Management, and Security, only this time they apply solely to the applications.

- Monitoring and Management is unique for every application. Chapter 7 describes the requirements and technologies used to management-enable applications, in general, and how to do so for ASP applications, in particular.

- The Application Operations function is conducted from an ASP's NOC and is closely related to Monitoring and Management.

- Customer Care is also application-specific. Traditionally, the ISV call-center/help-desks have been used for application sup-port. In other instances, the SIs who implemented these appli-cations offered a similar service. Most ASPs are using these approaches.

- Service Management is mostly about application SLAs, also discussed in Chapter 7 in more detail.

- Besides the opportunities of deploying the assorted security measures described later in Chapter 8, hosted applications may have their own unique security features built in. Manag-ing them is an application-specific challenge.

Pure-play ASPs also offer Professional Services, mostly those related to an application's life cycle. More about it is described in the next section.

Sampling of ASP Applications

Figure 6.11 borrows from an IDC research paper on ASP infrastructure software. It shows the top applications supported (hence, hosted) by ASPs and their relative popularity weights. These weights can be attributed to either nascent market demand or implementation feasibility of these applications over ASP versus the cost of direct ownership, or both. Note that the study and the ranking[17] "are based on a survey of senior technology executives for 29 ASPs." The report doesn't state if the 29 ASPs represent a statistical sample. Hence, the results may not be statistically relevant and are used here only for illustration.

Figure 6.11 *Top applications supported by ASPs.*

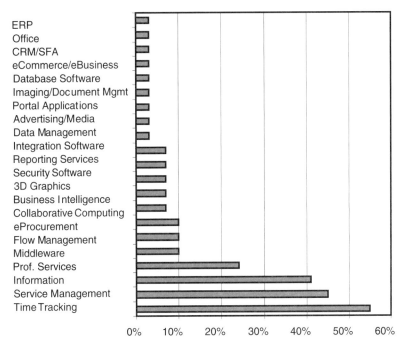

17. Amy Mizoras, Christian A. Christiansen, and Brian E. Burke, "Application Service Provider Infrastructure Systems Software," International Data Corporation report IDC #23083, September 2000.

ASP Application Taxonomy

Business applications are continuously evolving and growing. As business rules change and new technologies emerge—feeding on each other—the more complex the application landscape becomes: older applications get reworked for new business demographies (e.g., medium and small businesses), new applications get invented to address new and yet-untapped markets (e.g., e-commerce), and so on. The expanding computing diversity and platform convergence, as well as the newly discovered abundance of storage and bandwidth (discussed earlier in Chapter 3), all contribute to the complexity and feasibility of these application developments.

Designing taxonomy for a set of *any* entities is not an exact science. First, it is necessary to identify the set's salient characteristics and then arrange the entities along the dimensions of these characteristics. Numerous business application taxonomies have been defined in trade publications and market research papers on ASP. As Figure 6.12 shows, the three independent dimensions chosen for application taxonomy in this book are a Value Chain, Data Processing, and Analytical Applications.

Figure 6.12 *ASP application taxonomy dimensions: the horizontal value chain.*

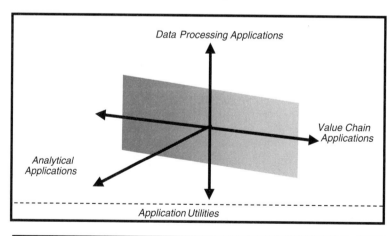

The Value Chain Applications dimension is the most important as it reflects on the key business functions—Supply Chain Automation, ERP, Finance, HR, Customer Services, Marketing, Sales, Customer Care, and others—all used to conduct and support the major business activities in a company. These applications fit within the various categories of a standard business value chain,[18] hence their name. The basic concepts of the value chain are described in the next section.

The vertical dimension is Data Processing. Commonly, the term "Data Processing" refers to an eponymous industry and a human vocation. However, in this chapter, it refers to business data and how it is processed in support of the Value Chain activities. Indeed, all Data Processing applications such as database software, imaging and document management, security software, middleware, and reporting exist for one and only one reason: to support business data and its processing. Still, despite this dependency, when speaking of the industry and vocation, Data Processing applications also have lives of their own. There is a caveat, though. For some enterprises, Data Processing is their core business. For them, different Data Processing applications will then reside within their Value Chain. For example, a multimedia production company will have multimedia applications throughout its Value Chain functional "containers"—from Inbound Logistics all the way to Service (see Figure 6.13).

Finally, the third dimension is Analytical applications. These applications also belong in Data Processing. Yet, the aforementioned Data Processing applications imply data manipulation: storage, movement, organization, presentation, and so forth. The Analytical applications process data to derive intelligence used for decision support. For example, in data mining, this intelligence is "extracted" from the hidden knowledge and relationships existing between the elements of the data. There are many examples of such applications: Web site visitation or click-through statistics are used to derive user profiles and for planning marketing campaigns,[19] product configuration engines[20] allow both internal personnel and external customers to configure products according to their criteria; data mining[21] helps identify hidden relationships to reveal trends; general purpose deci-

---

18. Michael Porter, *Competitive Advantage*, The Free Press, 1985, pp. 36–62.

19. Good examples are products coming from Broadvision www.broadvision.com and E*piphany www.epiphany.com.

20. For example, check www.firepond.com known for building car configurations for commercial sales, and so forth.

21. For example, IBM.

sion support tools[22] help analyze large data volume to arrive at the most relevant conclusions.

Value Chain Applications

About 20 years ago, Michael Porter of Harvard Business School invented the Value Chain as a tool for business analysis. Today, the Value Chain is used extensively as a framework for defining business activities and analyzing business strategies. Value Chains offer the following numerous analysis tools and applications:

- Terminology and Structure to *define* a business' activities and requirements;

- Methodology to *analyze* each activity within the Value Chain and its relationships with other activities (Porter calls these relationships "linkages");

- Techniques to *derive* cost and/or differentiation based strategies for competitive advantage, and so forth.

Figure 6.13 shows a classical Michael Porter's Value Chain. While its terminology is borrowed from manufacturing, the Value Chain concept has proven to apply to virtually any business. Both the Support and Primary Activities comprise multiple functional containers.

Figure 6.13 *Michael Porter's classical value chain.*

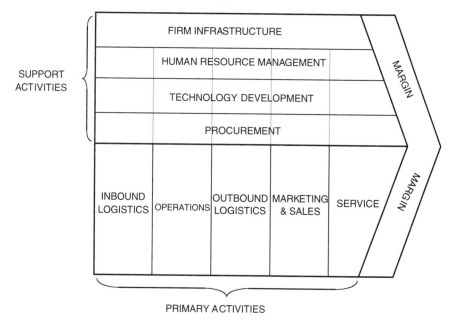

---

22. The new company, Network Decisions, was launched in late 1999. See "Former Novell Exec jumps into ASP Pool" by Deni Connor, *Network World*, Nov. 8, 1999.

The Primary Activities, in Michael Porter's words, are:

- *Inbound Logistics.* Activities associated with receiving, storing, and disseminating inputs to the product, such as material handling, warehousing, inventory control, vehicle scheduling, and returns to suppliers;

- *Operations.* Activities associated with transforming inputs into the final product form such as machining, packaging, assembly, equipment maintenance, testing, printing, and facility operations;

- *Outbound Logistics.* Activities associated with collecting, storing, and physically distributing the products to buyers such as finished good warehousing, material handling, order processing, and scheduling;

- *Marketing and Sales.* Activities associated with providing a means by which buyers can purchase the product and inducing them to do so, such as advertising, promotion, sales force, quoting, channel selection, channel relations, and pricing;

- *Service.* Activities associated with providing service to enhance or maintain the value of the product, such as installation, repair, training, parts supply, and product adjustment.

The Value Chain's Support Activities, also in Michael Porter's words, are:

- *Firm Infrastructure.* Firm Infrastructure consists of a number of activities including general management, planning, finance, accounting, legal, government affairs, and quality management.

- *Procurement.* Procurement refers to the function of purchasing inputs used in the firm's value chain, not to the purchased inputs themselves. Purchased inputs include raw materials, supplies, and other consumable items as well as assets such as machinery, laboratory equipment, office equipment, and buildings.

- *Technology Development.* Every value activity embodies technology, be it know-how, procedures, or technologies embodied in process equipment ... Technology development that is related to the product and its features support the entire chain, while other technology development is associated with particular primary or support activities.

- *Human Resource Management.* Human Resource Management consists of activities involved in recruiting, hiring, training, development, and compensation of all types of personnel.

Figure 6.14 shows Michael Porter's Value Chain as populated by the ASP Value Chain applications. Some of these applications come from the IDC report (Figure 6.11), and some from this author's primary Internet research and consulting experience. Obviously, numerous other applications can be added to this picture. The picture is not complete, nor can it ever be, due to the dynamics of market demand and changing application landscape.

Figure 6.14 *ASP's value chain applications.*

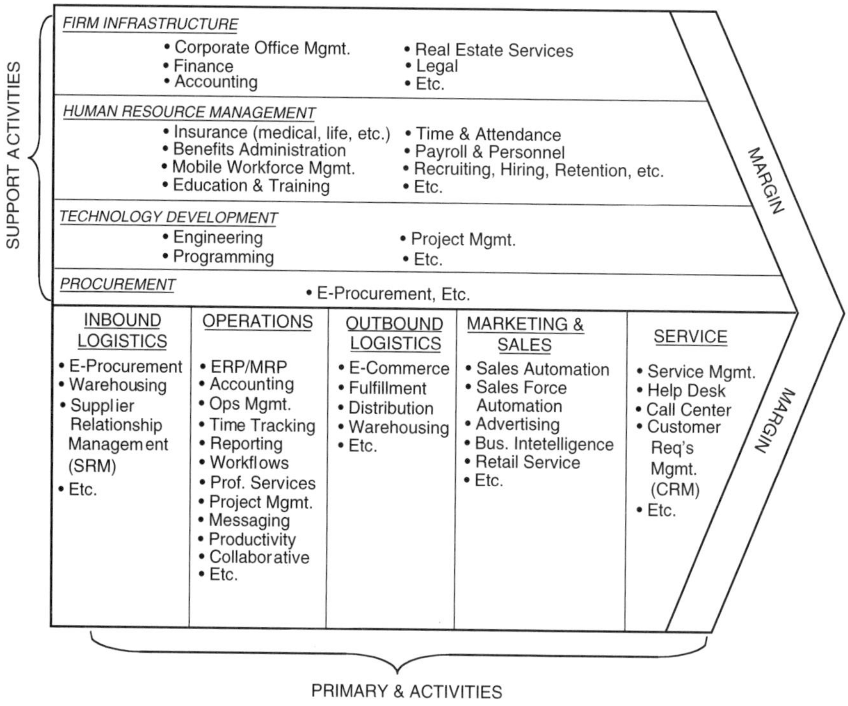

FIRM INFRASTRUCTURE				
• Corporate Office Mgmt. • Finance • Accounting		• Real Estate Services • Legal • Etc.		
HUMAN RESOURCE MANAGEMENT				
• Insurance (medical, life, etc.) • Benefits Administration • Mobile Workforce Mgmt. • Education & Training		• Time & Attendance • Payroll & Personnel • Recruiting, Hiring, Retention, etc. • Etc.		
TECHNOLOGY DEVELOPMENT				
• Engineering • Programming		• Project Mgmt. • Etc.		
PROCUREMENT				
		• E-Procurement, Etc.		
INBOUND LOGISTICS	OPERATIONS	OUTBOUND LOGISTICS	MARKETING & SALES	SERVICE
• E-Procurement • Warehousing • Supplier Relationship Management (SRM) • Etc.	• ERP/MRP • Accounting • Ops Mgmt. • Time Tracking • Reporting • Workflows • Prof. Services • Project Mgmt. • Messaging • Productivity • Collaborative • Etc.	• E-Commerce • Fulfillment • Distribution • Warehousing • Etc.	• Sales Automation • Sales Force Automation • Advertising • Bus. Intetelligence • Retail Service • Etc.	• Service Mgmt. • Help Desk • Call Center • Customer Req's Mgmt. (CRM) • Etc.

SUPPORT ACTIVITIES — MARGIN

PRIMARY & ACTIVITIES

Data Processing Applications

The roster of most typical Data Processing applications hosted by an ASP comes from the IDC report (see aforementioned) and this author's own primary research. This roster is not complete, nor can it ever be. Most applications included fall into the categories of data creation, storage, manipulation, presentation, and delivery.

- Database software;

- Imaging and Document Management;

- Data and Storage Management;

- Security software;

- Graphics;

- Multimedia, and so forth.

Analytical Applications

The dimension of Analytical applications is orthogonal to the Value Chain. Indeed, Analytical applications can apply to any Value Chain activity and hence be present in any Value Chain functional container. Figure 6.15 depicts an attempt to do just that. More and more new analytical applications are appearing on the market every day. For that reason, Figure 6.15 is just an example, a snapshot in time subject to change.

A few examples of the ISVs' analytical application vendors are: Firepond for Product Configurators; Broadvision for E-Commerce reporting, analysis, and planning marketing campaigns; E*piphany for CRM enhancements; Serviceware for Knowledge Modules; IBM (with its alphaWorks product) for Data Mining; and so on.

Figure 6.15   *ASP analytical applications.*

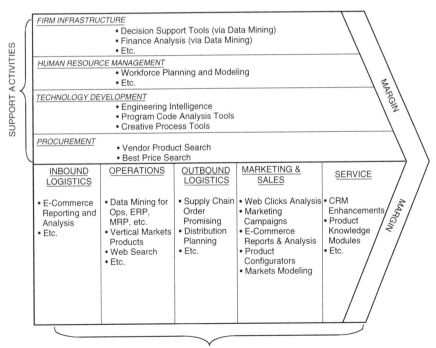

"Odd" Application Categories

There are some application categories that are difficult to place within the taxonomy, for example, personal productivity solutions, e-commerce tools and applications, and portals.

Personal Productivity Solutions and Portals

Personal Productivity solutions are not new. They have existed in the corporate world (e.g., word processing) even before the ascension of the Internet. Already available on the mainframe, their real inauguration came with the advent of the LAN. It was then when everyone with a PC linked to the LAN could participate in internal communications, share files, access common databases, and run common applications.

The arrival of the Internet added new dimensions to Productivity Solutions, those of faster implementations and an almost uniform accessibility. Now, a single Web site dubbed an Enterprise Portal could deliver productivity solutions to anyone also acting as a window to the entire spectrum of corporate information. The five Enterprise Portal functions are:

- Information Portal: By definition, this is a news portal. By design, it is not unlike popular consumer portals such as AOL, Yahoo, and Netscape's Netcenter. The major difference lies in that it emphasizes information that is of importance to the company.

- Knowledge Portal: By definition, this portal is essentially a window to all the data and information ever generated or accumulated by the company. By design, it typically provides directories and search capabilities over numerous internal Web sites that can be accessed on a need-to-know and right-to-know basis using passwords. Other, perhaps more sophisticated, access control means are also possible.

- Application Portal: By design, this is a collection of corporate applications accessed on a need-to-know and right-to-know basis with proper access security. Among these applications will also be enterprise/workgroup solutions such as workgroup and collaborative software (e.g., Lotus Notes Domino), universal messaging, and multimedia broadcast capabilities.

- Internal Expertise Portal: access to personnel and skills databases.

- Partner Portal: This portal exists on the extranet and is accessed by the enterprise's business ecosystems members, mostly customers and suppliers.

All types of portals can be built using Portal development tools[23] and then hosted by ASPs. A portal is not an application in and of itself. It is an umbrella or a placeholder connoting the multiple applications accessed by diverse user communities. Any enterprise application, from any dimension of the ASP application taxonomy, can be available through such portals.

Incidentally, Productivity tools are listed in the Operations container of the Value Chain. In reality, they may be placed in any cell where enterprise personnel use them.

E-Commerce

Strictly speaking, the term e-commerce doesn't describe business activities. It simply implies that various commerce activities are performed electronically, over the network, and increasingly, the Internet. E-commerce may therefore indicate any activities within the Value Chain involved in business information exchanges.

Still, the most common business activities supported by e-commerce are those conducted between the enterprise and outside partners: suppliers and customers. The former ones occur mostly within Inbound Logistics and Procurement, the latter ones—in Outbound Logistics, Marketing and Sales, and Services.

Summarizing Pure-Play ASPs

Pure-play ASP is a moniker for those ASPs dedicated to providing application services. Furthermore, it is reasonable to expect that over time pure-plays will dominate, as most underlying infrastructure will get commoditized.

Building and studying application taxonomies benefits all involved in the ASP business, especially ASPs themselves and their customers. It should help ASPs better plan their services, understand linkages to other activities and applications, and design clear business models and marketing strategies. In turn, ASP customers could better articulate their needs leading to their abilities to write better hosting requirements and develop more realistic expectations of the ASP's capabilities.

Application services are ultimately what ASPs are for. Everything else exists to support them. Keeping this in mind helps focus on what is really important for fostering the acceptance and evolution of the ASP.

---

23. A good example of a Web Portal Server is iPlanet's Portal Server. A quote from www.iplanet.com: iPlanet's Portal server ". . . is the platform and infrastructure for the secure, customized, and personalized delivery of any application or resource to users with merely a browser and an Internet connection."

ASP's Professional Services

Professional Services are not necessarily expected of ASPs, yet based on the ASP's early experiences, they are quite desirable, profitable, and well received by the customers.

The culture and heritage of Professional Services is very mature compared with that of ASPs. Professional Services can be highly diversified, differentiated, and much less subject to commoditization. Using these services, ASPs can complement their own offerings, ultimately enabling themselves to offer end-to-end services. The ASP's Professional Services may include business consulting (analysis, planning, marketing, financials, etc.), application life cycles services, systems integration, and education and training. And since most ASPs are young entrepreneurial companies with little consulting experience, they frequently rely on the alliances and partnerships with established consultants and SIs.

While mostly applicable to solving customer problems, Professional Services can also benefit ASPs themselves, and in a number of ways. First, professional consultants can help ASPs to better understand their own business, hone their own ASP business models, streamline internal processes, and build efficient internal organizations. Next, if properly packaged and managed, Professional Services promise ASPs to become a source of revenue with a high ROI. And finally, Professional Services can increase the ASP's market differentiation, making them look more like one-stop shops and helping to attract powerful and capable partners (consultants, vendors, and other providers alike).

To deliver Professional Services, an ASP must either build its own consulting organization or partner with established companies. Building its own professional services can benefit it for two reasons: control over their resources and the ability to grow and change the organization as the ASP business grows and changes itself. Also, if an ASP bundles the cost of Professional Services into its rental fees, it can offer one-stop shopping to its customers along with the economy of service integration at cost, not a market price. The disadvantages of building Professional Services organizations are long ramp-up times and high initial investments.

The second option, a partnership, can be achieved more speedily. By partnering with Professional Services organizations specializing in target markets and products, ASPs can rapidly gain the agility of selecting and pursuing these markets and products. A negative side of partnerships is the lack of control and the high cost of services that must be passed to ASP customers, resulting in a competitive disadvantage.

ASPs can offer many different services to their customers, including, but not limited to, the ones listed in the right stack of Figure 6.6. Without a claim of completeness, the stack's entries cover many facets of ASP's professional services. Some of these are detailed later.

Generally speaking, consulting offerings are independent of—or orthogonal to—the ASP hosting services. While there is a strong correlation between the types of hosting (co-location, MIP, AIP, ASP) and consulting services offered by such ASPs, no one is restricted from offering a much broader spectrum of consulting. As was indicated earlier, Professional Services can be very beneficial to ASPs, bringing in a market differentiation, higher ROI and revenue, and higher customer retention. Hence, many ASPs strive to maximize these advantages.

Application Life Cycle Services

So, what can ASP consultants offer ASP customers? The list of services can be pretty long. Here are some common tasks of an application (or systems) life cycle:

- *Application Requirements.* Consultants work with the customer to analyze their application requirements: the number of users, patterns of usage, capacities, and variances; and systemic qualities: reliability, availability, scalability, security, performance, and manageability.

- *Architectures.* Consultants design the application and systems architectures. For large architectures, this effort may be quite comprehensive and extensive, resulting in the designs for computing, storage, and networking infrastructures meeting a customer's application requirements and providing for systemic qualities as defined earlier.

- *Application Implementation.* Customers frequently develop their applications and/or customize/personalize purchased application packages using the equipment rented from the MIP. Whether involved directly in customer application development, or not, the ASP's consultants can then use this development cycle time to implement systems and application architectures.

- *Architecture Implementation.* Consultants implement the architectures: install hardware and software, interconnect them, and run tests. Concurrently, management probes and agents are installed and tested in this phase to ensure the future operational runtime readiness.

- *Installation.* Consultants install the application systems and conduct functionality tests.

- *Staging and Testing.* Consultants conduct overall application and systems QA, functionality, and stress tests. A very valuable service helping to optimize each application's resource requirements, it may lead to reduced fixed and variable costs factored into customer fees. Besides helping to determine the current capacity requirements, stress testing also allows planning for future capacities.

- *Operational Processes.* Consultants design operational processes and implement them.

- *Education and Training.* Consultants conduct customer training, and so forth.

Customer Planning

Planning services offered to ASP customers range from the basic planning of customers' future capacities to the most elaborate and sophisticated management consulting-style business, implementation, and operations planning. While the latter activities hardly represent an ASP's mainstream consulting offering, some ASPs believe they have the right wherewithal (in-house or contracted out) and extend such services to their customers.[24] These services may include:

- Customer Opportunity and Market Readiness Analysis;
- Business Planning and Business Model Analysis;
- On-line Presence and Brand Development;
- Architecture Strategy and Implementation Planning;
- Financial Advisory Services, and so forth.

Whether ripe for customer picking or not, the mere fact that such services are being offered may herald an interesting trend—that of ASPs becoming a major channel for different kinds of IT business services.

---

24. For an example, see Breakaway Solutions' Web site www.breakaway.com.

Planning for an ASP's success is a never-ceasing activity. After all, "plans are nothing, planning is everything," as President Eisenhower once said.

Implementation Templates

Implementation templates are collections of experience-based collateral materials applicable, with minor modifications, to many repeatable projects. Templates can be of different types and used during different phases of an application life cycle. There could be numerous analysis, design, programming, testing, monitoring and reporting templates.

ASPs that are directly involved with business applications and their hosting—Pure-Play ASPs, ASC/ASDs, ISV/ASPs, ASPs, FSPs, PSPs, ISPs, and AIPs (see Figure 6.5)—benefit more from the use of templates than the infrastructure ASPs. This is because application design has more variability than hardware. Templates that minimize this variability lessen performance and scheduling uncertainty, shorten implementation time, and improve the final product's quality.

Implementation templates owe their origins to life cycle methodologies. If an ASP has a comprehensive customer implementation methodology, it may be able to develop implementation templates. Templates are especially beneficial to ASPs that focus on functional or industry-specific applications. The use of templates is a direct contributor to the ASPs' economies of scope, and consequently, their bottom line.

Analytical Services

The section on hosted applications discussed analytical applications in the context of pure-play ASP offerings. However, any ASP itself can offer analytical services to its customers as a part of its consulting services. Such services may range from Web performance analysis tools to the more sophisticated customer analytics, marketing campaign management, Web brand establishment and maintenance, and real-time personalization. The ultimate product to the customer may be either enhanced B2C or B2B Web sites, or improved marketing and business decision support.

Education and Training

Since the ASP is a new and fledgling business, the two major tasks of ASP education and training are:

- Opportunistic education of markets; and
- Specialized training for ASPs, their customers, and ecosystem members.

Both are very expensive propositions, falling mostly upon ASPs themselves. Yet such is a fate of first movers in any new market or industry. It should be noted though that most trade publications, public and private educational organizations, as well as various industry advocacy groups, including the aforementioned ASP Consortium, have also stepped up to the challenge and have been doing a credible job. Nonetheless, the level of understanding of the ASP and its basic principles and implications to business still remain very low. The ASP education audience is very broad and includes:

- the general public;
- the business community (i.e., potential customers and users);
- the ASP ecosystem members (hardware vendors, Telcos, ISVs, SIs, consultants, other ASPs);
- the business professional community (legal, financial, investors, etc.).

The major subjects of ASP education, besides a greatly overfranchised theme of "value propositions," should be related to the following:

- Division of labor, IT economics, and the role of ASP;
- ASP economies (scale, scope, etc.);
- Provider/customer contractual relationships and SLAs;
- ASP's impact on its ecosystem (how ASP changes business SI's, ISV, vendors and others' business models)

Summary

The classification of ASPs provided in this chapter uses a stack of technology layers from a 3DF methodology defined in Chapter 5. Though developed by and borrowed from Sun Microsystems, the core ideas behind 3DF are, in principle, shared by many other technology vendors, ISVs, consultants, SIs and many commercial ASPs. The approach of defining the basic ASP types on an ASP stack (Figures 6.5 and 6.6) helps explain and analyze the services offered by real-life ASPs.

- The four basic types of ASPs defined are: a co-location ASP, an MIP, an AIP, and a pure-play ASP. The layers of 3DF technology stack don't overlap, so all ASPs also include non-overlapping sets of adjacent layers.

- All ASPs are interdependent, as each requires the services of other ASPs beneath it on the ASP stack (except co-location). Ideally, each ASP offers a unique set of services to a unique audience of customers. In reality, though, their services may overlap.

- Each ASP's services are based on its intrinsic core competencies. The higher the ASP on the ASP stack, the *more varied* the competencies it can have. They range from the simple basic computer room technology competencies (co-location), to computer technologies (MIP), to systems hardware and software (AIP), to applications (pure-play ASP).

- The lower the ASP on the ASP stack, the faster it can become a commodity. In fact, as at the time of this writing, co-location ASPs were already facing the onset of commoditization with all its attendant business consequences (see Chapter 9). Commoditization leads to cost-based pricing of services. On the same stack, the higher the ASP, the better it is positioned to charge fees based on value provided to its customers.

- Different ASPs have different intrinsic abilities to develop competitive advantages either based on differentiation or cost reductions.

- Different ASPs have different value propositions to their customers (Chapter 9 offers more details).

The terminology and definitions used for each ASP in this and other chapters are consistent with the terminology and definitions established and commonly used in the ASP industry at the time of this writing.

Managing ASPs

This chapter describes the comprehensive ASP management framework covering both the technical infrastructure management and ASP's professional services.

This management framework is built at two levels: it first defines the ASP management categories and then assigns the ASP management functions to each of these categories. Bundling management functions under categories is not absolute, however. It is subject to change, and should be considered prescriptive only.

The framework provided is merely an attempt to create a taxonomy of ASP management services—to "divide and conquer" the playing field and outline the challenges and opportunities inherent in ASP management.

ASP's Management Framework

Defining the ASP Management Framework

Numerous tangible and intangible assets fall under the ASP management umbrella. To simplify the analysis and design of the ASP management services, the ASP management framework uses the familiar "divide and conquer" approach by breaking all services down into the categories of functionally cohesive components. This categorization is performed in two steps by (1) defining the managed objects and then (2) identifying their pertinent management services.

The two objects the ASP manages are systems and people (Figure 7.1). Systems are further broken down into two categories: Operations and Monitoring and Management (or M&M), respectively. People's management services are also divided into those supporting the users and those supporting the business, i.e., Customer Care and business-Management Service, respectively.

This makes four categories, two for people and two for systems. The fifth category—security—applies to all four, and to virtually every component of the ASP architecture, services, and processes. Security may be very complex and is continuously evolving. Because of its ubiquity, complexity, and importance, the ASP security is described in detail in Chapter 8.

All management categories depicted in Figure 7.1 deal with the information assumed stored in a logical ASP information repository. All architectural components, services, and business processes must have access to this repository. The real repository may be represented by multiple physical databases.

Figure 7.1 *ASP management categories.*

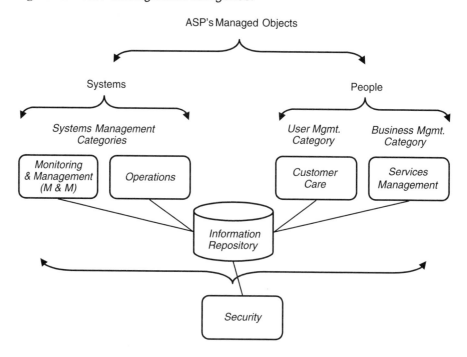

ASP Management Services

This chapter doesn't aim to become a reference to all ASP management functions and services. It strives, however, to assemble as many of them as possible, sort them by functional categories, and give them comprehensive definitions. The chapter describes these services first as if they belonged to an NC (in-sourced or outsourced), and then analyzes how they might change if applied to the ASP.

In general, management services apply to some or all ASP components: servers, networks, applications, auxiliary equipment, operations, customers and their users, and most importantly, ASP services. Most management services are well developed, with many practical guides, scientific papers, and books written about them. Many vendors sell comprehensive management platforms, and many consultants, armed with methodologies and "best practices," design and deploy these technologies for many successful implementations of ASP management. Figure 7.2 offers this author's version of the ASP management framework.

Figure 7.2   *Data center management frameworks.*

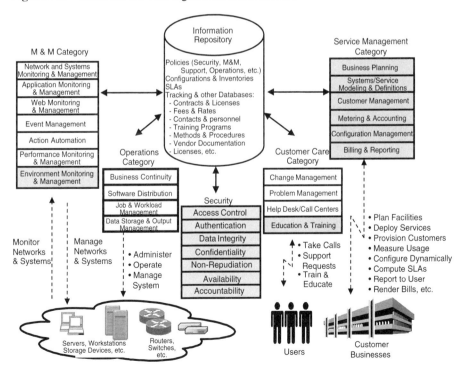

All management functions are relevant and important to the ASP. Yet a few of them, if not unique to the ASP, have some particularly ASP-specific content, for example, "systems and services modeling" or "metering and accounting." Such functions are shown shaded in Figure 7.2. However, there are no reasons why these functions could not be used by any business internally, even though it would imply that that business's IT department would formally contract with its internal customers for services rendered, write formal SLAs, and operate as a bona fide technology business using a P&L (real or phantom), and so on. Alas, as far as this author is aware, as of the time of this writing, this is rarely the case in the industry. In fact, it has been only recently that early adopter businesses have begun to consider applying the ASP model to their IT departments. Many requests for services to help implement the ASP model internally have been coming to various e-business integrators, such as Sun Professional Services and others.

All ASP management services in Figure 7.2 are assigned to five management categories: operations (day-to-day), M&M, customer care, service management, and security. The assignment is logical and doesn't imply how specific tools implement these management categories. The genesis of these categories was discussed earlier. Here are their more specific definitions.

Operations address typical business continuity and administrative services. The former ones consist of backups/restores, contingency plans, updates and changes to systems, as well as disaster recovery. The latter ones handle software distribution, storage and data maintenance, running scheduled jobs, and some others. Operations activities are planned, scheduled, and recurrent (day-to-day).

M&M manages all unplanned, sporadic, and random events through monitoring, analysis of these events, their correlation, and corrective actions, if applicable (manual or automated). These events also include the addition of new hardware as capacity demands.

Customer Care manages communications with customers and their users. The Help Desk and Call Center can also be viewed as cost of failure systems for problems reported by the customers and not caught by M&M, for creating, tracking, and following through with trouble tickets. Of course, if the customer is the one to report the problems first, M&M's capabilities are in question. Still, situations like this may arise and must be handled. At the same time, customer care is used for managing change requests and to support other customer services using mechanisms similar to trouble tickets' handling.

Service Management processes are the key to guaranteeing that the ASP services provided to the customers meet (or exceed) the agreed-upon SLAs. These processes range from service configuration, provisioning, change management, education and training, to assuring customer satisfaction. Also included are contractual relationships and all the diverse forms of communications between the ASP and its customers. The majority of service management activities are reflected in the ASP's ability to manage compliance with the SLAs.

Security activities consist of preventive, protective, detective, and response measures covering all facets of ASP security: confidentiality, data integrity, authentication, access control, and non-repudiation.

ASP M & M

M & M is a category whose functionality is similar to that of the old familiar NOC. However, in established management practices, the NOC comprises more functionality than M&M. That is why this book uses the term M&M.

For all practical purposes, M&M is a cost of failure system that handles all unplanned events and contingencies requiring monitoring, management, and corrective actions. It should be noted though that M&M is also used when the managed environment (e.g., ASP architecture) requires changes leading to reconfiguration. These changes are usually planned and scheduled.

M&M's major functions—the systems and network monitoring and management—work with the NC architecture's networks and servers and are very mature. Many products and practices have been developed for the NC's M&M and used effectively throughout the IT industry. Thus, this section doesn't aim to repeat what has been already written on M&M in countless volumes. What it does intend to do is give basic definitions to the M&M functions and then focus on whether these functions can work for the ASP and how.

Network and Systems M & M

Management Functions

NSM refers to the proactive monitoring of ASP resources—routers, switches, servers, storage systems, application infrastructure and applications themselves—in order to detect the imminent or already occurred faults so that remedial action can be taken. When an NSM is comprehensive, multiple managed devices and services are being monitored concurrently. When one or multiple faults occur somewhere within the components of the NC, all the devices and services impacted by the fault may generate events.[1] The NSM then feeds these events into the event correlation engines (see Event Management), first to discover what the real problem is—that is, the nature of faults that caused the rush of events—and second, to decide what cor-

---

1. In the parlance of NSM, these events are sometimes called alarms or alerts.

rective actions to take. These corrective actions could be manual, requiring the use of M & M's management consoles and operators, or automatic (hence, action automation); for example, reroute-the-traffic-around-the-failed-node or fail-over-to-the-standby-server or log-information-since-an-automatic-failover-already-occurred-but-also-notify-the-customer, and so forth. The second type of corrective action is problem escalation. If the M&M's Event Management determines it can create an automatic action for the problem at hand, it executes it and continues to track the results. It also sends information to Information Repository for data warehousing and analysis later. If the M&M's Event Management cannot create an automatic action, it sends the information describing the problem to Problem Management, which creates a trouble ticket to act upon it until the problem's closure.

The information related to trouble tickets includes a problem description (e.g., location, type, impact), references to the faults that may have caused it, methods to resolve the problem, procurement and deployment activities (if needed), and so on. For ASPs, trouble tickets should also list the customers affected by the problem and their SLA's impact on billing and accounting, and so on.

The fact that Problem Management belongs to the Customer Care category makes common sense, especially for ASPs. If a problem could not be fixed through automatic actions, resolution may be prolonged and hence impact the SLAs. Besides, when the customers discover the problem themselves, they are calling the Help Desk/Call Center or their Service Management representatives. ASPs should be aware of the situations when the customer knows of the problems before them; using customers as a first line of monitoring is not an effective approach to M&M.

Implications for the ASP

The aforementioned description already implies the existence of a customer, specifically an ASP customer. If so, what must M&M do to accommodate multiple ASP customers? There are two scenarios: customers with dedicated facilities (servers, network, routers, management network, etc.) and those sharing ASP facilities with others.

When an ASP customer uses dedicated facilities, management processes would not differ too much from managing the NC. Indeed, ASPs would create a management partition in their NSM system such as an HP Open View, IBM's Tivoli, CA Unicenter, Sun Management Center, or a combination of point products, and then assign operators to run it. Even then, managing ASP customer may present serious challenges. For example:

- Service management's databases—for configuration, change, problem, inventory, provisioning—must be able to identify with each customer.

- The information related to e-business management, customer portals, and contract administration must be created, stored, and managed separately.

- SLA management must be aware of the existence of multiple customers and collect, store, and process pertinent service level compliance information for all of them separately.

- The Customer Care and Operations functions must also distinguish among multiple customers to track user calls (or Web site hits), keep proper records for Systems Administration, know which processes to use for Business Continuity, and so on.

- And finally, Security must be configured to operate according to that customer's security policy, support its security architecture, and report either through the SLAs or other means on security events and compliance with the customer's policy.

Fortunately, the outsourcing industry had faced these challenges before so many practices and some tools were developed and successfully implemented to deal with them. However, evidence shows that most management models of outsourcing apply only partially to the ASP, largely due to the differences in technologies and architectures. And besides, they don't scale well in the new world of open systems.

If these challenges were not enough, the situation gets even more complicated for customers who share ASP resources. Even in a simple case when multiple customers run applications on a shared Business Logic tier server, these applications would need to be tagged somehow for tracking their resource consumption and for proactive monitoring and management for each customer and in accordance with that customer's SLAs. Doing this is not easy, which may explain why resource sharing is used only for relatively simple Web hosting applications in this young and budding ASP industry. It also explains why service pricing is not always linked directly to resources consumed but is developed on a cost-plus basis.

Application Monitoring and Management

Management Functions

Applications Monitoring and Management is the function of developing and tracking application availability, performance, and other metrics to accurately manage the application's behavior in its operational environment, including software servers (e.g., portal, Web, directory, application), other applications, operating systems, middleware, database engines, networks, and others.

For a long time application management was the "terra incognita" of systems and network management. Many vendors used to claim they offered application management solutions with their existing or new and forthcoming products, but in reality, many such products were mislabeled, leading to considerable confusion among the users. The reality checkbox outlines the key management market segments and its major players. Their use for application management is analyzed later.

REALITY CHECK

Group 1: Network and Systems Management (NSM)

Traditional NSM software vendors offer comprehensive, highly-scalable, and integrated multi-platform management solutions covering many management disciplines—albeit mostly for network components and servers—for example, monitoring and management of network, systems, performance and security; asset and inventory management; event correlation and action automation; tools for operations (e.g., backups/restores, job scheduling, software distribution); integration with customer care (e.g., help desks); SLA management. The heavyweights in this space—Hewlett Packard, BMC, Cabletron, IBM/Tivoli, Sun and Computer Associates—can also integrate other vendors' point products under their management frameworks. Examples of point products are legacy systems management (by Candle), user level Web performance measurements (by ServiceMetrix[a]), audit software enforcing security policies (by Axent), and so on.

Group 2: Monitoring Only

Vendors like Cisco, Micromuse, Opticom, Concord Communications, and others offer products to monitor, meter, measure, and report on the status of managed servers and networks.

Group 3: Application Monitoring

Application monitoring—somewhat a misnomer to begin with—offers status information on the applications' resources, not on the applications themselves. This information may include servers' status; CPU/Memory/Channel/Bandwidth utilization; summary statistics, and so on. Vendors include Cisco, Lucent Technologies, Computer Associates, and others.

Group 4: Application Monitoring

Finally, there is a new breed of sophisticated application monitoring and management tools. Besides observing each application's environment and resources, these tools literally talk to the applications to inquire about their status, analyze applications' logs, test applications' performance via low-invasion means (e.g., pings), and then use programmed logic to decide on corrective actions, if any, based on the applications' management policies. Vendors include: BMC, Hewlett–Packard, NetIQ, Tivoli, Dirig Software.

a. Acquired by Exodus Communications, Inc., in 2000.

In the past, unless an application itself was capable of reporting its status and activities, it could only be observed from the outside, from its environment, and not monitored and managed directly. By measuring the availability and performance metrics of the applications' external entities—for example, the servers that applications ran on and the networks they used—it was possible to estimate some metrics of the applications themselves (using mostly Group 3 tools; see Reality Check). But the results were superficial and because they were collected a posteriori (e.g., after the application-related events occurred), the metrics were useful only for the reactive, as opposed to a more desirable, proactive, management.

So, how should complex distributed applications be managed? Finding the solution to this question should start with the understanding of relationships among different applications, their interactions with their critical resources, and other dependencies within their environment. Ultimately, for the application to be managed effectively, two things must happen: the applications must be management-enabled and management tools must be "taught" to deal with the applications. Management-enabling the applications can be done in a number of different ways, from specifying the syntax and semantics of applications' logs, to developing applications' capabilities to respond to pings and other forms of testing them from the outside. As for the management tools, it must be possible to program them to conduct the measurements of applications' environments and to interpret application logs.

A major breakthrough in the field of application management occurred in 1995 when Tivoli Systems, an enterprise systems management company (later acquired by IBM), introduced the Application Management Specifications (AMS). AMS defined application management in the context of an application's environment—just as described before. The key benefit of AMS was in its approach to defining management-ready applications. This approach was not tied to a particular management tool but offered a generic application management paradigm. Here are excerpts from Tivoli's AMS, Version 2.0, published in November 1997:

> The Application Management Specification (AMS) provides a way to specify information about an application that is required for a management tool to manage the application.

> AMS enables management of the application throughout its life cycle, including the following tasks:
>
> - Application distribution
> - Application installation
> - Dependency checking
> - Application monitoring

- Application configuration
- Operational control
- Deploying updates and new releases
- Security Management
- Business System Management
- Application Response Time Management

In addition to defining the management requirements of a single application, it is often necessary to define how an application interacts with other applications and system resources to perform a critical business function.

AMS set the tone for application management, while itself remaining a point of reference for many other application management endeavors. Many companies have implemented AMS or similar application management frameworks.

Implications for the ASP

The next question is, "How should the applications be monitored and managed in the ASP environment?" With AMS (or similar schemes), different ASP customers and their applications can be managed in a segregated fashion. Furthermore, most of AMS would also work for the ASP applications that share resources.

For the ASP, application monitoring must be done by application by customer. Here, the ability to monitor the applications depends on the degree of resource sharing. For this monitoring one must ask the question, "What is the smallest unit of resources dedicated to this application?" For applications running on dedicated servers, a server is the smallest unit. For applications that share servers, a set of related application processes may represent an even smaller unit. Depending on what the customer wants and its ASP is able to provide, different tools from the Reality Check can be successfully used. Note though that in case of shared servers, application processes and customers must be carefully matched.

Another practical approach for the ASP is to management-enable the elements of application hosting environments—certain systems that applications depend upon or run under. Examples are the Web servers, application servers, database servers, email tools, and others. Monitoring and managing these systems may provide insights into the behavior of applications running under them even when these applications themselves are not management-enabled.

Web Monitoring and Management

Due to the rise of the Internet's popularity and an increasing use of its technologies for business applications—both in context of the NC and ASP—Web monitoring and management has become an important function of the M&M.

Web monitoring and management provides NC users (or an ASP customer and its users) with a means to track, and then act upon, collected information, to ensure that their informational and e-commerce Web applications perform according to their performance requirements.

The Web management solution offers the ability to capture response time data for customers' external and internal users and applications and other key metrics such as:

- Total response time
- Customer decision and browse time
- Network traffic
- Total server time
- Individual application and transaction response times
- Frequency of page views
- Paths taken to most popular Web pages
- How long an individual page is viewed, and so forth.

Most of this information is usually available to the ASP customers in numerous Web performance reports.

Performance Monitoring and Management

To satisfy the service guarantees (e.g., SLAs), ASPs must monitor performance and availability at multiple tiers and layers of a customer systems' architecture and then report the results to its customers. These reports usually cover the network (WAN, LAN), servers, routers, firewalls, and the elements of application environment: Web applications in the Presentation Tier, business applications in the Business Tier, application integration middleware in the Integration Tier, and even the information in the Resources Tier.

Here is a sample list of systems and network components and their features monitored for availability and performance:

- Networks are monitored for bandwidth use distribution patterns, bandwidth utilization by customer/applications, packet loss, errors, latencies, and so forth.
- Servers are monitored for processor(s) and memory utilization, disk systems' performance, operating system components' performance (processes, services, tasks, etc.), just to name a few.

- Business Applications are monitored for application response (both mean response time and standard deviations, which predict customer expectations), application self-healing incidents, and the reasons for those application processing exception logs.
- Web applications are monitored for response time, network time, browse time, and server time.
- End-to-end monitoring where a canned request is made of the entire system and compared against an expected response.
- The firewalls are monitored for security events and exceptions, security logs, and status.

Incidentally, when reporting on the availability and performance of the total hosted application—frequently measured from the point of view of end users across all tiers—an ASP must use the information extending as far as access to resources, lest its reporting be incomplete.

Environmental Monitoring and Management

Not all ASPs provide hosting facilities. However, those that do must ensure that the SLAs of the hosting environment are also included and satisfied. A sample list of what must be monitored and managed, locally and/or remotely, is provided here:

- Commercial power and contingency arrangements (e.g., redundant gas/diesel power generators), power grounding systems, and so forth
- HVAC and its distribution systems, redundancies, contingency designs
- Fire detection and monitoring systems, fire suppression equipment
- Building access, security guards, TV surveillance systems
- Seismic monitoring and control systems, seismic bracing

Many other environmental systems may also be included. Additional details on these services were already provided in Chapter 6.

ASP Operations Management Services

Software distribution, job and workload, data storage and output management are the disciplines within operations whose implementation is based on the extensive prior experiences of the traditional NC's operations management. The multicustomer nature of the ASP requires that all customers be treated separately, though. This may be relatively easy to do for customers with dedicated resources using traditional operations management tools and practices. However, it requires new and innovative approaches for dealing with those customers sharing resources. Chapter 10 offers insights into the technologies promising to provide each customer with a clearly identifiable set of resources and services managed independently, as if the customer had dedicated resources. The operations category of ASP management would be an apparent beneficiary of these technologies.

Data Storage and Output Management

Basic Functionality

Data storage and output management are two key operations of management functions within any data center and specifically within an ASP.

Modern data centers require comprehensive storage management solutions combining hardware, software, and management and operations processes. These storage management solutions (e.g., from IBM, EMC, Sun, Veritas) help implement, monitor, configure, and dynamically expand and manage storage systems to meet customers' ever-changing requirements for high-performance, reliability, availability, scalability, and security of their data. Chapter 10 gives more details about the specific storage and storage management solutions relevant to the ASP. Additionally, data storage management provides for a reliable, easy-to-use backup/restore and archival of data and software locally or over the network. These functions are normally performed automatically.

Output management tools implement "delivery" of customer output to multiple destinations including printers, plotters, fax numbers, email addresses, physical media (e.g., CD-ROMs or tapes), network ports, and Web/intranet sites. Additionally, outputs can be delivered to generic output facilities such as forms and storage management systems, content management and distribution systems, spoolers and report generation systems, and others. Most output management systems are driven by customer policies and can execute dynamic instructions telling them who to deliver the output to, when, and in what format. Finally, many output management systems can be, or already are, integrated with many application solutions such as ERP, CRM, Supply Chain, HR, and others.

Most output management systems come with sophisticated yet user-friendly tools allowing for viewing, scheduling, accounting, and control of all output functions and processes.

Implications for the ASP

The key ASP implication for data and output management is the avoidance of commingling data and operations. While mostly related to privacy (confidentiality), this concern is amplified by the fact that implementing it has negative connotations. One is the adverse impact on ASP economies and another is one of technological complexities. Examples are:

- Using separate backup tapes for different customers requires sophisticated tape management systems, multiple tape backup systems, and possibly manual intervention. This wastes tapes and storage space, and adds to equipment and labor costs.

- Using separate printers and fax machines within the ASP data centers has the same negative economic effect as the extra tapes and drives.

- Avoiding misdirection of output requires privacy protection and sophisticated detection capabilities.

Software Distribution

Software distribution is always a challenge, especially when delivering software to more than one operating system. It has therefore been an established practice to deliver software by OS types. Software distribution must provide for the installation and removal of software on all systems under its purview, support automatic upgrades to newer versions using patches, and be able to recognize and resolve software configuration conflicts.

Implications for the ASP are similar to those described for output management: avoidance of commingling and deliveries to wrong destinations.

Jobs and Workload Management

Jobs and workload management are traditional functions with their legacy in the mainframe world. Numerous tools exist and can be used successfully to implement these functions within an ASP. Similar to software distribution and output management, jobs and workload management within an ASP requires strong privacy protection and detection capabilities.

Business Continuity

Functionalities

Notwithstanding the amount of investment and the degree of reliability and availability built into the ASP systems and networks, accidents and malicious acts that can take the entire operational environments down or seriously impact their availability and performance do still occur. That's when the disaster avoidance plans are invoked. Yet, what are these disaster avoidance plans and what are their specific activities?

What used to be called disaster recovery has now become known as business continuity. While the former term assumes a period of time required to bring a failed environment back to life, the latter abides by the notion that recovery time for eBusiness is zero. Business continuity conjures up two components: the operational tasks required for successful operations under normal conditions; and the activities required to handle, and recover from, catastrophes. The first category is normally called operations, and the second, disaster avoidance.

Operations consists of mostly planned and scheduled tasks like those for data and software backup, data archival, managing offsite storage, computer jobs and workloads, hardware maintenance and upgrades, OS, and other software updates. Some of these were described before. Additionally, operations may include activities performed by customer request, such as restoring backed-up data or running special diagnostics.

Disaster avoidance (DA) is a set of activities for recovering from the consequences of unplanned and damaging events (contingencies), either man-made or caused by systems or networks. For really catastrophic events—defined as requiring extensive time for rebuilding—one common approach is building a hot-standby backup site. While it may be very expensive, many companies who cannot afford denying their users access to their services opt for this approach and demand that their ASP support it. So, ASPs must develop comprehensive DA practices and facilities.

To do that, ASPs may have to learn from, or partner with, the established business continuity services providers such as Comdisco, SunGard, IBM[2] or others. Following are certain types of services provided by such companies.

- Electronic Vaulting (Data)
- Database Shadowing (Data)
- Remote Journaling (Data)

---

2. See www.comdisco.com; www.sungard.com; www.ibm.com.

- Standby Operating Systems
- Standby Processing Systems
- Hot Network Nodes
- Data Staging
- Remote Disk Mirroring (Disk Monitoring)
- Server Replication Systems.

The DA activities are usually planned in advance and are exercised regularly for training purposes. There are several activities involved in planning DA including, but not limited to, the following:

- Identification of the most critical systems/locations/activities
- Assessment of systems and networks' vulnerabilities
- Assessment of the impact of operations' disruptions on business
- Detailed definition of DA activities
- Roles and responsibilities of DA teams and members
- Testing and exercising these DA activities

Implications for the ASP

DA brings to attention the whole spectrum of ASP activities discussed throughout this chapter. Security is one of the most important considerations for DA. The best ASPs have developed practices that outline and guide the process for designing DA for their customers. Nonetheless, in this young and evolving ASP industry, it is still the customer's responsibility to clearly define their DA plans and work closely with their ASP to implement them. In particular, the customer must decide on the monetary cost of various disasters and therefore the monetary value of various disaster avoidance approaches in order to decide what provides a reasonable return on DA investment.

ASP Customer Care

The help desk, call centers, change/request, and problem management functions are all well developed traditional components of customer care. Customer care's implications for the ASP are similar to those defined for M&M. They consist of the abilities to provide a virtual support environment for each customer according to their SLAs. There are many mature customer care tools available on the market today, especially for call center and help desk management. Many organizations and services providers, including ASPs, are already using them. Here are a few points related to the ASP change and problem management.

Change/Request Management

Change/request management provides processes by which changes are introduced into an operational environment such as the ASP Data Center, ASP network, ASP application infrastructure, and customer application environments. A change is defined as any activity that alters the configuration, components, or processes of the operational environment. This may apply to either a dedicated environment used by a single customer or the one established for shared use by multiple customers. In order to meet the levels of service from the systems and applications according to the written SLAs, change must arise from business and/or operational management decisions or specific customer requests; it must be thoroughly planned and communicated, be nondisruptive to users, and implemented to schedule and budget.

Changes are generally made either in response to a customer requirement, to fix a problem, to improve service, or perform an environment reconfiguration. In a complex ASP environment, even changes to a dedicated, exclusive, customer environment may impact other systems and processes. Stating that a particular environment is dedicated implies dedicated systems (servers, routers, firewalls, switches, etc.), dedicated networks, possibly dedicated management network, and even dedicated personnel assigned to this customer. Still, broader scope components, which are not dedicated, may be shared and can impact the overall ASP. Examples are power consumption, aggregate network bandwidths, shared personnel work loads, and so forth. It is therefore of paramount importance to analyze the effects of a change not only on those systems expected to change, but also on all others that may be impacted indirectly.

Problem Management

The two most essential ASP problem management functions are call tracking and problem tracking, both followed by resolution management. Problem management is usually invoked via a help desk or call center escalation.

Call tracking is targeted towards problems reported by customers and their users over the phone or Web. Calls can come from a variety of geographically dispersed locations and multiple customers and users, but must be handled for each customer uniquely, for example, according to its SLAs. While there are many tools available for working with multiple customers, as is mentioned already, it is customary for ASPs to assign dedicated customer care personnel to each customer, when warranted.

Problem tracking encompasses gathering and reporting of statistics and performance metrics for managed equipment and services, applications and customers. For an ASP, it is very important to provide for security and privacy of each customer's records as well their processing and reporting.

Both call and problem tracking are starting activities in the resolution management workflow. Resolution management addresses remedial work (tasks), roles, and processes (who, what, when, where, how, status) for operational systems. It may also be involved in managing the testing and staging for systems under development. Additionally, resolution management can be used to facilitate understanding and provide explanations of historical records when it is required for long-term business analyses, investigations, and education and training.

Education and Training

As is true for any new industry, effective education of ASP's markets is a major determinant of its future success. No matter what ASP types and services customers want and whether their applications are standard or custom, information exchange and knowledge transfer with their ASP should help both ASP and customers. In simpler terms, educated customers would gain more from their ASP (hence, leading to higher ROI) and ASP would find it easier (hence, less expensive) to work with them. Since education and training imply a direct contact with the customer and its users—in the "grand" spirit of customer care—education and training are included into the customer care management category.

ASP education and training takes on various forms. It ranges from educating a general business community to ASP-specific customer training; from technical and product training to an ongoing knowledge transfer within the life cycle of ASP customer applications. Here are just a few examples of education and training subjects gathered from a multitude of offerings by numerous ASPs and other members of the ASP ecosystem.

General Education

General education is dedicated to the benefits of ASP over conventional insourcing. The various forms of education are:

- Conferences, symposia, exhibitions, special courses and classes
- ASP consortia and various business associations' publications
- Magazine articles
- White papers and ASP's Web sites
- Marketing and sales collateral

ASP-Specific Training

Some ASP-specific training subjects are as follows:

- ASP customer's ecosystem and value chain
- ASP Internet applications and integration
- ASP customer's product and service definitions
- Strategic and operational opportunities with the ASP (e.g., value propositions)
- Customer business planning for the ASP
- ASP impact on a customer's organization
- Understanding the ASP contracts
- Understanding the ASP management services
- Understanding SLAs and related processes (data gathering, reporting, payments, etc.)
- Financial modeling and analysis for ASP customers
- Risk analysis and management

Technical Training

The technical training subjects are:

- ASP security issues
- ASP application integration
- Development technologies
- Middleware technologies
- Hardware and software scalability technologies (e.g., clusters)
- Management technologies (M&M, operations, security, service management, customer care)
- Networking technologies (e.g., Internet protocols), terminology, and options

Application and Product Training

This topic can be broken into application solution training (e.g., ERP, CRM, Financial, HR, e-Commerce, and integration of such applications) and specific product training (e.g., for products from Oracle, SAP, Ariba, Sun/iPlanet). Additionally, in the context of ASP's professional services (Figure 5.10), education and training are conducted as part of a formal, or not-so-formal, knowledge transfer during the life cycle implementation phase of each customer application, that is, during hosting requirements gathering, application modeling, development and implementation, and testing followed by the postimplementation customer care, upgrade procedures, and so on.

Service Management

Every service provider implements some form of service management. However, service management could remain a shallow concept if it doesn't have attached to it quantitative metrics of quality of service (QoS). These QoS metrics are parameters within the SLAs written between providers and customers. The SLAs play a critical role in ASP service management and have, for that reason, been mentioned repeatedly in previous chapters.

Before introducing the SLAs, it is necessary to explain what service management is and why it is important to the ASP. The key point is that the SLAs and ASP service management are tightly coupled in a cause-and-effect relationship, with the former (SLAs, the cause) driving the latter (service management, the effect).

To sum it up, since customers want service guarantees, these guaranties are quantified as QoS metrics within the SLAs; providers and customers write and sign the SLAs, which become binding agreements for service delivery; and finally, providers use these SLAs to design services and maintain them during the ASP operations.

This section consists of two parts, the first one describing the SLAs and the second one providing details on ASP service management, its process, and functions.

Service Level Agreements (SLAs)

The ASP Industry Consortium[3] in its SLA White Paper published on November 14, 2000, provided the following definition of an SLA (p. 4):

> Service Level Agreements define the services provided, the supported products, the performance levels, the measurement and reporting criteria and appropriate quality standards. In most cases, SLAs are typically complemented with other contractual documents that together cover multiple items such as corrective actions, penalty and incentive clauses, nonperformance, acceptable amount of service deviation, modification and change order procedures, reporting policies, termination criteria, intellectual property, and dispute resolution procedures. When taken in that broader sense, an SLA defines the complete set of responsibilities and obligations of a service provider and the user of that service.

Many ASPs, as well as many computer and software vendors, network providers, and professional services organizations—that is, all those who consider themselves members of an ASP ecosystem (see also Chapter 11)—have joined the ASP Consortium.

---

3. See www.allaboutasp.org.

Many of these companies have also contributed to the aforementioned SLA White Paper. It therefore makes sense to analyze some of the major theses about the SLAs provided in this paper and add a few new ones, as applicable. Overall, this SLA section addresses the following:

- SLA objectives
- Designation of an SLA as a contract or agreement
- Services, performance, and measureability
- SLA reporting
- Categories of the SLAs recommended by the ASP consortium
- SLA boiler-plate recommended by the ASP consortium

Note that an SLA is just the first, high-level definition of services and their qualities. Once written, the SLAs become a base for further negotiations. Defining and agreeing on the SLAs is but the first step in building a trusted relationship between ASPs and their customers.

SLA Objectives

It is commonly believed that SLAs are used mostly to set and manage expectations, both of customers and the service provider as well (e.g., ASPs). To define SLAs, it is first of all important to recognize their real objectives. Examples are as follows, such as:

- Set customer expectations.
- Set ASP's expectations.
- Identify service metrics to be measured.
- Determine the means of reporting on these measurements.
- Influence the service quality culture within both the customer and the ASP.
- Establish a base for building a customer/provider relationship.

All these objectives are addressed in the following discussion.

The SLA as an Agreement Between an ASP and Customer

In general, an SLA is a document describing the rights and responsibilities of its signatories. Yet there are two types of SLAs: contractual and advisory. Customers frequently view the contractual SLA as a lever to enforce provider commitments for services and quality. This enforcement should, in their mind, come in a form of rebates or penalty remunerations for the provider's failure to live up to its service commitments.

The major reason for the contractual nature of traditional SLAs has been a perceived need in the realm of public service providers to offer some form of service rebate capabilities against poor performance. To date, service rebates in the public domain have been nominal in nature.

These nominal rebates reinforce the view that the contractual nature of SLAs restricts the scope and usefulness of such agreements without adding any significant value to the process.[4]

Since it is a document about rights and responsibilities—a domain for lawyers—an SLA contract is prone to be misunderstood and misinterpreted. Sometimes, the parties in the contractual SLA may even become emotional and contentious, making arbitration and dispute resolution very challenging. This logic may explain why many service providers have, in the past, shunned writing SLA contracts, which in turn explains why the service industries' SLA culture still remains quite immature.

But the situation is changing for the better. Today, an SLA is not viewed as a one-sided contract favoring the customer and encumbering the provider. Today, the provider stands to benefit from a properly written and executed SLA as much as the customer, if not more. Why? Because a happy customer is a reference, and writing effective SLAs is a repeatable and leverageable skill.

Now, consider the SLA a partnership document. If these partners clearly understand their mutual roles and responsibilities, readily share the mutually defined procedures, consciously recognize the need for a service culture, and know each other's expectations, the SLA could become a powerful tool for a successful ASP and happy customers. This gives rise to a second type of SLA—the advisory one. While it also can be written, it is not a legal document. If the contractual SLA is an enforceable contract, the advisory SLA is based on good will. Nonetheless, the advisory SLA can still perform as well as the contractual one, if not better. The following quote (from the same book on service management as the previous quote) should further articulate the advantages of the advisory SLA over the contractual one, albeit without a total discounting of the SLA contract.

The time necessary to define and agree upon a service level agreement within a service provider organization poses an additional problem with the contractual SLAs. When contractual and financial considerations are involved, the process for ensuring that an SLA can be offered is almost always protracted. This has resulted in a slowdown in the development of the SLA to encompass additional service

---

4. Richard Hallows, *Service Management in Computing and Telecommunications*, Norwood, MA: Artech House, Inc., 1995, p. 61.

elements and higher service levels. The advisory SLA, on the other hand, *need not* to be subjected to the same process.

Moreover, the SLA should remain meaningful and continue to stretch the service provider organization to deliver a higher quality of services in as many possible areas of service as possible. The use of an SLA as a driving force for improved service is best achieved trough an advisory SLA within a service partnership.

To summarize, the enforcement aspects of the contractual SLAs and their distinctions from the advisory ones really count less than the implied partnership between the customers and the ASP. If established and properly managed, this partnership should enable providers to deliver their best-effort services that meet their customers' best expectations for services and quality.

Services, Performance, and Measureability

To design effective customer SLAs, an ASP must know its own capabilities.

Services. The services an ASP offers its customers are a function of ASP type (co-location, infrastructure management, etc.), its target markets (e.g., vertical or functional), and available expertise.

Performance Metrics. An ASP must maintain a list of service performance metrics it can measure, deliver, and include in customer SLAs. As was indicated before, all these metrics must be meaningful and defined clearly to minimize the potential for ambiguity.

Measureability. An ASP must clearly understand the measureability of metrics in terms of available instrumentation and reporting. Some instruments used in event monitoring and performance management, defined earlier, apply to the measuring of performance metrics for SLAs. Measureability is an important consideration that must always be shared with the customer. For every ASP service, there may be metrics that can or cannot be measured. Both types of metrics must be included in the SLAs and thoroughly articulated and explained in the ASP collateral literature and/or the SLAs themselves.

SLA Reporting

Reporting on the performance of SLAs is what makes them tangible to the customers. From reporting, customers can conclude whether service performance meets their expectations and whether they are getting their money's worth. For any type of reporting, especially for SLAs, the following key requirements should apply:

Accuracy. An ASP must assure its customers of the accuracy of its reporting. It can do so by demonstrating its tools and operations for monitoring, measuring, processing, and preparation of the SLA reports. Additionally, written (interpretive) reports provided by ASP to its customers must be objective and honest.

Relevance. The SLA reports must be provided to the types of people who are interested in them, qualified to judge them, and have authority to take actions, if any are needed. Likewise, ASPs must assign personnel to each report who can interpret these reports, explain them, and answer questions. This is also related to customer care management functions discussed earlier in this book.

Timeliness. The SLA reports must be recent and delivered per an agreed upon schedule. Another aspect of timeliness is contingent reporting. If a customer must respond to certain events or developments so that some actions can be taken, an ASP must apply its best efforts to avail the customer of these reports as early as possible.

In relation to reporting technologies, this subject has already been addressed in considerable detail within this book. Event monitoring, discussed in earlier sections, must capture enough data to be used for SLA measurements just as it was used for billing, and so forth. Reporting on the SLAs can also use the output management tools.

Categories of SLAs

The left part of Figure 7.3 is borrowed from the SLA White Paper from the ASP Consortium. The right part is borrowed from Figure 5.5. The figure shows how the elements of the SLA White Paper map into the NC architectural framework. In its turn, the White Paper's customer care can map into the same of the ASP management. The White Paper's dispute avoidance and resolution is a total new functional area and is not addressed in this book.

Figure 7.3 *Mapping ASP consortium's SLA categories to NC/ASP architecture.*

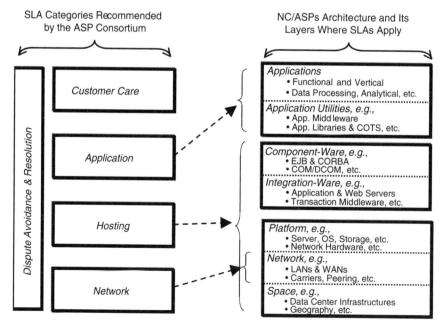

In general, not all SLAs apply to all customers. To be successful, an ASP needs to have an established set of SLA templates and processes to define them. The high-level process is very simple: First, the ASP and the customer must jointly determine what services and performance criteria are important to the customer. For example, for an interactive application (e.g., information Web site), network services and their performance—response time, throughput, etc.—are most important; for a financial application, data integrity, accuracy and confidentiality are important; for a customer care application, call center/help-desk responsiveness are important, and so on. In the second step, the ASP must select the types of parameters it can measure and deliver to the customer. And finally, the ASP and the customer must agree on the specific levels of measurement or provider commitments to be written into the SLAs.

Boiler Plate SLA Format

For most SLAs, the aforementioned ASP Consortium's White Paper recommends a format consisting of the following items:

- **SLA Metrics.** The metrics are used to measure service performance (see following).
- **Coverage.** Coverage defines the time and space scope of service provisioning (i.e., available metrics). For example, certain performance characteristics may be provided (or guaranteed) only between certain hours, for certain applications, for certain types of users.
- **Industry Ranges.** There may be certain industry standards established either historically (e.g., Telco network's reliability) or as the result of competition, but they may not always be available.
- **Importance Rating.** While appearing subjective at first sight, some importance ratings emanate from an industry consensus. For example, it is almost universally agreed that security and availability should reside at the top of the ratings list.
- **Reporting.** This item refers to the mode, frequency, and level of detail of SLA reports. The "tangible" (or objective, actual, factual) reporting modes are the same as described for output management, including hard copies, email, storage/archival, voice, paging, and others. Customer surveys offer a good example of the less tangible (or subjective, personal, particular) reporting.
- **Dependencies.** Within a complex ASP environment, dependencies are numerous. Internal dependencies are conditions for service delivery (e.g., availability of certain hardware or software); external dependencies may be written to protect providers against risks without the providers' control, including such odd ones as "acts of god," war, and others.

Not all categories described apply to all SLAs. They should be used with discretion.

Metrics

Metrics can be of two types: quantitative and qualitative. Examples of quantitative metrics are listed in Table 7.1.

Table 7.1 *Examples of Quantitative Metrics*

Metric	*Units of Measure*
Availability (of server, network, application, power, HVAC, etc.)	Percentage points, for example, 99.7%, 99.99%, or 99.999%
Response Time	Seconds of time
Network Throughput	A network capacity characteristic measured using telecom nomenclatures, for example, 64 kbps, DS3, OS12 links
Completion of Tasks	Percentage of time operational tasks are completed within predetermined time and on schedule (e.g., backup)
Notifications	Ability and timeliness of notifications for certain events demanding decisions within a predetermined time period
Software Upgrades	Accuracy and timeliness
Customer Care	Percentages of requests Customer Care (e.g., help desk) completed within a predefined time
Capacity on Demand	Time period within which a certain percentage of requests for expanded capacity are satisfied, and so forth

Qualitative metrics don't have specific units of measurement. Most of them describe the ASP's commitments. Examples of qualitative metrics are:

- Architecture design commitments (e.g., using a particular framework)
- Certain security commitments (e.g., access control, presence at the data center of motion detection devices and security cameras, the use of certain encryption standards and certain types

of encryption key management procedures, responsibility assignments)

- Deployment of redundant equipment: servers, network, power, and so on
- Types of customer care support availability
- Assignment of dedicated staff to the customer account
- Accountability for other members of the ASP ecosystem (e.g., if an infrastructure ASP uses the facilities of a co-location ASP, its SLAs carry the responsibility for co-location)

Summary for SLAs

An ASP is a member of a broad ecosystem (for details, see Chapters 3 and 11). Together, all members of this ecosystem organize into an ASP value chain. Yet an ASP is but one member of the value chain with a direct contractual relationship with the customer. This positions it to be ultimately responsible for all services and qualities, even those provided by other value chain members. To assume such a role, this ASP must contractually bind all those other value chain members into formal relationships for sharing responsibilities and risks.

The SLAs used by ASPs and other types of service providers have a much more expanded scope and scale than the traditional SLAs in the Telco world. While there can be many possible SLAs—some defined in the aforementioned ASP Consortium's White Paper, at the time of this writing—SLA writing is more an art than a trade. The industry is evolving and so are the service culture and diverse practices for defining realistic, accountable, and dependable SLAs.

ASP Service Management Process

There are many functions ASPs perform to design application (and other) services and manage their provisioning to customers. The complete cycle involves building an application hosting infrastructure, designing application services, procuring customers, signing SLAs, allocating resources for a customer's systems according to the SLAs, ensuring compliance with the SLAs during operations, billing and reporting to customers, and so on. The functions repeat for each new service and new customer and there exists a certain cyclical process which could show how these functions are interrelated, in what sequence they execute, what components of hosting infrastructure they impact, and who manages them. The material here addresses these functions (and their process) in detail. Later,

Chapter 10 will describe specific products that enable the functions of this process.

So, what does this process look like? Answering this question requires an impartial analysis of a large body of available empirical data including the countless publications by market research firms (e.g., Gartner Group, Forrester Research, IDC); numerous White Papers obtainable from public and private sources; vendors' marketing collateral, advertising materials, and product data sheets; and especially the commercial ASPs themselves, their experiences and needs. Defining this process is tedious, yet there is no escaping it. Unless the subject is very abstract, like a mathematical problem, the design must begin with an idea, followed by a prototype, reinforced by value analysis, and concluded with a formal model. It can be argued that at the time of this writing the state of the design of this process loomed somewhere between value analysis and formal model. Without the redundancy of further explanations, the ASP Service Management process can be depicted as shown in Figure 7.4 consisting of two sets of functions: implementation and operations, respectively, with each set, in turn, comprising three unique functions on either side of the vertical bar.

The three implementation functions are business planning, systems and service definition, and customer management. They deal with planning the hosting environment; setting up the systems, services, and writing SLAs; and the provisioning of customers. The three operations functions are metering and accounting, configuration management, and billing and reporting. These functions measure the consumption of services and usage of resources. They also configure and reconfigure the operational environments to better meet customers' QoS expectations, and perform bill rendering and reporting to customers and ASP management.

The ASP service management process looks like a "wheel." The wheel is always spinning as it is energized by the nonstop development of implementation functions (e.g., new business plans, new services, new customers) and continuous innovation of operations (e.g., new metering technologies, new methods of dynamical management, new data mining capabilities for reporting and new pricing programs for billing, etc.). The following sections offer more detailed explanations of the ASP service management process and its functions. Later, Chapter 10 will provide additional descriptions and technology and vendor/product references for Service Management.

Figure 7.4   *ASP service management functions—the "wheel."*

Business Planning

The function of business planning depends on an ASP's business models and financial capabilities. Additionally, it uses the empirical data resulting from the application of metering and configuration management. Specific components of business planning are:

- Business modeling: what markets to attack, what ASP type to become, and so forth

- Services' marketing mix: what applications and other services to offer, how to price them (e.g., prepaid services, flexible pricing, usage-based, tariffs), what marketing channels to develop, and so forth

- Investment planning: for facilities, systems, processes, personnel

- Engineering of facilities and systems

- Feedback analyses: cost reduction analysis and design to leverage sharing in a pursuit of economies of scale, scope, learning, focus, and logistics

- Fraud and churn management

The key message here is that business planning is a continuous function dependent on technology and market trends as well as the dynamics and performance of each ASP business.

Systems and Service Definition

Systems and services definition is related to the business modeling and services marketing mix. Service definition brings together all the elements that make up an application service, including:

- Applications themselves

- Application infrastructure (J2EE containers, APIs, transaction and database middleware, etc.)

- Hosting infrastructure (servers, storage systems, routers, switches, security systems, components for redundancy, etc.)

- Management infrastructure (management networks, consoles, service management tools, etc.)

- Customer management infrastructure (tools for customer care, customer contracts, etc.)

The key message here is that systems and services definition addresses the design of the entire ASP infrastructure and management domains in order to provide and ensure provisioning of services in compliance with customer SLAs.

Customer Management

Customer management involves two activities: the initial customer pipeline and customer provisioning.

Customer Pipeline

To better plan resources and evaluate potential business, companies and organizations wishing to become ASP customers are submitted to a customer pipeline process. Each potential prospect must transition through various states before becoming a bona fide customer. Every ASP has its own versions of this process and states. Sample states are a prospect, a qualified prospect, a candidate, a qualified candidate, and finally a customer. Each state reflects a prospect's level of readiness to engage in ASP business and each transition between states requires passing through a certain "gate" to justify the ASP's investment of resources. Here are a few activities an ASP must conduct on behalf of each prospect:

- *Request for Hosting.* Receive a prospect's request for hosting, submitted by ASP sales or a marketing channel. By this time, the customer has gone through a formal process of initial qualification (due diligence) covering a prospect's financial stability, technical skills, and finally, an overall fit for the ASP.

- *Requirements.* Identify a prospect's technical and service requirements for hosting and/or renting applications. The technical requirements may include CPU cycles, disk capacities, communications bandwidths, APIs, security, network and systems management needs, middleware, and service management needs (e.g., types of billing). The service requirements are captured as QoS for the SLAs.

- *Value Propositions.* Define and prioritize value propositions to all parties involved: the customer and its users, the ISVs whose applications will be hosted or rented, the channel, the ASP itself, and others.

- *Business Model.* Help customers with their business models and formal bidding. The business model's elements include partnership and marketing programs, pricing and revenue models, and SLAs, as well as the rules of engagement for all involved members of the ASP ecosystem.

- *Implementation Plan.* Assemble the elements of a customer's implementation plan including schedules of events (e.g., bringing the customer's systems into ASP); various project activities, deliverables, and milestones, approval and acceptance processes, and so on.

- *Contract.* Conduct contract negotiations and execute a binding agreement for services including all detailed SLAs.

Customer Provisioning

Provisioning helps subscribe customers (and their user) to ASP and provision required services. It further itemizes and applies customer-specific technical and service requirements (second bullet in Customer Pipeline section) to configure the required services. Itemized technical and service requirements and decisions about what is needed usually include:

- Application choices (for rentals, from the ASP's portfolio)

- Application-related components (print queues, shared files, notification email accounts, etc.)

- Systemic qualities (performance, scalability, availability, etc.)
- User security profiles, hierarchies, tools (access, subscription, self-management, etc.)
- Pricing and charge plans
- Customer care levels, and some others

Metering and Accounting

The successful operation of an ASP as a revenue-producing business depends heavily on its ability to collect usage data from which to bill customers, report performance, measure utilization of the ASP and customer assets, and plan for future activities and upgrades. To perform these activities, ASPs must collect event data representing the various operational and resource-related systems and network parameters measured in time and space. There are several sources of such data:

- *Application Events.* Data collected by applications (ERP, CRM, supply-chain products, etc.), all of which are known to generate transaction statistics.
- *Integration and Component-Ware Infrastructure's Events and Logs* (Figure 5.5), generated by such systems as:
  - Application Servers (e.g., BEA's WebLogic, iPlanet iAS, IBM's WebSphere)
  - Integration Services (e.g., iPlanet's BuyerXpert and SellerXpert)
  - Web and Portal Server (e.g., iPlanet's Enterprise and Portal Servers)
- *Network/Server/Storage/Systems logs* and data generated by M&M tools, ranging from simple SNMP to middleware (e.g., RPC) and Java-based products.
- *Security Events.* Data from systems logs, firewalls, routers, servers, and so on.

Following are examples of event data categorized by their sources:

Application Systems Events

- Users for exclusive application, by customer, and by time
- Customer and end users for shared applications
- Transaction counts by application, client and server, time period, and so on

- Monetary values of transactions and volumes in a billing period
- Product catalog size

Server Utilization Logs

- CPU loads and time distributions
- CPU usage by process and process threads, and by time

Network Usage

- Bandwidth usage (traffic volume)
- Size of transfer units (e.g., files and transaction size)
- Time of usage (clock and period: peak or not)
- Traffic distribution over time and space (e.g., trunks, routers)
- Web site access statistics (hits, pages requested, distribution of requests and hits, etc.)

Storage Statistics

- Disk usage for HTML pages, XML scripts, Java Server Pages, Java applets and servlets, user registries, content for delivery, software distribution files, databases, and so on
- Backup/restores

Messaging Statistics

- Number of email accounts
- Mailbox size
- Messages sent/received
- Message sizes
- Unsolicited bulk email

Security Events

- Directory entries, for example, users by applications
- Certificates issued
- Passwords generated
- Utilization statistics by customer of firewalls, intrusion detection systems, special security features like shared SSL hardware accelerators
- Virus software runs
- Size of log files by entries or bytes
- Executions of the log file analysis software
- Numbers of security reports per period of time

Configuration Management (Static and Dynamic)

Inventory and configuration management are traditional mainframe and client-server functions. For the ASP, they can be divided into two groups: static and dynamic. Static management helps set up and monitor the facilities in a conventional, incremental fashion, requiring human intervention and decisions. Dynamic management operates automatically on the basis of data collected in real or near-real time to make configuration decisions driven by policies and specific service requirements (i.e., SLAs).

The next two sections—Inventory Management and Configuration Management—describe the static functions for ASP service management. The third section—Dynamic Configuration Management—details configuration and reconfiguration capabilities driven by the ASP's changing conditions.

Inventory Management

Every organization implements inventory management, although to varying degrees of sophistication. Many inventory management systems have been developed and become available to support a broad range of functions for tracking, management and maintenance of inventories, and the purchasing functions for customers/vendors/users. They cover the following components:

- Server and networking hardware
- Networks and network equipment
- Software and applications
- Maintenance and support
- Training programs
- Installation and changes
- Vendor information
- Purchase orders

The more sophisticated inventory and provisioning systems are integrated with monitoring, configuration, and other management categories and functions, usually via some form of an information repository, as depicted in Figure 7.2. Additionally, many inventory and provisioning systems also support automatic inventories through network discovery functions and audits of configurations (also see M&M category and Configuration).

Extensively used and developed by traditional outsourcers, these systems can support multiple customers—like ASPs—with diverse security capabilities. Newer inventory and provisioning systems are also Web-enabled and support open protocols (e.g., HTTP, SSL, XML) and interfaces (e.g., SQL) to other management systems, integrate with multiple vendors' systems, and provide for advanced presentation graphics.

Configuration Management

Configuration management is a well-developed, albeit very complex subject. Its legacy lies in the ISO[5] standards that established the comprehensive conventions and facilities for managing networks to begin with. However, many principles and methods of network configuration management are also applicable to systems and applications. Configuration management is used "to monitor the state of resources and their interrelationships (for example, to describe network topology); and to change the state of, and relationship between, resources[6] . . ." The functions of configuration management are as follows:

- Identify systems and network resources (including applications)

- Define and name these resources

- Monitor and control these resources

- Initialize, operate, reconfigure, close down, and/or delete them, and

- Collect data about their (resources) operations (performance, availability)

The term configuration management is also used for software version control. Typically, software configuration is implemented in a program tool that maintains versions and variations of software source, object, or executable code in time. The tool tracks changes and allows for dynamic updates, retrievals, and audits of versions and variations. Obviously, this tool can be used to manage configuration of any type of content.

Configuration management is tightly integrated with M&M. Nonetheless, it is assigned to the service management category to emphasize ASPs' responsibilities for setting and maintaining customer-specific network and systems configurations. Implications for the ASP for configuration management are similar to those for M&M: maintain different customer configurations securely and consistent with the customer SLAs.

---

5. ISO—International Standards Organization.

6. Morris Sloman, *Network and Distributed Systems Management*, Reading, MA: Addison-Wesley, 1994, p. 72.

Dynamic Configuration and Management

Dynamic configuration management uses real-time, or near real-time, data collected by metering and runs sophisticated algorithms for managing the elements of ASP's *operational* environment:

- Compute the real ASP's operational conditions.
- Match them against those required by customers' SLAs.
- Change parameters of managed elements, as needed.

This function is, perhaps, the most complex of all as it implies dynamic modeling of the entire managed environment with major allowances for demand randomness. The major elements this function manages are routers, switches, Web and application servers, databases, firewalls, load directors, and applications themselves. For example, when a Web server performance falls below a certain level, traffic may be rerouted to another Web server. Or, as in another example, when customers have different performance requirements, traffic for some may be throttled to satisfy the requirements of others with higher performance SLAs.

Billing and Reporting

Billing and reporting applications are essential to ASPs and their customers as they help recognize their ROI in the ASP. Billing and reporting is more than just preparing reports and rendering bills to customers. Reporting also implies data mining to derive patterns of usage trends and growth requirements for business planning. Billing uses multiple pricing plans by customer, applications, and other variables. Billing applications support three essential activities:

- Billing Data Collection. An ASP converts the event data to billing data and then packages it for use by billing services.
- Bill Generation. Next, the ASP uses the billing data to create customer bills and invoices using the rules and fee schedules for each customer.
- Bill Presentment. Finally, the ASP generates bills and uses the diverse means of bill delivery to its customers. For that, the ASP may use Output Management services.

Additionally, the ASPs must support other functions associated with billing including:

- Customizable bills
- Customer account management (to define bill computation rules)

- Interfaces to customer care applications (e.g., help desk) so that ASP's customer account reps can determine the status of individual accounts, make adjustments, resolve disputes, and perform other customer support functions

- Notification ability, for example, sending emails, pages, voice mails, and faxes to customers notifying them about the bill available for viewing and delivery

- Payment interface that enables customers to make payments using credit cards, checks, and so forth.

Summary of Service Management

This is a brief recap of how ASP SLAs are related to ASP service management. Each function of the ASP service management process described in this chapter uses, or is impacted by, the SLAs.

- If ensuring higher QoS requires bigger investments, SLAs must be considered directly or indirectly for *business planning*.

- Designing hosting systems and services (hence, systems and service definition) is like designing multiple and shared NC architectures using the varied quality requirements described in Chapter 5 and listed in Figure 5.6.

- Customer management helps discover QoS requirements leading to the SLAs. It subsequently uses the understanding of service levels to design and provision the right resources and services.

- The SLAs determine which parameters to watch, measure, meter, and account for, directly contributing to *metering and accounting*.

- The SLAs directly drive dynamic *configuration management* decisions for better meeting customers' QoS requirements.

- *Billing and reporting* is performed according to customer SLAs.

Summary

A solid business model, capable organization, and sophisticated service infrastructure are all required but are not sufficient ingredients for an ASP's success. All must be monitored, analyzed, and managed—continuously, persistently, and comprehensively.

The scope of ASP management disciplines is very broad. It ranges from the "ungrateful" costs-of-failure topics to the "mundane" data center operations processes to the "tricky" customer satisfaction issues to the complex contracts administration practices, in addition to the vast diversity of security concerns. An ASP's ability to build and execute these disciplines greatly determines its ultimate success. If it sounds like a tall order, it is. Customer expectations and requirements, technology innovation, legal and regulatory developments—all are changing rapidly, impacting these disciplines in the most profound, yet unpredictable ways. For these reasons, the ASP's need for management will, over time, only grow more pronounced and important. Addressing ASP management early should then translate into improved services to customers, lower costs, better market acceptance and, ultimately, a high growth potential for the entire ASP industry.

Chapter 8

ASP Security Services

For organizations looking for benefits through electronic commerce and other uses of the Internet, ASPs offer enormous promise. But to fulfill this promise, ASPs must overcome the disbelief and fears of the business community. One such fear is security. When outsourcing, a business transfers some of its physical and intellectual assets to an ASP and gears up to use the Internet—an entirely public medium. The fears stem from the concerns for access to these assets, confidentiality and integrity of data, and systems availability. Another critical concern is security related to legal protection of the business' diverse assets (e.g., physical and intellectual, brand identity, good will). This causes many enterprises (especially large businesses) to think twice before outsourcing, as they trust their legal departments more than those of ASPs'. If a subpoena comes in, who will represent the company in court? This and similar security concerns are among many that ASPs must strive to assuage.

To address these concerns, the ASP must offer customers a comprehensive security program and demonstrate its abilities to implement and manage it.

There exists a formal, traditional approach to designing security for a computing/networking system. It can just as easily apply to the ASP. Its basic steps are as follows:

- Analyze threats.
- Identify vulnerabilities.
- Assess risks.
- Determine measures to allay risks.
- Quantify the cost of the measures versus the cost of the risks.
- Design and implement a portfolio of security measures.

This chapter on security, however, does not intend to become a formal manual on how to design ASP security. Instead, it is a compilation of security measures deployed by many existing ASPs. It also offers material with some forward-looking, ASP-specific, security ideas. Here is a brief overview of what this section provides:

- Formal definitions of security policy and security architecture
- Common security architecture frameworks applicable to the ASP
- Sample ASP security architectures for the 3DF architecture (see Chapter 5)
- Brief descriptions of major security measures (technologies and practices)
- Unique requirements for ASP security management
- ASP security management issues

The purpose of this chapter is twofold: it helps analyze the ASP impact on the traditional security disciplines and establishes the relationships between these disciplines within the ASP environment.

Additionally, this chapter widely uses the term "security measure." A security measure is a combination of the most appropriate technologies and best practices to support a certain aspect of systems or network security. Examples of technologies used in security measures are firewalls, intrusion detection systems (IDS; e.g., Snort[1] system), log analysis software, network filters, security test software (e.g., Nessus[2]), directory services, and so forth. The best practices used by

---

1. See www.snort.org for a Snort: "a lightweight network intrusion detection system, capable of performing real-time traffic analysis and packet logging on IP networks. It can perform protocol analysis, content searching/matching and can be used to detect a variety of attacks and probes, such as buffer overflows, stealth port scans, CGI attacks, SMB probes, OS fingerprinting attempts, and much more."

2. See www.nessus.org for Nessus—a security scanner software provided to the Internet community for free and used to audit remote Web sites and networks to determine whether they are vulnerable to malicious attacks or misuse.

security measures may be those for building a secure (hardened) version of operating systems or using architectural methodologies to segregate networks and systems into independent domains, and so on.

Security Is NUMBER ONE Concern

Security was identified in Chapter 5 as an important systemic quality within the NC (and ASP) frameworks used for analysis and design. It was also defined as being complex both in the business and technical sense. Nobody should ever understate or underestimate the importance of security for an organization in general, especially when the organization conducts business online or over the Internet. Security becomes an even greater concern for the customers of ASPs. Most market analysts and trade writers agree with this theory and some even go as far as to declare security as the *first concern* of every customer engaging the ASP to run their applications: [3]

> In selecting an ASP, your first concern should be security. If you are going to trust someone to handle your financial, ERP, and customer-relations applications, you darn well better make sure your data is in good hands. The ASP you choose should have a security officer, a written set of policies and regular security audits, and all audit results should be available for your inspection. Some ASPs go as far as to do background checks on their staff members who will have access to your data. Your ASP should be checking on you, too. Upon receiving a request for new users to access sensitive data, the ASP should contact your staff to verify the request.
>
> Along with physical security and employing technology such as VPN, firewalls and intrusion-detection software, ASPs must provide safeguards to ensure that each customer sees only its own data . . .

This statement conveys the importance of ASP security in a very charismatic way. It can be summarized as follows:

- Security is an ASP customer's number one concern.

- The ASP security program must address the key issues such as a security officer overseeing customer systems' security, written sample policies, measures to ensure security, audit and reporting, and others.

- ASPs must provide security SLAs to its customers defining mutual roles and responsibilities of the ASP and customers/users.

- ASPs' security SLAs must also address cross-customer confidentiality issues within the ASP environment.

---

3. Art Wittmann, "Is there an ASP in Your Future?" *Network Computing,* June 12, 2000.

What Is a Security Policy?

Every organization, big and small, is expected to have a certain understanding of security issues related to its business activities. "A Security Policy is a set of rules which apply to all security-relevant activities in a security domain. A security domain is typically the set of computer and communications resources belonging to one organization. The rules are established by an authority for that security domain".[4] Some organizations express this understanding in their formal security policies. Others implement security measures without a policy.

Notwithstanding an organization's attitude toward security, when it becomes an ASP customer, it falls to that ASP to provide security. Again, the first question the ASP asks is about the security policy. If it doesn't exist, the ASP may help to define or, at least, formalize it. However, a security policy is only a starting point for designing a customer's security architecture for deploying over an ASP. The ASP needs to address many other security issues. They are as follows:

- Many security issues flow from an ASP's sharing nature. This ASP may be sharing a data center's floor space, network bandwidth and equipment (e.g., LAN switches), management network and management systems, professional and management staff, and even servers and applications.

- Others issues emanate from an ASP's complex service-provider and business-user relationship with its customers. These relationships may be team-based or arms-length but always contractual, therefore requiring a continuous business and technology vigilance and reporting on the SLAs.

- Finally, each ASP is a bona fide business, with its own business and marketing strategies. These strategies define the types of customers to whom it provides services and what security it may want to deliver. Also, customers usually have heightened expectations of what this ASP provides as opposed to what they could do themselves.

Whoever the ASP, one thing is clear: ASP security architectures can be more sophisticated than those that customers could implement on their own. Here are a few reasons why:

- By leveraging its intrinsic economies of scale and scope, an ASP can use the best-of-breed technologies and practices such as using two or more different firewall types, or services such as Counterpane,[5] to monitor system and network activity.

---

4. Warwick Ford and Michael S. Baum, *Secure Electronic Commerce*, Upper Saddle River, NJ: Prentice Hall, 1997, p. 95.

5. See www.counterpane.com for dynamic managed security monitoring services offered by the eponymous company (Counterpane).

- By dealing with its customers contractually an ASP can ensure a customer's security with possible monetary remunerations or other forms of compensation for losses sustained due to security failure.

- By being a multicustomer service provider, an ASP provides for customer privacy protection against other customers. This privacy protection (e.g., confidentiality) is something the customer's security policy may not even be addressing. Without an ASP, this might leave the customer vulnerable to attacks when hosting in-house.

- By constantly updating its security measures (technologies, tools, practices, etc.), an ASP can deliver state-of-the-art technologies and practices to its customers and do so in a timely fashion.

It is universally accepted that security architecture is a custom product and no two organizations have the same architecture. This statement, however truthful, doesn't bode well for most ASPs' strategies towards maximizing economies of scope and focus. It is therefore conceivable that an ASP, with a clear business model and focused marketing strategy, may develop multiple security architecture templates applicable to different customer types. These customer types may depend on an ASP's market segmentation; other classification schemes may be based on security strength, focus, function, or other criteria.

What Is Security Architecture?

Security architecture is an end-to-end, structured, integrated, and standards-based assemblage of hardware, software, network components, and operational and business practices working together to meet (and exceed) the security requirements expressed in the customer's security policy. Security architecture is unified, comprehensive, and coherent. Besides providing for prevention, protection, and detection, it is also designed to ensure:

- Lower cost of future systems and network implementations

- Ease of systems and network management

- Properly balanced security functionality and management flexibility

- Ease-of-use by end users

- A customer's strong sense of confidence in the ASP's provisioning of security leading to high overall customer satisfaction

Security Architecture Design Frameworks

Prevention, Protection, Detection, and Response

When analyzing failures it is customary to think of how they could be prevented, how to protect against them, how to detect them as soon as possible after they happen, what caused them, and how to respond to them. These four key functions of security—prevention, protection, detection, and response—can be aligned along the axis of time to become a *temporal* dimension of security measures. Indeed, prevention is done before a failure takes place; protection—when attempts to cause them occur, and detection and response—is done after the failures.

In the world of NCs and ASPs, security is a key quality called upon to guarantee a system's uninterrupted operations. So, the NC and ASP security measures can also be characterized as preventive, protective, detective, and response. Or, more specifically:

- *Preventive* measures are used to forewarn, deter, and hence evade security breach attempts. Examples are administrative control over distribution of authorities or a timely installation of systems patches.

- *Protective* measures provide dynamic deterrents to discourage attacks by making the costs of perpetrating them higher than the potential gain (e.g., through encryption which may require tremendous computing resources to crack the keys).

- *Detective* measures are used to analyze the results of security breaches or the attempts at them. Key objectives here are to find failures faster and, since many security breaches frequently go unnoticed and unchecked, to ensure finding as many of them as possible. Examples are analyzing intrusion detection and systems logs. *Detective* measures also help design the improvements to all prevention, protection, detection, and response measures

- *Response* measures are activities undertaken by the parties injured after the attacks have been identified. When an attack occurs, an established (and hopefully tested) attack response protocol is engaged. Its activities may include, but are not limited to, the following:
  - Stem the attacks.
  - Alert all involved.
  - Engage security analyst(s).

- Launch *remedial* measures that isolate damage, reassign resources (e.g., via a switchover of redundant systems), and reinstate lost controls.
- Follow *remedies and healing* measures to help restore damaged resources, compensate for losses, and rebuild capabilities (e.g., by installing new equipment).
- Collect data required by security insurance and file claims for (1) loss of or damage to information assets resulting from a breach of security and/or (2) interruption of business due to loss of use.
- Track the intruders and investigate their activities.
- Improve preventive, protective, detective, and response measures.

Characterizing security measures as preventive, protective, detective, and response may be confusing at times. This is especially true when trying to discern the preventive and protective effects of a security measure. But no matter what causes confusion—semantic interpretations or the timing of when the measure is used—it is still very useful to think about the temporal aspects of the security measures. There may be situations when investing in a preventive measure helps alleviate operational vulnerabilities rather than trying to catch security breaches in real time or live with the consequences. For example, hardening the OS mitigates risks of systems takeovers during runtime. Or, vice versa, prevention may be expensive to some, so they may prefer to invest in less expensive protection or detection. For example, sharing systems and network resources rather than buying dedicated ones saves costs but may create security exposures. Encrypting transactions at runtime may then be a viable means of protection in a shared environment.

Security thus becomes an economic concept. Costs establish a subtle balance between the gains from security breaches and the means to perpetrate them. It is a leapfrogging game of hacking schemes and countermeasures controlled, directly or indirectly, by costs. Incidentally, even when clever hacking schemes or security measures are just inventions of brilliant minds, there is an assumed cost proxy for them all. More specific examples of hacking ideas—controlled by costs—are:

- It is possible to crack any encryption (even public key) given enough computing power. In fact, schemes using thousands of computers linked over the Internet have been tested to prove this feasible.
- Schemes for eavesdropping on fiber optical cable have been written about. It may be very expensive—yes, but possible.
- Personnel screening can be thwarted by falsifying documents and by altering or deleting records. The cost of doing so may

be either monetary, or implied, for example, that of breaking the law and the dubious "pleasure" of dealing with unsavory helpers.

Thinking about how to battle such hacking schemes, one cannot help but appreciate how expensive it might be. Here then are examples of high-cost security measures:

- Traffic filtering for prevention of, or protection against, Distributed Denial Of Service (DDOS) attacks becomes increasingly expensive on the high-speed network backbones, if economically feasible at all. The faster the traffic (and it may be multiple Gigabits), the faster the filtering capabilities must be. Besides some technical problems—such as synchronization for existing and dominant high-speed technologies (SONET)—this would also require extremely powerful computers. Hence, high costs!

- A similar problem occurs with the firewalls. The faster the traffic, the faster the firewall analysis must be performed or else the firewall may become a performance bottleneck. Hence, expensive servers may be needed to run the firewalls.

- Physical access security may require biometrics, which is an expensive proposition in and of itself.

Domains and Facets

There are many different ways to look at and analyze the ASP model for designing security architectures. Many people and organizations have tried their hands at it. They include the national and international standards groups, general purpose and specialized boutique security consultants, numerous organizations' own security teams, and so forth—all trying to design the unique security frameworks for providing the best security architectures and measures, at costs that are commensurate with the benefits. Notwithstanding the differences among them, all these frameworks have one goal—to safeguard the systems and network environments from attempts to thwart their normal operational mode.

This chapter and those later in the book use two popular security frameworks described by many different researchers and employed by many practitioners and ASPs themselves. These two frameworks are called domains and facets. They are described here.

Domains. One popular approach to building security architectures is to view the environment it must safeguard as consisting of three distinct domains of tangible components: physical infrastructure, networks, and systems.

- *Systems* security is about controlling the security aspects of hardware and software to ensure they are accessed and operated by authenticated users possessing proper authorizations.
- Security for *physical infrastructure* deals with access to the ASP data centers and other physical facilities.
- *Network* security covers all security aspects of data moving across diverse networks: LANs and WANs.

These tangible dimensions of the NC and ASP architectures are frequently shown as rows in a matrix and mapped against key functional requirements in the matrix's columns, such as authentication, authorization, administration, accounting, audits, planning, and training. Then the matrix cells are filled in with the security measures. Once completely filled, the matrix is expected (assumed!) to provide for comprehensive security.

Facets. Many security professionals promote, and many have written about, the five major facets of security: access control, authentication, integrity, confidentiality, and non-repudiation. By now, there exists a large consensus on this classification that is best expressed in Part 2 of the OSI Reference Model.[6] This consensus leads to the belief that the five security facets (some call them services, categories, types, etc.) are overarching in their ability to cover and incorporate, in a comprehensive manner, a majority of the salient security requirements and capabilities.

This author accepts that the facets are indeed comprehensive yet still suggests two more: availability and accountability. This is similar to other authors' opinions[7] and has survived the test of time. The seven facets are defined below and used later as benchmarks to check the completeness of the ASP security architecture. The seven facets are:

- "*Access Control* defines who (or what) may have access to some object... The Access Control problem is essentially one of authorization, rights, and privileges . . .
- *Authentication* means establishing proof of identity. Usually it involves one of a combination of something you are, something you know, and something you have . . .
- *Data Integrity* refers to the current condition of data as compared to their 'pure' and original state . . ."[8]

---

6. ISO-7498-2, 1988.

7. Phillipe A. Janson, "Security for Management and Management of Security," IBM Zurich Research Laboratory.

8. Larry J. Hughes, Jr. *Actually Useful Internet Security Techniques*, Indianapolis, IN: New Riders Publishing, 1995, pp. 10–13.

- *Confidentiality* refers to the assurances of privacy for information stored, processed, and communicated over the network. Mostly defined through the use of cryptography, *confidentiality* can be achieved by other means too (e.g., through physical security).

- *"Non-Repudiation* ensures the availability of sufficiently strong evidence to support the speedy resolution of any"[9] situations when legitimate users may repudiate a communication or transaction.

- *Availability* is the facet of security reflecting on the security architecture's ability to provide service in the face of "disruptions, perturbations, abuses, or misuses" of network and systems components and resources.

- *Accountability* is the facet of security that establishes the means for holding some individual accountable for the actions or events taking place in the systems. It is also used for billing services.

Both domains and facets are used for designing ASP security architectures. Different security measures may support multiple domains and map into multiple facets.

Sample Security Architecture for ASP

Domains, Facets, and Security Architecture

The design of the ASP security architectures uses both the domains and facets frameworks. It uses domains to segregate the ASP architecture into security architecture views, for physical infrastructure, network, and systems. It next uses facets to verify the completeness of each view of the security architecture. It does so to ensure that every view has measures that map into every facet.

In describing the security measures for different security architecture views, every attempt is made to be comprehensive. While a difficult proposition—the progress in security technologies never stops—this should nonetheless help analyze which security measures apply to the ASP and which need to be changed as the security landscape changes.

---

9. Warwick Ford and Michael S. Baum, *Secure Electronic Commerce*, Upper Saddle River, NJ: Prentice Hall, 1997, pp. 99–100.

Systems Security Architecture

The Systems' security architecture enables and controls all security measures for the computer and communications systems (servers, routers, switches, storage devices, etc.) located within data centers. Figure 8.1 provides a view of a systems security architecture built over a hypothetical customer's five-tier, 3DF-based systems architecture (see Chapter 5). The notations used for differentiating the security measures from systems components are as follows: all security measures are annotated in upper case letters and shaded while all systems components appear in lower case letters.

Table 8.1 lists the most common systems security measures recommended for ASPs. Column 1 of the table defines the security measure. Column 2 explains the functions each measure performs and the components it consists of. Column 2 also includes in each explanation the verbs *prevent*, *protect*, *detect* and *respond* in reference to the temporal aspects of security measures described in the

Figure 8.1   *Systems view of security architecture.*

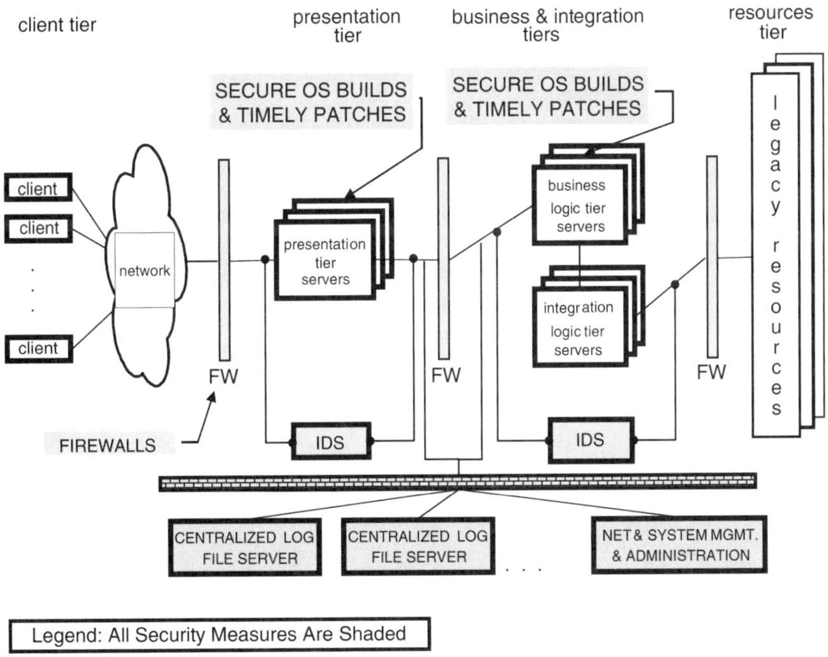

Security Architecture Design Frameworks section. Finally, Column 3 provides the view on which facets each measure maps to. Note that Figure 8.1 doesn't show all the security measures described in Table 8.1.

Table 8.1 *Common Systems Security Measures*

Measures	*Explanation (Prevention, Protection, Detection, Response)*	*Security Facet*
Systems & Network Architectures	*Prevents* exposure of data among customer networks. The N-tiered architecture approach—like the one used by 3DF, in Chapter 5—segments the network into tiers. Untrusted networks must not access any tier except presentation protected by various access controls (e.g., routers, firewalls, servers) and communicating to other tiers via access control systems for those tiers. ASP management network (not shown in Figure 8.1) must be trusted to have access to each customer's network.	Access Control
IP Access Control	*Protects* against unauthorized network access. Follows the policy "that which is not specifically allowed is denied." May be implemented with firewalls.	Access Control Authentication
Host-Level Access Control	Same as IP access control for systems with an IP stack: routers, switches, servers, and others.	Access Control Authentication
Encryption	*Protects* against interception, modification, and exposure of networked content. May be implemented with SSL at the presentation tier; 128 bit digital certificates for interserver communications; tunneling (e.g., IPSec) for administrative access; and so forth.	Mostly Integrity, but also: • Authentication • Confidentiality • Non-repudiation
Systems Logs	*Detects* breaches that have occurred or attempts thereof implemented • On remote log servers • With special software *Response* protocols are engaged following detection.	Access Control

Table 8.1   *Common Systems Security Measures (Continued)*

Intrusion Detection Systems (IDS)	Monitors network traffic to *detect* and report security breaches or attempts thereof in real time and possibly engage *protection* measures. Can also predict breaches by examining IDS logs. Host-based IDS helps *detect* changes to systems binaries and/or configuration files. *Response* protocols are engaged following detection.	Access Control
Secure OS builds	*Protects* systems OS by limiting functionality to the bare minimum via removal of certain packages and features and adding security software, like: • SSH to encrypt data connections between systems • Host-based access control mechanisms (see above) • Software integrity checks (see host-based IDS) • Patch installation management tools	Access Control Confidentiality Integrity Availability
Patch Installs (timely patches)	*Prevent* exploitation by malicious parties of known vulnerabilities on systems that lack security patches.	Access Control Confidentiality Integrity Availability
Administration	*Prevents* spread of authority beyond that which is absolutely necessary.	Access Control Authentication Confidentiality
Password Services	These services include password generation, secure distribution to applications, and availability throughout the ASP. *Prevents* the use of aged passwords that may be divulged and/or guessable. Prevents encrypted password collection (e.g., through "match-only" access to LDAP-based password stores). Prevents password snooping.	Access Control
Virus Detection	*Detects* viruses that infested the systems. Virus detection is implemented as software scanners operating on incoming messages, inspecting transactions, and checking files. *Response* activities always follow virus detection.	May affect any facet but mostly: Availability Accountability

Physical Security Architecture

The physical view of security architecture is provided in Figure 8.2. It shows the major physical components of a hypothetical ASP data center and security measures, pointed to with arrows.

There are many other security measures not shown in the diagram but defined and categorized in Table 8.2. Note that there is an image of systems security architecture, from Figure 8.1, "nested" inside the physical infrastructure under the headings Customer 1, Customer 2, and Customer N.

Table 8.2 lists the most common physical security measures recommended for ASPs. The columns in Table 8.2 have the same meanings as those in Table 8.1.

Figure 8.2   *Physical infrastructure view of security architecture.*

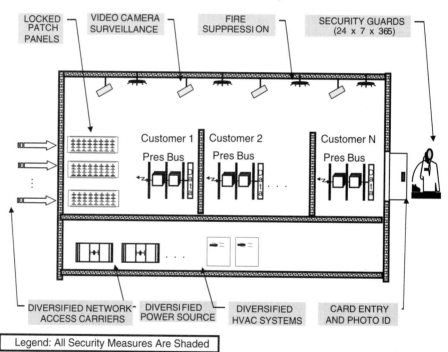

Table 8.2   *Common Physical Security Measures*

Measures	Explanation (Prevention, Protection, Detection, Response)	Security Facet
Preauthorized Visits	*Prevent* and *deter* unauthorized access to the data center facilities.	Authentication
Personnel Screening	*Prevents* granting access privileges to personnel who fail security screens.	Access Control
Recordkeeping	Helps *detect* unauthorized access to and activities performed at the data center. *Response* activities always follow a physical security breach detection. Implemented with systematic and detailed record accounting with scheduled and random audits.	Access Control Authentication Nonrepudiation
Administrative Console's Access Restrictions	*Prevents* and *deters* unauthorized access to administrative console devices. May be implemented using Terminal Access Controller Access Control Systems (TACACS+) protocol.	Access Control
Card Key Entry with Photo IDs	*Protects* against unauthorized access. Usually implemented with mechanical locks, electronic-magnetic entry cards, or biometric access systems.	Access Control Authentication Accounting
Video Surveillance	*Detects* unauthorized entries and activities. Video security observers are expected to *respond* to detected unauthorized activities.	Access Control Authentication
Guard on Duty	*Protects* against unauthorized people, maintains physical access records, mans video surveillance, and is on defense against other types of physical security breaches.	Authentication Accounting Accounting
Locked Patch Panels, Cabinets, Cages	*Protects* and *deters* unauthorized attempts at access to locked facilities. May be implemented with technologies similar to card entry: mechanical locks, electronic-magnetic entry cards, or biometric access systems. Also may use single-key system (customer gets one key; backup key is sealed and kept at ASP, available for customer inspection at any time).	Access Control Authentication

Table 8.2 *Common Physical Security Measures (Continued)*

Fire Suppression	*Detects* fires and prevents its damage as much as possible. *Response* activities follow an established protocol (including a possible switchover to backup site).	Access Control (availability) Integrity
Diversified Network Carriers	*Protects* against the loss of network communications.	Access Control (availability)
Diversified Power Sources	*Protects* against the loss of power. Implemented with backup power systems such as battery-based, natural gas, or diesel powered UPS.	Access Control (availability)
Diversified HVAC	*Protects* against the loss of environmental conditions required for computing and networking assets' normal operations.	Access Control (availability)
Cable and Wiring Management Systems	Helps *prevent* wiring/cabling mistakes.	Access Control Integrity Confidentiality
Raised Floors	By not exposing wires and cables, raised floors help *prevent* tampering and hence help *deter* unauthorized access to communication and power lines (provided barriers between locked rooms are maintained under floor).	Access Control Authentication
Seismic Bracing	*Protects* against damage caused by earthquake tremors.	Access Control (availability)
Construction Architecture	Helps *prevent* unnecessary construction. Architectural solutions suggest the overall design of data centers to improve the ease of operations, management, and customer privacy. The requirements specify special topologies for rooms and facilities in the data center buildings, wall designs, floors, door, windows, and so forth.	Access Control Authentication Confidentiality
Disaster Recovery	Mostly, *response* measures of *remedial* nature (damage minimization, control reinstallment, etc.) and *healing* measures (restoration, loss compensation, rebuilding, etc.).	Integrity Confidentiality Availability Accountability

Network Security Architecture

The network view of security architecture is depicted in Figure 8.3. It shows conceptually the major network components of an ASP and major network security measures. Not all network security measures are shown in the diagram but they are defined and categorized in Table 8.3. The physical infrastructure—the data center and a component of a hypothetical systems security architecture—are shown "nested" inside the network security architecture. The network security architecture may connect to multiple data centers.

Figure 8.3   *Network view of security architecture.*

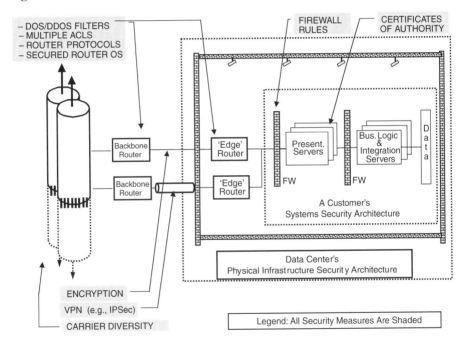

Table 8.3 *Common Network Security Measures*

Measures	*Explanation (Prevention, Protection, Detection, Response)*	*Security Facet*
Router and Firewall Access Control Lists	Programming routers to maintain secure access control lists (ACLs) of customer specific IP addresses and transport layer ports and services (e.g., HTTP), helps *prevent* unauthorized network access. Additionally, packet filtering helps *prevent* common spoofing and "man-in-the-middle" exploits. Finally, for less secure ports and services (e.g., sendmail, telnet), routers must be programmed to support secondary, less secure ACLs.	Access Control Authentication Confidentiality
Firewalls	Defining firewall rules helps further *prevent* and *deter* unauthorized access to ASP customers' data and systems.	Access Control Authentication
Secure Hardening of Router OS	*Protects* networks by limiting routers' acceptance of non-secure exchanges and services (typically provided by default).	Access Control Confidentiality
Router Protocols	Router Border Gateway Protocol 4 (BGP4) Routers use BGP4 to advertise IP network routes. ASPs must manage routers to support only route topologies with authenticated customers. This helps *prevent* and *deter* unauthorized access to the ASP network. Hot Standby protocols (e.g., Cisco's HSRP) Hot standby protocols allow building networks in which surviving routers take over the jobs of failed ones. Enabling these protocols helps *protect* against failures.	Authentication Access Control (availability)
Network Level Authentication, Authorization, and Accounting	Implementing special high security systems like TACACS+ helps *prevent*, *deter,* or *detect* attempts at any unauthorized access to, and performed activities on, the networks and systems via administrative consoles (see also physical security architecture above for administrative console's access restrictions). *Response* may involve a switchover of network facilities.	Access Control Authentication
Network Encryption	Usually achieved via Secure HTTP (SHTTP), Secure Socket Layer (SSL and HTTPS), or tunneling (e.g., IPSec), encryption helps *protect* data integrity and confidentiality.	Integrity Confidentiality

Table 8.3   *Common Network Security Measures* *(Continued)*

Detection and Protection Tools against (Distributed) Denial Of Service (DOS and DDOS) Attacks	*Prevents* (1) denial of access to the customer site and (2) prevents the exploitation of this site as a proxy to attack others. There are many DOS and DDOS profiles and corresponding tools: • Traditional firewalls. • Packet filters installed on the "edge" of the ASP backbone to customer networks to prevent customer sites from becoming puppet sites to attack others. • Packet filters to limit ongoing attacks. • Packet filters to detect on-coming attacks.[a]	Access Control (availability)
VPN Services	A customer's multiple corporate site may be connected via VPN. Using VPN *protects* data integrity and confidentiality	Integrity Confidentiality
Diversity of Network Carriers	See physical security architecture.	

a. An interesting example of Denial of Service is a simple "SYN Flag" attack in which TCP packets arriving at a site have SYN flag set so as to request the establishment of new sessions that never occur. The receiving computer allocates resources and waits. If more TCP packets with SYN flag arrive, more resources are allocated until the computer is out of resources and hangs.

Additional Security Services

In addition to tangible products and processes related to ASP security as described, ASPs may provide many other security-related activities. Sometimes ASPs perform these services themselves; sometimes they contract them out. Such services may include, but are not limited to, the following:

- Code review services that employ tools and techniques used to search for, identify, and recommend changes to code to eliminate potential vulnerabilities. Additionally, when source code is not available, application testing helps stress applications under varying conditions for application security design problems.

- Training ASP customers to expand their knowledge and understanding of security issues and various security tools and methods.

- ASP customer architecture security assessments, studies, and tests.
- Customer's industry-specific security assessments, frequently conducted by vertical industry ASPs or by industry experts contracted by them. For example, health care industry customers must abide by certain federal, state, and local rules and regulations in handling patient and treatment information. The Healthcare Insurance Portability and Accountability Act of 1996 (HIPAA) is one such federal regulatory document.

Quantifying ASP Security

Many service providers, as well as customers who in-source their information technology, have all historically used a cost-plus approach to valuing security. Things should change, however, for the ASP. Security is the ASP customer's number one concern and it behooves ASPs to become more serious about quantifying it. While the customers are wary about security, they are still very sensitive to fees. So ASPs must provide the best-of-breed security but also run a tight ship. How can they do it?

Microeconomics to the rescue! Attach a price tag to each security measure, not based on what it costs, but on its value to the customer. Assemble all such costs, use their sum as a benchmark, and see how it all plays out in the market. This way the ASP may become more competitive and enjoy better control over its own costs.

A good idea? Yes, but it is easier said than done. How does one find these values? Every measure addresses only certain particular aspects of security. Yet, in a good security architecture, security measures are interrelated. So when one fails (or is thwarted), another one takes over. There is a certain pattern and sequence to how this happens and it is determined by the security architecture itself. If an ASP understands this sequence (or sequences), it might then analyze how much security it provides its customers and what to charge for it. Different architectures will result in different sequences, hence, different numbers. Thus, the main benefit to the ASP will be its ability to create certain security templates and know in advance their safeguarding abilities, their costs, and their value to the customer.

The following is a brief insight into how such an analysis, given a particular security architecture, can be performed.

At What Cost Security?

A formal analysis of security architecture, consisting of multiple security measures, would ask questions about the relationships among the measures, about how they work, or how they impact each other. Other questions would be which security measures the customer relies on first, which ones second, third, and so on. Combined with the understanding of the customer's specific security needs, answers to these questions would provide critical insights into which security measures are absolutely necessary, which ones are just useful, and which ones are merely nice-to-haves. Additionally, such analyses would help value the losses the measures ensure against, price the measures, and decide on the priorities of implementing them.

If the answers to these questions are available, it is possible to establish a notation to describe the relationships among the measures and their overall impact on security. The easiest notation is a simple English-like pseudolanguage. Imagine there is a hypothetical environment with four security measures (M_{1-4}) available to safeguard it (for example, packet-filtering routers, firewall-based packet filtering, OS-level network hardening, and application level connection filtering). Then, the application of these measures can be expressed as follows:

> **Apply M_1 security measure**
> **IF < M_1 fails> THEN Apply M_2**
>   **IF <M_2 fails> THEN Apply M_3**
>   **IF <M_3 fails> THEN Apply M_4**
>   **IF <M_4 fails> THEN Declare a Security Failure.**
>   **ELSE Continue**
>   **ELSE Continue**
>   **ELSE Continue**
> **ELSE Continue.**

Next, if it were possible to obtain (or conjecture) the probability of each measure being breached—for example, P_1, P_2, P_3, or P_4—then it is possible to derive the reliability (P) of the entire security architecture. Indeed, given P_1 the probability of M_1 failing, the probability of both M_1 and M_2 failing is P_2*P_1, the probability of both M_1, and M_2, and M_3 failing is $P_3*P_2*P_1$, and so on. Then, P can be calculated as follows:

$$P = 1 - P_4 * P_3 * P_2 * P_1.$$

It is useful, if at all possible, for an ASP to review security measures offered its customers using the above approach. It may open some eyes within their own organizations as to:

- Which security measure to develop to better meet security requirements of the market segments this ASP is serving

- What security measures to offer to which customers

- How to price the security measures reflecting the value of safeguarding they provide
- How to better define the security-related value propositions to customers and partners
- How to better build the security architectures, both for the ASP as a whole and customers
- How to better design and contractually define the security SLAs

If an ASP implements the above approach, it may develop security architecture templates consisting of multiple security measures and then apply them to the customers' security architectures. By doing this, the ASP would stand to benefit both operationally, by leveraging its processes, and strategically, due to the ability to offer customers better articulated and understood security architectures, security measures, security SLAs, and eventually clearer, value-proxy-based, competitive pricing.

Analyzing Security Architecture

Figure 8.4 shows the approach to how the architecture, with four security measures, M_{1-4}, can be analyzed.

Figure 8.4 *Approach to analyzing security architecture's security bastions.*

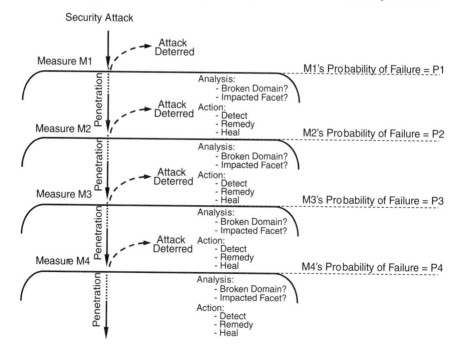

The diagram in Figure 8.4 shows four security bastions, one for each measure, and a hypothetical security attack. At each bastion, the attack can succeed, resulting in penetration, or it can be deterred. For each potential attack penetration, the approach recommends to analyze which domain it broke through (e.g., systems, network, physical) and which facet it impacted. Next, actions are designed. Since penetration already occurred, prevention is of no use now. Here, the approach advocates the use of detective and response actions: first detect the nature of attack and damage done, next search for remedies to limit the damage and neutralize the attack, and finally, decide on healing.

Example of Security Architecture Analysis

Figure 8.5 shows an example of how a real attack could occur. Here, four measures are a router, a firewall, a hardened OS, and data encryption at the application layer. The attack is very savvy. It breaks through the router's access control, "fools" the firewalls whose rules could not identify the attack's profile, and then breaks into the OS.

Figure 8.5   *Example of security architecture under security attack.*

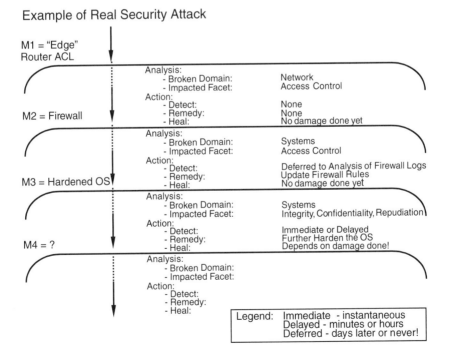

At this point, the attack's damage can be very severe depending on the attacker's intent and, perhaps, other security measures. The attacker may read the data affecting confidentiality, or alter them affecting integrity, or destroy them, thereby affecting availability. Or, the attacker may place in time bombs, or computer worms and viruses. The attacker may want to use the system to launch attacks against other Internet sites. Finally, the attacker might use this customer's systems to attack other customers hosted by the same ASP. This is especially dangerous if shared resources are not safeguarded by applicable security measures. Or, the attacker may want to simply sabotage the site by slowing it down or deface its Web pages. Once the attackers are in, the way it is described here, their options are very open.

If it were possible at this point to determine the value of the violated facet, for example, of integrity and confidentiality (both applied to data), the customer could have reasons to pay more for better design of router ACLs, or more powerful or reprogrammed firewalls, or stronger OS security, or choose to deploy other measures such as encryption of databases, and so forth. Many other considerations would arise here too:

- Encrypting databases would require faster server processors or extra encryption acceleration hardware.
- If availability is very important, replication sites may be needed.
- Intrusion detection may be needed to analyze attack patterns in order to protect against them in the future.
- (Distributed) Denial of Service prevention filters may be installed.

What is really enlightening about the approach and especially the hypothetical example above is that its scenarios are very possible: IDs and passwords are guessable; firewall rules are not perfect; OSs cannot be completely "hardened"; encryption can be cracked, and so on. And so, as the ASP business evolves and grows, and ASPs recognize security as a value proposition, many questions would still and always remain. What security measures are needed? How to sequence them in the architecture? At what cost security?

Security Management

All security domains, facets, and measures discussed above aim at safeguarding the ASP customers. However, the very environment that needs this security the most is the ASP management environment itself. Figure 7.1 showed this very explicitly. There, security, as a category of ASP management, uses a horizontal brace to show that it applies to all other management categories: M&M, operations, services management, and customer care. Indeed, the ASP management environment depends on security more than, or at least as much as, any ASP customer. For this brief insight, it suffices to say that since an ASP supports multiple customers, its own security capabilities must exceed, or at least match, security requirements of its most demanding customers (in many cases, such as co-location ASPs, this is due in part to the fact that customers can install any equipment into the data center and have all privileges on their own equipment, making it a potent platform from which to launch an attack).

Figure 8.6 attempts to provide a simple visualization of the relationships among security, other ASP management functional categories, the ASP, and its customers. Arrow 3 shows that the same security (or more as was just mentioned) applies to the ASP management as it does to ASP customers.

Another critical aspect of ASP security is the integration of security into the broader context of the ASP management environment. After all, security must be managed too (Arrow 4 in Figure 8.6). Brief descriptions of basic security management needs that may or may not be integrated into the overall ASP management framework follow here.

Figure 8.6   *Security within ASP's management framework.*

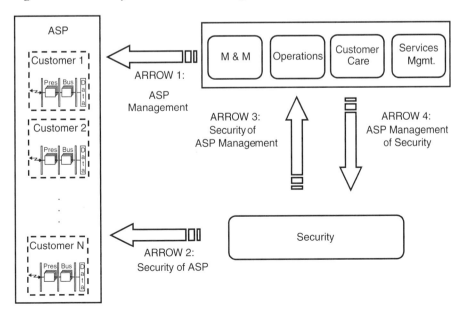

Security Organization Management

The very first rule of security management in the ASP is that it should not be confused or combined with other forms of management. A common mistake, for example, is to combine network management with network security management. The former is concerned with "feeds and speeds," that is, making sure that connectivity and performance are maintained. The latter is concerned with potential vulnerabilities.

When such roles are combined, the result is usually inadequate attention paid to security. In such cases, a common security fault occurs when network managers, in an attempt to troubleshoot a network problem, turn off access controls on network equipment. The result is, at best, a temporary vulnerability, and more often a permanent security lapse.

As a result, security management should always be separated from other forms of management, such as network and server management. Taking this a step further, many security experts strongly recommend separating security hardware from other forms of hardware. For example, if a packet filtering router is being used in place of a firewall (for cost reasons), the recommendation would be to use two routers, one for packet filtering and one for traffic routing, rather than combine the two functions on one piece of hardware.

Access Control Management

Managing ACLs and other access control attributes of multiple systems (e.g., routers, firewall, hosts) is perhaps one of the first concerns of any NC and ASP. This management must cover the following functions: centralization, storage, safeguarding, distribution, creations, and modifications across multiple systems and networks, for multiple customers as well as for the ASP itself. To safeguard these lists and attributes against tampering and disclosure – in violation of integrity and confidentiality facets—ASPs must develop appropriate management strategies, policies, tools, and procedures. ASPs also manage physical security such as:

- Access control systems and access cards for data centers and customer facilities (e.g., vaults)
- Personnel security screening
- M&M of environmental and power controls or interfaces with those who do it to help network and systems problem resolution
- M&M of video surveillance

Encryption Key Management

Encryption key management functions are key generation, distribution, storage, update, archival, and destruction. While the research and innovations related to these subjects continue, with many issues still open and outstanding, many solid tools and practices have already been created and implemented. Since cryptography is outside the scope of this book, interested readers are referred to a huge body of security literature where the theory of cryptography and key management functions are described in more detail and with scientific accuracy. As for ASPs who must manage keys for multiple customers, both they and others (e.g., certificate authorities) may be involved in handling key management for ASP customers.

Authentication Management

Authentication management is based on cryptography and key management as described before. Yet, its challenges go beyond key management. One of them deals with the so-called proxy and forwardable certificates of authority – essentially required for delegating authority for getting and using certificates on behalf of others. Other authentication management issues are single sign-on (SSO), use of dedicated workstations, smart cards, and so forth. ASP management may handle these challenges by itself or delegate them to others. In either case, ASP management must remain in control.

Non-Repudiation Management

Another subject requiring a deeper inquiry, non-repudiation is managed by providing digital signatures in public key infrastructures (PKI). Again, an ASP may manage nonrepudiation itself, as some do, or outsource it to specialized security service providers.

Audit Management

Already mentioned earlier for all types of systems logging (servers, routers, firewalls, etc.), intrusion detection systems, and on-line event monitoring, audit functions are critical for ensuring continuity of security operations. On-line monitoring can be protective since, once it detects security violations, it may undertake the remedial and healing actions. When analyzing logs, audit looks for patterns inconsistent with the ASP or customer's security policies and hence may raise alarms.

Summary: Implications of Security for ASP

It was stated earlier that all security measures described in this chapter were derived from a collection of security offerings of existing ASPs. As such, they are the real security measures implemented by the real ASPs for their real customers. Conversely, one might easily notice that nothing in their descriptions identifies these measures with an ASP. Any NC—an informational Web, a portal, a trade exchange, an auction site, and so forth—might as well be using the same measures.

So, why talk about these measures at all in the context of ASP? Only because some ASPs offer them? Well, not only for that reason. It is not the measures, but how they are packaged and managed for ASP customers that really count. ASPs mainly advertise the functionality of security measures they offer, yet internally they manage the many unique aspects of ASP security not present in the NC. These unique aspects of security flow from an ASP's aspiration to maximize the sharing of resources by multiple customers, a commitment to manage each customer's qualities per their SLAs, and a need to meter consumption of services by each customer for accounting and billing. The shared resources and the necessary ubiquity of complex management tools deployed throughout the ASP environment together heighten the relevance of intercustomer security facets, especially those of access control, data confidentiality, and accountability. It is then up to ASPs themselves to establish security philosophies and policies and develop appropriate implementation practices for delivering adequate security to their customers. Following are two guidelines—*need-to-know and right-to-know policy* and *partitioning*—which should help address, albeit only partially, the intercustomer security facets in a shared ASP environment.

Need-To-Know and Right-To-Know

An ASP must design and implement a comprehensive *need-to-know* and *right-to-know policy* for managing customers' security. Need-to-know is a concept related to information confidentiality controlled through information sharing policies. Every social and business organization has implied and written rules defining the roles and responsibilities and, hence, the scope of information dissemination and sharing. Right-to-know is also related to roles and responsibilities but in the context of required knowledge to perform the roles and maintain responsibilities. Right-to-know may also be a legal issue stipulated by different societal laws and/or an organization's by-laws.

The ASP *need-to-know* and *right-to-know policy* must apply to all ASP personnel in general, the ASP personnel dedicated to specific customers in particular, and to all customer personnel. This policy covers the following:

1. All customer security information management functions including information creation, distribution, storage, archival, updates, and destruction. The representative objects these functions operate on are:

   • ACLs on all shared access-control, authentication, and authorization devices such as routers, firewalls, and Web servers

   • Encryption keys

   • Firewall rules

2. Physical facilities management:

   • Rooms, vaults, cages, fire alarms, video cameras, motion and sound detectors

   • Access control devices—both electromagnetic and biometric—and issuance and management of access control cards

   • Console access privileges of customer and ASP NOC personnel

Partitioning

Several issues related to partitioning of ASP security management are (1) customer network design, (2) software tools partitioning, and (3) partitioned processes.

1. Network partitioning is a design-time issue. Just like the measure "Systems and Network Architectures" in Table 8.1, network partitioning must protect a customer's network from the untrusted Internet and allow for access by the ASP management network. Additionally, it may have to protect against access from other customers' networks by limiting the use of shared networking resources such as V-LANs, and so forth.

2. Partitioning of software tools is a runtime issue. ASP security management tools must allow for partitioning by the customer.

As of this writing, few tools are capable of this and many tool publishers are working to accommodate this requirement. The following must be partitioned:

- Collection and processing of systems and IDS logs by the customer (this requirement holds of course when IDS is shared)

- Systems and data backups for each customer to customer-dedicated database partitions or separate tapes

- Customer care systems (e.g., call centers, help desk)

- Systems and Network M&M tools that collect data on faults and performance used to compute the SLAs

3. ASPs must implement operations and support processes that are segregated by customer, for example,

- Backup/restores

- Disaster recovery

- SLA reporting

- Problem escalation (including security breaches)

Summary

This security discussion may be used as a point of departure for designing an ASP security—its strategy, policies, architecture, service offerings, pricing, etc.—yet, as was indicated earlier, this discussion has been derived from a compilation of security services of existing ASPs at the time of this writing. As time goes on and the new technologies, tools, and methods are developed, each ASP will need to conduct its own analysis and design of security measures and decide for itself how much security it needs and how much to offer its customers. Ultimately, that decision would depend on each ASP's business model, marketing focus, its incumbent knowledge and experience, as well as the general market trends and conditions.

This chapter started by positing security as an ASP customer concern number one. As such, it should end on the same note. It is naïve to expect that absolute security—whatever it is—will ever be achieved. Security is and will increasingly remain one of the most complex, expensive, and dynamic aspects of ASPs, and hence must always be heeded with serious consideration and due respect.

Chapter 9

Strategic Analysis of ASP Types

How can an ASP create sustainable competitive advantages, which are so needed for every business to survive, grow, and prosper? What markets—by industry, function, customer type, or size—should it pursue? What types of services should it offer? What partnerships should it seek? What technologies should it use? What business processes should it develop? Where should it focus its energies and direct its investments? These and other questions should all be addressed in a specific ASP business plan. This chapter is not such a business plan, but rather an attempt to generalize on the types of competitive advantages that can be derived from the real nature of the ASP based on the analyses of its architectural types, services offered, and applicable and enabling technologies.

Approach to Analyzing the ASP Services

By definition, the "two basic types of competitive advantages a firm can possess are low cost and differentiation."[1] Both low cost and differentiation are reviewed for every type of ASP in the text that fol-

---

1. Michael Porter, *Competitive Advantage*, New York, NY: The Free Press, 1985, p. 11.

lows. There are six sections in this chapter. The first section establishes analytical frameworks for analyzing and deriving ASP's competitive advantages. First, it offers a framework for analyzing differentiation-based competitive advantages. Next, it reintroduces (albeit, briefly) the frameworks from Chapter 4 to analyze cost-based competitive advantages. Finally, it develops a simple framework for deriving ASP's value propositions.

The next four sections are each dedicated to a particular type of ASP. Differentiation-based competitive advantages, cost-based competitive advantages, and then ASP type-specific value propositions are included in each such section. The sixth section, the summary, offers a synopsis of ideas and findings uncovered throughout this whole chapter.

Three Frameworks for Four ASP Types

While an ASP develops its competitive advantages for business success—cost-based or differentiation-based—it never forgets who makes this success possible, its customers. For this reason, the ASP must also develop the compelling customer value propositions, which have become commonly known and called in the industry exactly that, the value propositions, or simply VPs.

On the one hand, an ASP's competitive advantages and VPs are very different. The former ones are focused on the provider, the latter—on the customer. Yet, on the other hand, they are tightly coupled and interrelated. A particular ASP service only becomes a competitive advantage when the customers perceive it as such. To raise customer awareness about it, the ASP must determine customer benefits from its services and then formulate the appropriate VPs.

Figure 9.1 shows the application of three different frameworks to the four types of ASP:

- Framework One is derived from Michael Porter's teachings and used to derive differentiation-based competitive advantages.

- Framework Two is for the VPs. Its simple description is also given.

- Framework Three is the ASP economies framework from Chapter 4.

Together, the application of three frameworks to four ASP types produces a comprehensive picture of ASP's competitive advantages, cost economies, and value propositions theoretically achievable

Figure 9.1 *Analysis frameworks, ASP types, and ASP competitive differentiators, cost savings, and VPs.*

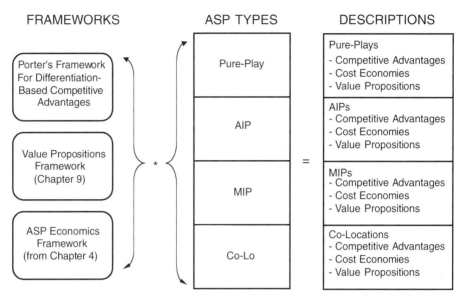

Three Frameworks multiplied by four ASP types produce 12 descriptions

through decisions on ASPs' business strategy, technology choices, and business processes.

The remaining material in this section defines the framework for competitive advantages and then the framework for VPs.

Framework One – Competitive Advantages

Michael Porter says the following about competitive advantages through differentiation: "The sustainability of differentiation depends on two things, its *continued perceived value* to buyers and the lack of imitation by competitors." The "lack of imitation by competitors" is further broken down into three conditions for success: "*uniqueness of offerings, multiplicity of the sources of differentiation,* and *switching costs.*"

Uniqueness of offerings is achieved through "*proprietary learning, linkages, interrelationships, and first-mover advantages.*" Many forms of learning arise from the development of effective processes within an enterprise, ASPs included. Linkages, in Porter's terms, imply optimization and coordination between the different activities of an enterprise's own value chain. First-mover advantages contribute to brand awareness, market capture, and good will.

Multiplicity of the sources of differentiation is interpreted as follows: "differentiation that results from coordinated actions in many value activities will usually be more durable, since it requires wholesale changes in competitor behavior to imitate."

Finally, *switching costs*—fixed costs of changing suppliers by customers—arise out of how customers use products and services.

In summary, the analysis of the ASP's competitive advantages uses four criteria (key words bolded):

- **Value** that is continually perceived by customers
- **Uniqueness** of offerings: proprietary learning, linkages, interrelationships, and first-mover advantage
- **Multiplicity** of the sources of differentiation
- **Switching** costs

All the dimensions of competitive advantages due to differentiation are analyzed for each type of ASP in the subsequent sections.

Framework Two – Value Propositions

Generic Value Propositions

The media, market analysts, and ASPs themselves use the term "value proposition," or simply VP, very broadly and generously. Typically, VPs originate in an entrepreneurial business plan, which also includes various analyses to justify investments in technology. All entrepreneurs, including ASPs, write business plans in which they articulate their products and services and why the markets should like and buy them. These entrepreneurs use their business plans to raise funds and run their young business when launched. One thing they all do from the get-go is to vigorously promote and advertise the benefits they promise their customers. Then, marketing takes these benefits and turns them into what has commonly become known as customer value propositions.

Incidentally, VPs are not only used to attract customers. Different VPs may be created for a business's partners, investors, and even the general public. Here is a list of the most common, albeit random, VPs used by the media and ASP's marketing:

- Faster time to market
- Reduced Total Cost of Ownership[2] (TCO)

---

2. A good TCO analysis covers more than just the cash flows for payroll, real estate, depreciation, and so forth. It must address many indirect or hidden costs such as management involvement, opportunity costs of faster time-to-market, impact of service quality on the quality of a business's product and services, morale, and others.

- Quality implementations: procurement, deployment, and operations
- Timely updates and upgrades to software and hardware
- Less concern about hiring talent in-house
- Access to expertise on an as-needed basis
- Access to best-of-breed, latest technologies, for a fraction of the cost
- Access to best application functionality at a fraction of the cost
- Access to the best application life cycle management capabilities, for a fraction of the cost
- High service qualities: reliability, availability, scalability, performance, security, flexibility, accessibility, usability
- Best customer care and support
- Scalability on demand
- Peace-of-mind due to a contractual nature of the customer-ASP relationship (due to SLAs)
- Mind-your-own-business attitude (e.g., customers can focus on their core competencies instead of their IT)

The list is not normalized and it can be very long. There are duplicate messages but they should be tolerated as long as they help maximize customers' awareness of and their interest in the ASP.

VP Analysis Framework

After a thorough analysis of a large body of marketing literature, several major categories of VPs have crystallized into the following taxonomy:

- **Strategic advantages**: timeliness, mind-your-business, impact on own product quality
- **TCO issues**: staff reductions, less need for scarce talent, opportunity costs
- **Peace-of-mind**: single point of contract, SLAs, access to functionality and resources
- **Qualities**: reliability, security, availability, scalability, manageability
- **Support issues**: customer care, morale
- **Miscellaneous and Intangibles**

Other taxonomies are possible too. Yet, this one has already been used successfully to produce foundation benefits for all types of ASPs (see the following) interpretable into viable marketing VPs. And as long as it produces constructive results, it should help ASPs to better understand themselves as well as their customers.

Incidentally, but not accidentally, each entry in the VP taxonomy is aimed at a different audience within a customer's organization: Strategic VPs aim at the CEO, TCO—at CFO, Peace-of-Mind—at COO, Qualities—at CIO and CTO, and Support—at middle management. This taxonomy is used throughout this chapter to derive VPs for all ASP types.

REALITY CHECK

Current Costs of ASP

One misconception that has crept into the culture of VPs is that ASP services should cost less than running an in-house IT. So, some customers check the discounted cash flows of their fees and discover that ASP may have cost them more than they used to spend before. This makes them wonder if they made the right decision going with ASP. However, lowering direct costs is just one value proposition to ASP customers. It is the value returned for cost that really matters, plus other crucial propositions such as time-to-market, reduced TCO, quality of service, and importantly, mind-your-business VPs. In fact, many customers would willingly trade costs to take advantage of some of the other VPs. For example, a growing interest in ASP shown lately by large corporations has proven this point. That came as a surprise to many ASPs who targeted mostly small and medium businesses (SMB). Yet, the main reason large enterprises liked ASP was that having experienced difficulty running their complex IT themselves, these companies finally recognized the possibility of outsourcing their applications to somebody else while focusing their energies on developing their own competencies and running their own business (the mind-your-own-business VP at work!).

Expectations for Future Costs of ASP

Then, there is even better news. While some ASP services may cost more today (on the net present value basis) this should change in the future. Specialization, leverage of scale and scope, learning, focus, and logistics will inevitably drive the ASP costs down. Eventually, the savings should pass through to the customers. If one believes the laws of economics, this is exactly what has happened with all other service industries and there is no indication that the same laws of economics should not apply to the ASP.

Co-Location Competitive Advantages

Co-Location's Competitive Differentiators

Following are the competitive advantages based on differentiation available to co-location providers.

1. **Geographical Coverage** is the first obvious differentiator with a continued perceived value to customers. Customers with multiple sites may be able to find provider's data centers near their locations. By working with a large provider, they can also get larger discounts and enjoy the simplicity of dealing with a single point of contact and support.

2. **Quality Real Estate** is another differentiator with a continued perceived value. Its advantages flow from its physical/geographical location, building design, seismic bracing, building access, parking, and common other amenities, as well as data center floor features: vaults, enclosures, fire and flood protection.

3. **Environmental Controls** and power are critical to a co-location provider's success but are difficult to quantify. The absence of problems—such as HVAC breakdowns, power outages, flood—is not proof of these systems' reliability and performance. While real estate location and broad geography advantages are obvious at first sight, environment, power, and security must be proven both on paper and in action when handling disasters. This is a tall order, but a powerful means of a perceived-value-based differentiation.

4. **Quality Customer Care** is always a major deciding factor in choosing service providers. It is important for the ASPs to look into the vast well of expertise, experiences, processes, and metrics of traditional call centers and help desks and leverage them for their own benefit. This differentiator is a combination of the perceived value and learning types.

5. **Network Services.** A co-location provider cannot avoid offering access to networking services. However, just having NSP's POPs at its data centers may not be enough. For access to bandwidth, the provider must heed the requirements of network service diversity, scalability, and second sourcing, mentioned in the description of co-location in Chapter 6, and be able to manage these capabilities per customer demand. This differentiator clearly flows from the interrelationships with the NSPs.

6. **Security** can be a major differentiator of a perceived value type. However, just like the environmental controls, it must be proven in action. Unfortunately, the Internet is filled with hackers. Therefore, once the customer site is on-line, it doesn't usually take a long time to prove the efficacy of security measures.

7. **Content Services** can be a major differentiator for the co-location providers. The differentiator is based on the interrelationships with content services vendors and ISVs. However, it may also be a first mover advantage differentiator. At the time of this writing, offering content services was very new and very promising. Numerous providers (e.g., first mover) rushed to establish relationships with the ISVs and other content service providers resulting in major partnerships and alliances.[3]

8. **Strong Vendor Relationships**—for all the gear co-location providers buy—offers strong differentiation of the linkage type. Becoming a value-added reseller for specific hardware vendors adds to this VP by giving the customer a one-stop shop for both machines and hosting.

9. **Expansion Abilities**. Many co-location providers pride themselves in their abilities to select geographies for data centers (marketing learning), or build and set them up quickly and efficiently (processes-related learning).

10. **Effective System Deployment**. For the ASP's value chain, linkages are present in having proper processes for the customer systems deployment to help save operational costs or in the frequency of reporting to customers to improve customer education and satisfaction and reduce support costs. Interrelationships are about partnerships with the NSPs, ISVs, SIs, and others.

11. **Customer Education and Training.** Broad and effective customer education and training contribute handsomely to switching costs and hence increase customer retention. Higher switching costs, in the case of ASPs (co-location and other types), however, are less related to customer capital and more to spent variable costs, for example, those related to customer involvement in the ASP's business processes and learning. Thus, customers' higher switching costs may result from an increased interaction with them, such as customer learning of providers' processes, technologies, SLAs, reports and bills, and vice versa. The more comfortable a customer is that the ASP

---

3. For example, Digital Island announced its Sun and Inktomi partnership in 2000, a move that combined Sun servers, Inktomi caching services, and Digital Island's content delivery service.

understands its processes and needs, the higher the perceived switching costs. Achieving higher levels of customer retention is every ASP's goal.

Some of these differentiation-based advantages (e.g., Real Estate, Environmental, Network Services, Security) are absolute musts for a co-location provider, while others are add-ons or nice-to-haves (e.g., Education and Training, Content Services). Each advantage is achieved by a certain value activity such as building up the real estate, buying network capacities, investing in security expertise, developing educational curricula, and so forth. By combining different value activities, a co-location provider may develop an offering that would attain the synergies of its components and thus assume a new competitive advantage that is difficult to imitate. This competitive advantage would then be achieved due to the multiplicity of the sources of differentiation. An example could be a provider that focuses on high-bandwidth backbone, which it uses primarily for streaming media content distribution marketed to media companies.

Commoditization

"The process of 'commoditization'—the descent into entrenched price warfare that erodes profit margins and chokes off funding for innovation—is inevitable in any industry."[4] Co-location and other types of ASP represent one such industry that is not immune to this process. The fact that the bulk of co-location services flows from a co-location provider's physical assets—buildings, floors, rooms, cages, vaults, environmental and fire systems, security systems, human guards, and so on—makes these services relatively easy to itemize and price and, therefore, easier to replicate but harder to differentiate. However, moving up the ASP stack—to MIP, AIP and Pure-Play ASPs—one would find more variable or intangible elements, such as server platform and OS, middleware, application components, support and consulting services, which would make the services these elements support more unique and differentiable. As time goes on and the ASP industry grows and evolves, commoditization process should be expected to be moving up this ASP stack.

Factors that impact the pace of commoditization are "overall economic expansion, growth in demand, intensity of competition, capacity, and the pace of technological change." All these factors have an impact on the commoditization of co-location services. For example, demand for co-location, at the time of this writing, exceeded avail-

---

4. Caroline T. Chauncey, "A Model for Maturing Markets," Technology Review, *MIT Magazine of Innovation*, Nov/Dec 1997.

able supply. Whenever and wherever a new data center opened its doors, it had already been booked to capacity. This was a seller's market, yet probably not sustainable for a long time. Indeed, several econometric analyses conducted by market analysts and ASPs themselves in the year 2000 predicted that within 12 months supply would finally meet demand. That's when the battles for competitive advantages, differentiation or cost-based, would begin in earnest.

Likewise, the pace of technological change is a source of standardization leading to commoditization, too. Indeed, a new technology to ASP-enable business applications, or tools to improve ASP service management, or more reliable power conditioners, or more sophisticated content technologies—all innovations that complete, automate, or just simplify the provisioning of ASP services would lead to standardization.

REALITY CHECK

Commoditization Process Model

"Henry Birdseye Weil, a senior lecturer in the Strategic and International Management Group of MIT's Sloan School of Management, has created a computer simulation of the commoditization process that can be adapted to any industry. Weil already used his simulation to model the airline, telecommunications, oil, and chemical industries. "He hopes next to turn his attention to mobile telecommunications service providers in Hong Kong, an 'adolescent' industry just beginning to grapple with the dynamics of a maturing market."

Reality of Commoditization

"Weil has used his simulation to identify strategy options for companies facing maturing markets and his models have generated some counterintuitive solutions. Traditionally, for example, established companies have tried to limit total capacity in an industry by forcing new entrants to duplicate established companies' investments. This strategy is based partly on the belief that, once competitors have entered the field, the need to earn a return on their investment will force them to keep prices high. 'History has shown that that's absolutely incorrect logic,' Weil asserts. 'Once the capacity is in place, it's a sunk cost and people will compete very aggressively to fill it up.' According to his models, established companies may even find it to their advantage to offer capacity to new entrants. For instance, one British telecommunications company recently decided to lease excess network capacity to newcomers to the market rather than force them to build their own networks; the leases have become a substantial new revenue source."

By reviewing the Reality Check on commoditization, it is easy to conclude that Weil's words turned auspicious for the ASP. At the time of this writing, numerous big co-location business players—Exodus, ATT, Quest, and others—had, for all practical purposes, become wholesalers of their co-location capacities. They let their facilities to numerous higher-level ASPs—MIPs, AIPs, and Pure-Plays—and other co-location providers alike. The latter fact may appear odd, considering the commoditization trend. However, reasons vary. One may be that some co-location ASPs may simply need data center space at new geographical locations in order to satisfy demands of their customer's distributed applications.

Wouldn't be interesting to apply Weil's model to the new budding ASP industry? While not negating the premises of competitive advantages, simulation-based ASP strategies may turn out to be quite deviant from those driven by conventional wisdom. These strategies may then spell even more extraordinary consequences for the development and maturation of the ASP industry following all the prophetic predictions of its future that are alluded to in this book and, possibly, many other publications.

Co-Location's Analysis – Cost Economies

Internal Economies of Scale

Using the ASP economics framework developed in Chapter 4, four applicable categories of economies of scale are Specialization, Substitution, Fixed Factor or Overhead, and Laws of Geometry.

Specialization. Specialization flows from a business's size. This is a division of labor phenomenon. When a co-location provider is big enough to dedicate personnel to specific roles and responsibilities, specialization happens. But it doesn't happen by default. It requires continuous management focus, refined business processes, and rigorous training. Examples of specialization abound. Many have already been spoken to before, such as prospecting for data center locations, building data centers, customer provisioning, operation of environmental control systems, security systems, and customer training.

Substitution. Substitution of larger systems/facilities for smaller ones is dependent on a marketing strategy. If an ASP targets larger customers, economies of scale can be enjoyed in building larger facilities and partitions (economies of scale due to the laws of geometry; see the following), purchasing fewer larger systems than many small ones, for example, secure enclosures (economies of scale built into acquired products' pricing), and in direct savings in sales, marketing, and operational overhead.

Focusing on larger customers, though more attractive, increases the co-location ASP's dependence on such customers. While lowering direct costs, this approach increases business risks.

Substitution-based economies of scale for co-location also flow from volume discount purchases of assets or services. Eschewing the simple examples of buying MRO[5] products and services, substitution applies both to capital equipment and services for resale. Here again, strategy drives economics. If, for example, an ASP targets a certain market, larger volume discounts for equipment (e.g., vaults) can be negotiated for longer term purchase commitments. Or, if the ASP is buying bulk network capacities for resale to customers, knowing which capacities to buy may considerably increase resale margins.

Substitution is easiest to develop for a co-location ASP. There are, however, limits as to how far the ASP's scale can be stretched. At the time of this writing, the optimal data center size was fixed at about 20,000 to 25,000 sq. ft. After that, most overhead expenses— personnel, climate control, power, and so forth—are duplicated. New technologies and management processes improve these economies of scale, which should result in higher numbers for the optimal data center size.

Fixed Factors/Overhead. A simple euphemism applicable here is reuse. What can a co-location ASP have (purchase or develop) that can be applied across multiple instances of certain assets, services, or customers? Good examples are found in software: customer account management, customer care systems, and systems and network management tools. These systems can be used for all customers, regardless of the size and nature of their business.

Laws of Geometry. This is simple and perhaps only applicable to co-location. Building larger facilities may theoretically yield lower costs per foot, because doubling the data center dimensions quadruples its footage and increases its volume eightfold. Also, as was already mentioned before in substitution, buying larger systems for larger customers yields obvious cost savings.

Internal Economies of Scope

There are three categories of economies of scope: standardization, technology reuse, and knowledge reuse. While the advantages of standardization are well known, the material here focuses mostly on the two types of reuse.

---

5. Products used for management, repair, and operations (MRO).

Standardization. By heeding industry standards, co-location ASPs can enjoy savings in purchasing equipment (standard products tend to become commodities), training of technical personnel, and on installation and maintenance processes.

Technology Reuse. This is similar to reuse discussed for economies of scale in fixed factor/overhead. It is similar, but not the same. Technology reuse for economies of scale applies fixed costs to multiple instances of the same kind, for example, customers. For scope, technology reuse must apply to different entities; in this case, customers and suppliers. This means that if the word supplier (or partner) can be substituted for customer in software titles, such as customer account management, customer-care systems, the economies of scope are achieved.

Knowledge Reuse. This economy flows from people and their knowledge, or what is sometimes referred to as packaging "best practices." Higher-level ASP services—MIP, AIP, Pure-Plays—are rich in knowledge reuse. Still, co-location has options of its own. Project management metrics used for installing the ASP's own equipment can be used for customer deployments. Training materials used for internal personnel can be used with customers. Many other examples are possible. In fact, some co-location ASPs are already known to package their knowledge on security audits, professional services, installations, and diverse management practices for resale. Packaging and selling knowledge related to the data center design and operation promises to become a lucrative business for the ASPs. These, and other co-location knowledge reuse opportunities, should be sought out, developed, and leveraged.

Internal Economies of Learning

Economies of learning are easier to obtain for more mature industries than for the ASP. Nonetheless, the key rule of learning that relates a reduction in unit costs to accumulated volume (see Chapter 4) can be applied to co-location ASPs too. Tracking the unit costs—for example, deployment time per customer or system—can reveal many secrets about the factors that influence learning in an attempt to leverage the positive factors and curb the negative ones.

External Economies: Focus and Logistics

Economies of focus and logistics are external to the ASP arising from the relationships with its ecosystem: suppliers, vendors, and partners. Both types of economies—focus and logistics—must be driven by well-thought-out strategies. An economy of focus is based mostly on the ASP's own strategy while logistics requires a collaborative implementation of strategies of ASP and others. Thus, a co-location ASP may focus on:

- Specific markets—by size, industry, application, geography (e.g., large customers only, or insurance industry only, or United States only, or a combination thereof)
- Select suppliers and/or technologies used for building data centers (e.g., secure enclosures from Lamperz)
- Preferred hosted technologies (e.g., Sun Servers for running network management tools)
- Certain services (e.g., content management and distribution, ultra-secure vaults, high bandwidth network pipes)
- Marketing channels (e.g., by computer supplier, systems integrator, value-added reseller)
- Network types provided to customers (e.g., high bandwidth IP for streaming media, for sports events distribution)

Any focus, if properly implemented, holds the potential for incremental economic benefits. These benefits can be manifested through faster time-to-market; fewer staff, hence, lower cost; improved systems availability; higher quality customer service; and so forth. These benefits can be used as customer VPs for marketing and sales purposes and also render tangible cost savings that, if passed to customers, can create sustainable competitive advantages.

Co-location's economies of logistics emanate from coordinated strategies similar to the following:

- Work with industry associations to better understand competitive climate, market trends, customer needs, and partner's strategies
- Involve vendors in joint innovative marketing and selling campaigns
- Partner with vendors and suppliers to get early-bird notifications for their new products and services, test them early, and rush to market sooner
- Joint venture with network providers for preferred rates

Co-Location's Value Propositions

By applying the VP framework defined earlier, the true benefits to co-location customers for co-location ASPs are summarized in Table 9.1. Each of these benefits can be used as a VP. Key words for each benefit (or a VP) are underlined.

Inevitably, the table echoes the logic of building competitive advantages through cost or differentiation as described previously.

Table 9.1 *Co-Location Value Propositions*

Category	*True Benefits to Customer Usable as VPs*
Strategic	Customer <u>managers are freed</u> to focus on core competencies of their business (mind-your-business) <u>Capital is freed</u> from the data center construction to investments in core competencies <u>Faster build-ups</u> of facilities speed up implementation of customer's own business plan <u>Faster time-to-market</u> for eBusiness applications (such as CRM, Supply chain, business-to-consumer, etc.)
TCO	<u>Capital savings</u> on facilities <u>Variable cost savings</u> due to one-stop shopping for data center equipment and technologies <u>Expensing</u> rental fees No need for facilities and network services operations personnel (hence, <u>staff reductions and no new hiring</u>)
Peace-of-Mind	Clear, mutually agreed upon and enforceable <u>service guarantees</u> spelled out in the facilities SLAs Co-location facilities are always <u>state-of-the-art technologies</u> <u>Timely upgrades</u> to hardware and software fall <u>under</u> co-location provider's purview, for example, network routers, security systems, and so on
Qualities	<u>Choices of network</u> providers ensure high availability of services <u>Reliable</u> facilities <u>Scalable</u> facility and bandwidth <u>Superior security</u> for networks and facilities
Support	<u>Superior support</u> (customer care) via ASP's help desk and call center Access to <u>superior facilities management personnel</u> Possible assistance up the stack of ASP services offered by the co-location ASP <u>professional services</u>, such as enhanced security services (e.g., security audits), preferred systems integrators, and systems and network management
Miscellaneous	Convenient facility locations

MIP Competitive Advantages

MIP's Competitive Differentiators

The four criteria for competitive advantages—value, uniqueness, multiplicity, and switching costs—are applied here to the five specific areas of MIP services:

- Systems: services related to the procurement and deployment of a customer environment's hardware components—servers, storage systems, routers, switches, hardware firewalls, and other network equipment—along with their operating software (OS, etc.)
- Management services
- Network services
- Professional services
- Miscellaneous services: ISP-based email, Web hosting

Each MIP's service area is analyzed. All differentiators are numbered continuously throughout the following sections.

Systems Services

To differentiate an MIP from a co-location ASP, one simply needs to look for managed hosted systems (servers, routers, switches, etc.) and related services. The MIP's competitive differentiators arising from these systems services are:

- **Strong Vendor Relationships** for preferred deliveries of hosted systems and support.
- **Proven Implementation Skills**. Besides referring to generic technical and procedural skills, this differentiator implies the ability to deliver special designs such as high availability computing using redundant servers and High Availability (HA) clustering[6] technologies.

Management Services

MIPs can offer many quality management services: capable network and systems management, sophisticated event correlation and action automation, reliable customer care and support, robust operations, and comprehensive services management. However, there is little novelty in these services; effective management tools have been designed, marketed, and successfully deployed, numerous systems

---

6. Veritas or Sun Microsystems are two vendor examples of HA Clustering technology.

and network objects have been management-enabled, methodologies and practices developed and proven, consultants educated, and operators trained. Barriers to entry offering such services are low. Overall, most of these services are viewed today as commodities and are therefore hard to differentiate. One type of management service, however, is promising. It is the ability to write SLAs (and, obviously, to gear up and deliver on them). Another type of management service, with a great potential for differentiation, is service management. It was already defined in Chapter 7 and will be addressed in more detail in Chapter 10.

As of this writing, ASP's SLAs have not fulfilled their promise of an ironclad service contract between the customer and provider. SLAs have been written, signed, then broken, argued about, litigated, and so on. There have been customer complaints, recorded in the media, about providers' hidden agenda to use SLAs more to protect themselves rather than their customers' interests, and so on. In this unstable climate, an MIP that can write aggressive SLAs, with more balanced terms, can achieve a major market differentiation.

An SLA is aggressive when its terms and conditions exceed the industry's prevailing averages. For example, the SLA may define an outage as a degradation in service by a certain percentage lasting a certain number of minutes. If the percentage and duration are lower than prevailing averages and the SLA also stipulates a remuneration plan (e.g., money back, service credit), this SLA is definitely aggressive.

Aggressive SLAs are true competitive differentiators. They clearly state their commitment to service and hence are attractive to customers. Their competitive advantages stem primarily from the value perceived by the customers and the elements of extra risk and increased business discipline (learning, linkages, interrelationships).

Network Services

The network is the MIP's major asset and a source of sustainable differentiation. The three potential differentiators derived from the network are:

- **The backbone's** physical topology, capacity, and manageability (customer's perceived value).

- **Diverse peering** arrangements coupled with traffic **QoS guarantees** by the MIP's networking partners (linkages as a sustainable differentiator).

- **Effective skills and proven practices** of its network engineering staff for designing and managing customer networks (learning as an entry barrier).

"Physical topology, capacity, and manageability" respectively refer to the backbone's geographical coverage, bandwidth, and facilities for providing flexible capacity, routing, and other forms of management. "Diverse peering" implies strong partnerships with other carriers (e.g., NSPs) so that after maximizing the use of its own network for reliable routing, the MIP can hand-off customer traffic to its peering partners with the same guarantees of high QoS. The MIP's ability to build effective customer networks implies more than just a powerful network management, it implies the "effective skills and proven practices" for designing such networks over an MIP's own backbone and its peers' networks.

One might ask what constitutes a well-designed customer network. The answer is simple: low transmission latency and low packet loss. To lower transmission latency and packet loss, MIPs can do some of the following:

- Design the network with the least number of node hops on its own backbone.

- Employ traffic congestion monitoring and avoidance techniques.

- Implement traffic priorities by customer and/or data types, for example, streaming media.

- Reserve "headroom" for improved dynamic-on-demand bandwidth availability and planned bandwidth scalability; and manage it proactively.

- Provide dedicated access to customer sites—point-to-point leased line capabilities for connecting customers' enterprise networks directly to the MIP's backbone and then to the Internet.

To sustain differentiation, MIPs must continuously evolve their backbone, improve management facilities, and enhance their own organizations' professional skills and network engineering practices.

Professional Services

Professional Services can be a source of very strong differentiators:

- Perceived value may flow from the known **reputation** of MIP's professional services.

- Uniqueness of offerings can be concealed within the systems and application **architectures' linkages**, both developed by the same professional services groups.

- Switching-cost differentiators are derived from the **unique implementation methodologies or proprietary technologies**. While the former differentiators may be sustainable, the latter are not. They are unstable and hence not advisable.

Miscellaneous Add-On Services

This area of services offers a very broad range of opportunities for competitive differentiators. Some differentiators may arise from a deeper exploration of a particular MIP's service area, while others come from venturing entirely outside the MIP's service domain. The two examples here prove these points.

- An example of an **in-domain specialization** is a focus on content distribution, which dovetails with MIP's capabilities such as OS version maintenance. For that, an MIP may invest in building a content distribution infrastructure and establishing partnerships with content distribution ISVs and providers (learning and interrelationships).

- An example of an **out-of-domain specialization** is an MIP that has moved up the ASP stack to offer data processing services from the portfolios of the pure-play ASPs. These services may include database software, imaging and document management, data and storage management, security software, graphics, and multimedia (learning, linkages, first-mover advantages).

Many other examples are also possible:

- Basic **Internet applications:** email, general Web access, news, chat, Web hosting (perceived value).

- **Specialization**: streaming media services including encoding, live production, hosting and broadcasting, satellite downlinks, pay-per-view applications, bandwidth and use of state-of-the-art production facilities (learning).

- **ISO 9002 certification**. This differentiator is based on learning, linkages, interrelationships, and perceived value.

MIP Cost Economies

Internal Economies of Scale

Just like they were used for the co-location provider, the applicable categories of economies of scale are used for the analysis of the MIP's cost-based competitive advantages.

Specialization. MIP's specialization can be developed within the various functional domains of the 3DF platforms layer (Figures 5.9 and 6.6). The most obvious is specialization in technologies. This refers to systems, networks, management, and professional services alike. The larger the organization, the more specialized groups handling different technologies it can have. This spells savings. However, reducing the number of vendors and other suppliers reduces the number of such groups and may lead to higher purchase discounts, more training per person, and a lower overall training budget. The ultimate results are lower per-customer purchase, procurement, deployment, and support costs.

Substitution. Like the case for co-location, substitution of larger systems for smaller ones depends on the MIP's business model and marketing strategy. That is, it is very much determined by how and to whom the MIP markets. Are there a few very large customers or many small ones? Do they require rapid scaling-up of resources? What are their other critical quality requirements?

Buying larger systems (e.g., UNIX servers) saves money due to a vendor's economies of scale in pricing. Also, larger systems used for processing (or routing, or switching, etc.) can be deployed and managed for less per unit of their resources. For a single-tenancy large customer, it all works fine as long as the underlying technologies are inherently scalable (see Chapter 5). But what happens when the systems are used for multiple tenants? Will substitution work when multiple customers use larger systems together but have different, unique, and varying requirements for availability, scalability, performance, management, security, and support? Will the overhead of supporting the virtual or quasivirtual environments for these customers exceed the savings from substitution? The answer is simple... it depends. It depends on how widely customer needs vary, how mature the virtualization technologies are (see Chapter 10), how complex and diverse the applications that customers run are, as well as on the types of tools their MIP uses.

The real picture is not always so bleak, though. There are many MIPs that are successfully running multitenancy customers. However, the scope of the issues just listed still remains very broad and the answers are not so clear—for now anyway.

Fixed Factor/Overhead. Known as "reuse," fixed factors or overhead can apply across multiple instances of similar assets, services, and customers. Good examples can be found in software (customer account management, customer care systems, management services and tools) or in certain processes (updates and patch installs on the OSs of different systems, running security audit software against systems logs).

Internal Economies of Scope

Standardization. In a nutshell, the use of standards across multiple platforms and applications adds to the economies of scope. Protocols are kings of standardization. The Internet owes its success to the standardization of TCP/IP, HTTP, and HTML, just to name a few.

Technology Reuse. Perhaps the most convincing example of technology reuse is the portability of management services and tools across multiple customers and multiple technology platforms. Many management technology vendors such as BMC, HP, Sun, IBM/Tivoli, and others have products that work cross-platform. Hence, monitoring and management of NT and UNIX-based systems and applications can be performed using the same systems: Only one type (or even instance) of the management tool may be needed, and operations personnel must learn only one set of management processes. Further, the concept of technology compatibility is nothing more than a tribute to technology reuse and interface standardization. Java code runs on multiple platforms and can be made portable. Many storage devices are portable across different server platforms. With the advent of SAN and NAS,[7] data storage and access have become standardized. SAN and NAS can contribute handsomely to the MIP's economies of scope.

Knowledge Reuse. Already alluded to before and in the description of knowledge reuse for co-location, procurement and installation, operational and management processes, and project management metrics used for installing the ASP's gear can apply to customers too. The same applies to the ASP's internal training materials.

Internal Economies of Learning

What can an ASP learn from customer interactions and multitenant operations? This question is rhetorical as it points clearly to where to look. It is all in the processes related to these interactions and operations! "Knowledge reuse" explains how to leverage processes. Learning helps define and refine them. Following is a list of learning sources related to the MIP business processes. By no means is this list complete! This is just the beginning:

- Defining customers, channels, partners
- Qualifying customers
- Customer procurement pipeline
- Finding the hand-off points between qualification, requirements gathering, pricing, procurement, and installations
- Finding integration points with data centers' systems, management tools
- Planning delivery of technical capabilities
- Tracking costs, time, and motions
- Creating fixed-price services based on time-and-materials pricing combined with experience-based efficiencies
- Capturing and leveraging the learning from failure postmortems and lost bids
- Handling of walk-in customers

7. SAN and NAS are new technology abbreviations: Storage Area Network and Network Attached Storage, respectively.

Technologies and customer needs change rapidly. Yet, the established business processes within an ASP (MIP and others) can be *reliable* and *sustainable*. They are *sustainable* because it takes a technology revolution, not evolution, to impact business processes. They are *reliable* because a commitment to processes is an ASP's management's internal decision, not impacted from the outside.

Refining business processes can create considerable economies. Examples abound. A library of standard responses to customers' RFI/RFQ/RFP[8] improves an MIP's marketing efficiency (see Bullets 2 and 3 in the list of learning). Another example could be experience-based implementation time and effort metrics, assessment of a project's technical skills requirements, and many others.

External Economies of Focus and Logistics

In terms of its flow, the discussion here is similar to the one given for co-location earlier. The economies of focus are based on internal decisions while the economies of logistics require mutual cooperation with the MIP's business ecosystem. Just like in co-location, MIPs may focus on industries, applications, and geography; computer and networking equipment vendors (e.g., Sun and Cisco); management tools; select services, marketing channels, network types, and so forth.

Further, the benefits of focus for co-location described earlier also apply to MIP, perhaps, even with a stronger punch. They are: faster time-to-market, fewer staff, higher purchase discounts (similar to specialization), "privileged status" vendor support, and others. Some benefits sound like the VPs and truly many of them are.

Focus-based strategies tend to be sustainable yet are not as reliable as those of learning. To be sustainable, both the MIPs and its vendor's business strategies must be harmonized. MIPs must always strive to work closely with all of its vendors.

The MIP's economies of logistics must be coordinated with its ecosystem's members too, that is, with vendors, network carriers, ISVs, SIs, other ASPs. They must also:

- Work with associations, consortia, and industry groups for better understanding of the needs of customers and partners as well as for education and promotion.

- Include vendors into the MIP's business plans. For example, ask them to accept payment for equipment not when it is installed but when it is used—similar to how Sun Microsys-

8. RFI/RFQ/RFP are Requests for Information, Quotation, and Proposal, respectively.

tems implemented it with its multiprocessor systems which are delivered fully loaded yet charged only for the processors used ("Capacity on Demand").

- Partner with the hardware vendors and ISVs to beta-test and be the first-to-market with their innovations, such as new flexible SAN and NAS technologies, high-availability clusters (e.g., Veritas and Sun), new XML-based network and systems integration and management tools, streaming media, and so on.

MIP Value Propositions

MIP's value propositions are summarized in Table 9.2. These are detailed VPs. They essentially explicate what the more aggregate VPs really mean. For example, the popular "Faster Time-To-Market" really translates into multiple smaller VPs. Likewise, "Lower Cost of Ownership" translates into cost savings and staff reductions.

Many VPs for the MIP may appear the same as co-location's. While their words might be similar, the content they apply to varies significantly.

Table 9.2   *MIP's Value Propositions*

Category	*True Benefits to Customer Usable as VPs*
Strategic	Customer <u>managers are freed</u> to focus on core competencies of their business (mind-your-business)
	Hardware and software <u>capital is freed</u> for investments in core competencies
	<u>Faster systems/network procurement/deployments</u> speed up customer product development and marketing
	<u>Faster time-to-market</u> for eBusiness applications (e.g., CRM, Supply chain, business-to-consumer, etc.)
	<u>Service commitments</u> may be <u>shorter</u> than systems' duty cycles or depreciated lives
	<u>Best-of-breed technologies</u> for a fraction of the cost
TCO	<u>Capital savings</u> on hardware/software purchases
	<u>Expensing</u> rental fees for systems, networks, and management services
	<u>Reduced personnel</u> requirements for operations and systems and NOC services all leading to staff reductions and lesser need for in-house talent

Table 9.2 *MIP's Value Propositions (Continued)*

Peace-of-Mind	<u>Single point of contact</u> for all systems and network services
	Clear, mutually agreed upon, and enforceable <u>service guarantees</u> spelled in SLAs for operations and management
	Hosting infrastructure components (servers, routers, switches, their OSs, etc.) are always <u>state-of-the-art technologies</u>
	<u>Timely upgrades</u> to hardware and software for all operational and management systems in hosting infrastructure
Qualities	Benefit from <u>robust architecture designs</u> (especially when using fail-safe redundancies and cluster technologies)
	<u>Sophisticated management services</u> (see Chapter 7) can guarantee major systemic qualities:
	<u>Higher availability</u> due to failover designs and contingency plans
	<u>Rapid scalability</u> for systems/network capacities, when needed (requested or even dynamic)
	<u>Performance</u> M&M and dynamic reconfigurations
	<u>Sophisticated security</u> (see Chapter 8)
	<u>Best-of-breed</u> choices for vendors and products
Support	Multiple levels of <u>quality customer care</u> for systems and networks—high quality, experience-based, and well-equipped
Miscellaneous	See co-location

AIP Competitive Advantages

AIP's Competitive Differentiators

The AIP's competitive advantages emanate from its abilities to host customer applications by leveraging the capabilities of 3DF's component-ware and integration-ware layers (see Figures 5.5 and 6.6). The same differentiating criteria—value to customers, uniqueness of offerings, multiple sources of differentiation, and switching costs—

that were used for co-location and MIP are also applied to the AIP to derive its specific competitive differentiators.

AIP is the most technologically complex type of ASP, but also the most promising. Recalling the concept of "complexity hiding" (related to middleware) helps realize the true potential of AIP's technologies that ensure availability, performance, and scalability, and thus liberate application designers from worrying about them. Likewise, AIP's application integration capabilities, like those embodied in the application integration brokers (Chapter 6), prove the points about both the complexity and attractiveness of the AIP.

So, AIPs focus on complex technologies and attendant implementation services required for the delivery of application infrastructure hosting. It is, however, very common for AIPs to "encroach" on and offer the MIP services as well. This allows AIPs to combine their application infrastructure's software with an MIP's hosting infrastructure's hardware. Some reasons why many AIPs make inroads into the MIP services territory are as follows:

- **Hardware-Software Interdependence**. There still exist, although diminishing, computer hardware and software interdependencies, especially where the delivery of systemic qualities (e.g., scalability, availability) is concerned. These interdependencies also allow the combined AIP/MIP to build the hardware/software packages—templates, ready-to-deploy hardware-software units, and so forth—to meet their customers' varied requirements.

- **One-Stop-Shopping** for customers whereby an AIP selects a combination of hardware and software most appropriate for a customer's needs.

- **Simplified Partnerships**. In the parlance of business strategy, an AIP/MIP is a vertically integrated business. This means one less relationship in the ASP's overall vertical stack. All that an AIP/MIP must do to complete the stack is to contract for co-location.

The descriptions of AIP competitive differentiators, which are by no means complete, are given here. Each description assigns a differentiator's criteria and a judgment about its sustainability. All differentiation-based competitive advantages are numbered.

1. One of the first claims AIPs make is that they use "the best-of-breed" products and services. These products and services come from the **industry-leading suppliers**, the best brand names. There are three key types of ASP suppliers: systems vendors, ISVs, and Internet consultants/SIs. Systems vendors supply physical computer and networking "gear"—servers,

routers, switches, and pertinent OSs. ISVs deliver the entire spectrum of middleware products, for example, Web and application servers; test, deployment, operations, management, and security software; transaction middleware; development and runtime platforms (e.g., J2EE[9]); application integration brokers; and others. Internet consultants and systems integrators (SIs) deliver customer life cycle application solutions; services may be end-to-end including business and application architecture strategy, technology choices, analysis, design, deployment, testing, and operations. The value of the relationships with these suppliers also extends into AIP's common activities such as procurement, deployment, hosting, and operations management. As a competitive differentiator, relationships with **industry-leading suppliers** are interrelationship-based. These relationships represent a sustainable advantage, as was indicated earlier.

2. **Proven implementation skills** are needed for the development and integration of customer applications within the AIP infrastructure. Proven implementation skills is a very important, if not *the* most important, differentiator. Indeed, how competitive can an AIP be if it fails to integrate a customer's application into its infrastructure? Proven implementation skills are based on the AIP's intellectual property (IP). This IP consists of reliable methodologies, proven practices, reusable templates and patterns, effective training programs, and clever personnel policies (e.g., promoting and retaining talent). Extensive learning and well-oiled linkages within the AIP organization establish proven implementation skills as a competitive differentiator. Once built, this differentiator is very sustainable.

3. **Timeliness** refers to the delivery of development and integration projects to the customer. While appearing as a viable independent differentiator—easy to understand and promote—it is subordinate to the proven skills. Likewise, it can be sustainable.

4. **Qualities of products/service** refers to a host of customer deliverables. It is a very complex differentiator based on learning, internal linkages, and external interrelationships (e.g., with network carriers). Examples of how qualities are delivered are architectures designed with redundancies (assuring availability), capacity on demand (scalability), contingency and disaster recovery processes (business continuity), superior security measures, and many others. Consistent successes can

---

9. J2EE stands for Java-2 Enterprise Edition.

give an AIP a measure of good will, that is, the value perceived by its customers. An AIP's reputation for quality is sustainable, but may be fragile and fickle, as a single negative story may destroy all the accumulated good will.

5. **Proprietary Integration Technologies**. In the age of open standards, the term "proprietary technologies" has a negative connotation as it harkens back to the times of closed architectures and vendor lock-ins. However, the business of ASP is very young. It presents AIPs with many technological and business challenges. And before any standards and portable technologies addressing these challenges are available, AIPs must use the best means possible to meet their customers' requirements. So, AIPs develop custom solutions and reapply them to multiple customers. Proprietary technologies may be AIP's own or provided by ISVs. They may include the deployment and support automation activities, application integration brokers, customer and end-user self-provisioning capabilities, and access control management applications. Chapter 10 addresses some of these technologies in detail.

6. When hosted applications use proprietary technologies, customers' propensities to switch providers drastically decrease while switching costs dramatically increase. Thus, proprietary technologies are a powerful "switching costs" differentiator. However, their sustainability is suspect.

7. AIPs known for their **aggressive SLAs** can use evidence of their "100% scheduled uptime guarantee"[10] and other superior service qualities as a powerful competitive advantage. The ability to write aggressive SLAs relies on an AIP's use of proven implementation skills and qualities (see earlier). This advantage is synergistic and, due to the multiplicity of the sources of differentiation, helps the AIP. Sustaining this advantage may be difficult but not impossible with a continuous focus on underlying abilities.

The aforementioned differentiators emanate from an ASP's architectural view and therefore are AIP-generic. There can also be differentiators stemming from an AIP's business and marketing strategies, such as:

8. **Technology Focus**. Technology focus differentiates an AIP when it focuses on a particular suite of technologies, for exam-

---

10. From the Web site of Loudcloud, Inc.—a "premier software infrastructure services provider" that is, using the definitions of this book, a bona-fide AIP (albeit also offering the elements of MIP services).

ple, the Wintel[11] or UNIX platforms, certain suites of middle-ware such as iPlanet's complete product portfolio, or J2EE. This differentiating focus is sustainable.

9. **Functional Focus.** Some AIPs may accumulate experience in hosting and integrating specific business functional applications. Examples of such applications could be financial, ERP, MRP, human resources, and, of course, eCommerce. Like the industry AIPs, this differentiator is based on internal learning and linkages and is sustainable.

10. **Industry (Vertical) Focus**. Some industries have strong requirements for unique types of applications. Focusing on and learning about these applications can render AIPs sustainable competitive advantages. For example, the oil and gas industry has very distinct requirements for services of so-called acquired data service providers (DSP) and derived DSPs. These terms are defined in the article, "Knowledge Management and New IT Architecture."[12] Written by the researchers of Landmark Graphics, Inc.,[13] a Haliburton company, this article's conclusions may have an auspicious value. The paper states,

> *Acquired* DSPs would be organized around major data types that share common characteristics: *seismic* surveys, *wireline logs*, etc. Contractors such as Western Geophysical, PGS, CGG and Veritas would supply all of their raw geophysical data to an independently-managed *seismic* DSP. Oilfield service companies such as Schlumberger, Haliburton, and Baker Atlas would provide downhole data to a common *wireline* DSP... *Derived* DSPs of the future would be organized along two lines: type of data and customer. While many companies could share the costs of archiving and accessing one copy of raw data, there would be no economies of scale or scope for derived and interpreted data. Five companies using the same data would generate five maps. They might also reprocess the survey in five different ways. Unique variations among derived data form the basis of healthy competition and value creation. Therefore, the five interpretations would need to be stored securely in one or more remote *derived* DSPs...

> DSPs will significantly lower overall industry costs, funneling that money into more worthy investments.

---

11. Wintel is a merger of the words Windows (alluding to Microsoft and its OS, e.g., NT) and Intel (alluding to Intel or compatible processor technologies).

12. John Gibson, "Knowledge Management and new IT Architecture," *World Energy*, 2: Energy Group, Vol. 3, No. 2, 2000.

13. See www.lgc.com.

AIP Cost Economies

Internal Economies of Scale

All categories of economies of scale used earlier for co-location and MIP apply to the AIP to derive cost-based competitive advantages.

Specialization. The discussion of competitive advantages due to differentiation implies diverse types of specialization. Focusing on certain functional or industry applications, or suppliers and proprietary integration technologies, to name just a few, helps narrow down the range of activities for the AIPs, leading to more refined roles and tasks and more specialized tools. Thus, a deep understanding and leverage of AIPs' activities may render them additional cost-based competitive advantages. To repeat some of the lines written for the MIP earlier, larger AIPs can become more specialized by dividing themselves into more focused groups using more specialized tools and techniques. Smaller AIPs must carefully choose their focus to better use their resources and maximize the possible cost economies due to specialization. As was indicated for the MIPs, the ultimate result would be lower costs for AIPs themselves that can be passed to the customers.

Substitution. For pure AIP services—those derived from the component and integration layers—substitution becomes a question of scalability. For example, if there are middleware products such as application and Web servers, application integration brokers, or transaction monitors/managers that can support larger scale applications, or more application processes, or more sessions with each other, then substituting them for those less endowed may become a feat of improved economy of scale using substitution. While theoretically possible, substitution of this sort may though become expensive, far-fetched, and impractical.

Furthermore, the advent of complete development and runtime platforms, like J2EE, helps create the fabric of distributed application environments that is infinitely more scalable and functionally extensible, rendering substitution a moot point. For the AIP services, however, extending into the MIP territory, substitution becomes more viable. Like for the MIP, for example, buying larger systems (e.g., UNIX boxes) may result in additional economies, albeit with the same caveats as those discussed earlier for MIPs.

Fixed Factors/Overhead. AIP shines at reuse when its capabilities are applied to multiple instances of similar assets, services, and customers. "Hunting" for, identifying, and leveraging this reuse must be, and as experience shows has been, on the minds of many AIP managers whose ASPs have successfully implemented various types of middleware—servers, monitors, brokers, and so forth—to support multiple instances of similar applications, services, and customers using them. Moreover, these same middleware packages could be shared by different entities—assets, services, and customers—constituting the reuse for the economies of scope...but that is discussed later.

Internal Economies of Scope

Standardization. Just like the standards in the MIP domain are able to add to its economies of scope, so can the existing de facto, or de jure, standards within the AIP layers improve its economics. What are these standards? Leaving the argument of de facto or de jure out, the standards arise from the omni-functional power of the distributed application development and runtime platforms such as J2EE, COM/DCOM, and others.

Another extremely powerful and standard protocol that is emerging as a power to reckon with is XML. As of this writing, the momentum behind XML is tremendous and its future is bright. The leverage it is capable of providing cannot be underestimated. It then falls to AIP managements to assess its value and implement XML for many beneficial reasons, including the economies of scope due to its standardization.

Technology Reuse. Simply put, the use of varied middleware types across multiple instances of dissimilar assets, (application) services, and customers represents technology reuse. The more the same middleware is used for multiple customers, the better. The same middleware software can handle multiple jobs simplifying installation, deployment, operations, and management. One caveat, though, remains. It is the issue of software licenses. Typically, licenses are charged by processors, user seats, or other physical units of usage. The more innovative licensing involves fees per transactions, use time, resource consumption, and so forth. These new approaches promise to benefit both AIPs and ISVs while charging customers for what they use, thus supporting the premise of the rental nature of ASP.

Additionally, and similarly to the MIP, AIP's reuse also comes from the leverage and portability of management services and tools across multiple assets, services, and customers (similar and dissimilar).

Knowledge Reuse. The amount and sophistication of AIPs' knowledge must not be underestimated. Being the most technologically complex of all ASP types, the AIP's success, to a great degree, rides on its knowledge, expertise, experience, and efficiency methods, for example, methodologies and practices. All these must be recognized, captured, and continuously developed.

AIPs' knowledge reuse can be easily spotted. The use of recognized subject matter experts (SME) saves time and money and enhances the AIP's reputation—all the while contributing to the AIP's competitive advantage of proven skills and, of course, the economies of scale and scope.

Internal Economies of Learning

The earlier description of learning for MIP alluded to a number of areas to accrue the learnings and develop efficiencies based on them. The same logic applies to the AIP and, in addition to business processes—the focus will also be on the architectural development, integration, deployment, and operations of services arising from the component- and integration-ware layers of 3DF. Again, as in several instances before, the key to learning comes from proven implementation skills. To leverage this learning, an AIP must recognize repeatable patterns, templates, code, and so forth, in the application of AIP skills to meet customer requirements. While these patterns, templates, code, and other repeatable practices may appear as scope and scale-based reuse, reuse it is, this time leveraging the application of AIP knowledge. Examples of internal economies of learning are easy to find, for example, the design of application architectures, metrics for middleware deployment, personalization/customization efforts; reusable beans developed for a particular functional and/or industry focus area; resource allocation to each customer's application; and so forth. Note that the "reusable beans" here is not an example of pure *reuse* for scale or scope. It is created from the learning in order to enhance the AIP's decisions about how to design customer application configurations. Once implemented and proven, these beans then become *reuse*-able for the purposes of economies of scale or scope.

External Economies of Focus and Logistics

The above materials already outlined differentiation-based competitive advantages flowing from the industry, function, or technology focus. The bases for success of focused strategies are rooted in learning as just described. The same logic described for MIP equally applies to AIPs, including a call to harmonize AIP suppliers' and AIP's own strategies, working closely with industry-independent bodies such as associations and consortia, and collaborative marketing. As with MIPs, cost advantages from focused strategies are sustainable but not as reliable as learning alone. Learning is totally controlled by AIPs. Focused strategies are dependent on others.

AIP Value Propositions

Table 9.3 holds AIP's value propositions. Many of AIP's VPs are similar to MIP's VPs. The definitions may be similar, but the content is different.

Table 9.3 *AIP's Value Propositions*

Category	True Benefits to Customers Usable as VPs
Strategic	Customer <u>managers are freed</u> to focus on core competencies of their business (mind-your-business)
	Integration software <u>capital is freed</u> for other investments
	<u>Faster development and deployments help</u> speed up customer's own products' time-to-market
	<u>Feasibility of application integration</u> using integration brokers
	Faster <u>time-to-market</u> for eBusiness application development and integration
	<u>Service commitments may be shorter</u> than middleware's duty cycles or depreciated lives
	<u>Best-of-breed</u> technologies for a fraction of the cost
TCO	<u>Capital savings</u> on the acquisition of development and runtime integration systems (middleware, and possibly hardware/OS for AIP/MIPs)
	<u>Variable costs savings</u> for application development and runtime integration systems by leveraging the efficiencies of AIP's proven implementation skills
	<u>Reduced personnel</u> for application development and runtime integration
	<u>Expensed rental fees</u> cover the use of runtime middleware
Peace-of-Mind	Use of <u>state-of-the-art</u> development and runtime integration systems (middleware, etc.)
	<u>Timely upgrades</u> to all of the aforementioned
	Use of AIP's <u>proven implementation skills</u>
Qualities	Use of <u>scalable and functionally extensible</u> development and runtime integration platforms, for example, J2EE
	Enjoy <u>high availability</u> due to software failover designs implemented in the middleware
	Ensure <u>intercustomer/interapplication security</u> due to the use of virtualization technologies (see Chapter 10)
Support	See MIP and co-location
Miscellaneous	See MIP and co-location

Pure-Play Competitive Advantages

Pure-play ASPs offer customers application services. They choose the markets, select appropriate ISV applications, and then contract with other ASPs for hosting them. They host these applications on top of application infrastructures provided by the AIPs, over physical infrastructure hosted by the MIPs, and space and networks supplied by the co-location providers. In reality, however, pure-plays usually deal with a single provider for all such underlying services.

Pure-plays' relationships with application ISVs vary. Some pure-plays act as ISV's customers and buy software licenses outright for renting the software to *their* customers. Others develop revenue-sharing partnerships in which ISVs get paid only when pure-plays' customers pay. In this latter arrangement, pure-plays and ISVs establish a sharing plan based on certain service accounting metrics such as customer's user seats, application usage terms, transactions, general resource consumption, or any combinations thereof.

A partnership approach has been touted as the most advantageous both to ISVs and pure-plays alike. The key benefit to pure-plays is a divestiture of risk. The young and budding ASPs, always strapped for cash, do not need to buy software licenses now but may pay for them gradually when the revenue comes in. Both the pure-play ASPs and ISVs can now enjoy the many benefits of a tighter collaboration in sales, marketing, gathering market intelligence, product development, testing, and customer support. But ISVs are the biggest winners. Their numerous benefits, or essentially, the VPs from pure-plays to ISVs, are as follows:

- **Continuous Revenue Streams**—a financial stability of smooth revenue flows rather than hard-to-predict license sales driven by capricious markets and seasonality
- **Expansion Into New Markets**—access to broader markets, for example, medium/small businesses who could not afford expensive applications before but would readily pay for sophisticated application functionality by renting it
- **Increased Integration Options**—with other software, either performed by the pure-plays themselves or jointly with the AIPs
- **Reduced Time-To-Market** for ISV's software: for testing, deployment, and customer adoption
- **Leveling Of Competitive Playing Field**—smaller ISVs have the same access to end customers as their big competitors (the Web being an equalizer)

- **Centralized Controls** from the ASPs' NOCs for version control, updates, centralized management, customer care, and so on
- Ability to focus on the development of an application core (**Mind-Your-Business,** see earlier) and be less involved with deployment, integration, and even marketing and channel management.

Once understood, the advantages of hosting applications for rent compelled many industry-leading ISVs to get into the ASP business themselves. Some prominent examples are Oracle's Business-On-Line[14] (BOL) initiative, J.D. Edwards' JDe.sourcing,[15] and many others. Additionally, many ISVs themselves approached AIP ASPs with offers to jointly manage hosting of their software for rental access. In these latter cases, while the financial arrangements vary, the relationship bolsters collaborative marketing and shared revenue.

Pure-Play's Competitive Differentiators

ISVs sell application licenses to their customers. ASPs get these licenses from them somehow (see earlier) and offer customers access to the same applications on a rental basis. Thus, ASPs simply change the mode of how the customers access application functionality and then enjoy the same competitive advantages as the ISVs. This may be a true statement, but it is also cursory and somewhat short-sighted. There is more to how ASPs host the ISV's applications. Some of these unique characteristics are analyzed here.

The pure-play ASPs essentially intermediate between the customers and ISVs. They front the customers and thus effectively take customer "account" control away from them. (This was already alluded to in Figure 3.1 titled "How an ASP changes roles of vendors/providers of IT products and services" in Chapter 3. By developing this logic further, it is easy to see that eventually customers won't need to know the ISVs and will choose applications only on the basis of their functionality, and ASPs—on the basis of service qualities, contractual terms, support, and pricing. However, while this might happen in the long drawn-out future, for now, customers are still very concerned about the brands of applications their ASPs offer. Therefore, pure-plays' competitive advantages (differentiators) should still have a strong relationship to their ISVs.

As done before for other types of ASPs, the competitive differentiators are assigned criteria of perceived value, uniqueness, "switching

---

14. See www.oracle.com.
15. See www.jdesourcing.com.

costs" or multiplicity of the sources of differentiation, as well as the subjective judgments of their sustainability. All competitive advantages are numbered.

1. Like AIPs, with which they are tightly linked, pure-plays thrive on hosting the "best-of-breed" applications from the best brand-name **industry-leading ISVs**. However, this claim alone is not sufficient for ASP success. Pure-plays must explain why renting "best-of-breeds" is advantageous:

   - Sophisticated application functionality

   - Ease of use, deployment, configuration, customization, personalization, and management

   - Linkages to, or integration with, other applications: whether within the same ISV's suite of products or with a cross-vendor; the latter could be achieved using the varied means of application integration described earlier for AIPs.

2. Note that while some features clearly come from ISVs, the advent of others is due to ASPs, for example, an integration with other vendor products. The competitive advantage of **industry-leading ISVs** flows from such interrelationships.

3. **Proven Implementation Skills and Timeliness** refer to the effectiveness of a pure-play's customer procurement and deployment processes (see also MIP and AIP). Learning and linkages within their organizations define pure-plays' competence and hence its competitiveness. Proven implementation skills and timeliness are both sustainable competitive advantages.

4. **Functional and Industry Focus**-based competitive advantages are always ISV dependent. Whatever markets pure-plays select and whatever software they buy, they serve. However, in this context, pure-plays can excel the most. Many pure-plays are ISVs themselves. They write their own applications for the customers in the markets they know the best, integrate them with other appropriate applications, and then contract for hosting them to their customers. Some such ASPs are not even pure-plays at all. Many host their applications themselves and since they offer *remote* application services, the location of the data centers and NOCs is totally irrelevant to their customers. A prominent example of such an ASP is one of the oldest pure-plays named Employease.Com.[16] Here is a simple description of what the com-

---

16. See www.employease.com.

pany does, obtained from its own Web site:

> Employease.com takes full advantage of the Internet's power to facilitate communication and connectivity between you and your employees, managers, and service providers… HR experts from Employease will demonstrate the ease of using the Employease Network to:
>
> - Enable Employease Life Events to automatically administer employee events such as marriages, promotions and terminations
> - Automatically connect with service providers, such as insurance carriers, payroll providers and other benefits providers
> - Enable your employees to find information about their benefit status and update personal information without a single piece of paper
> - Enable line managers to process and track status (such as salary history) of their direct reports.
>
> The end results are satisfied and productive employees.

5. Pure-plays who write **aggressive SLAs** can also gain considerable competitiveness provided they successfully abide by the underlying services' providers promise to stand by the same promises of qualities and service guarantees. Aggressive SLAs are mostly built-in interrelationships.

Pure-Play's Cost Economies

Pure-play ASPs derive their services from two layers of 3DF: application and application utilities. Both are leveraged in the discussion of costs economies here.

Internal Economies of Scale

All categories of economies of scale used earlier for co-location, MIP, and AIP equally apply to pure-play to derive the cost-based competitive advantages.

Specialization is a function of scale. Not the absolute scale of investments but the scale of the ASP's commitment. What this means is that when an ASP decides to specialize in a particular business function or industry, it can potentially develop the economies of scale from specialization. Indeed, the fewer the domains the:

- More concentrated the investments in personnel education, with potentially lower overall training costs, more specialized tools and techniques
- Higher software licensing discounts, as more software licenses are purchased
- Better vendor support, possibly resulting in ASP's lower support costs
- Faster and more effective the learning (see following) for the same investments

These economies of scale can be measured, first to establish a baseline and then to compute the effects of specialization.

Substitution. Are there two applications similar in functionality but different in scalability? What does different scalability actually mean: the ability to support more customers, or transactions, or database channels, or communications sessions for the same software license; or for the same copy of code; or for the same amount of required resources such as the CPU, memory, disk, and so forth? How does the difference in capabilities impact the price? Is it skewed in favor of one vendor or another? And then, whose product is cheaper per customer, transaction, channel, session? Do these relationships change when more copies of software are purchased; or are more deployed resulting in increased capabilities; or deployed on larger servers? What are these products' scalability cost curves (see Chapter 5) and how do they differ? And so on... There are many dimensions to application scalability and its impact on costs. If some of these questions can be answered, the case for substitution in application software can be made. And indeed, this happens. Customers are known to switch from one ISV to another, provided the functionality is similar, if the new product offers a higher scale from the get-go and/or more when needs increase. This is one realistic example of economies of scale due to a substitution in application software.

Fixed Factors/Overhead. Like its underpinning AIPs, pure-plays can also benefit from reuse. It mostly comes from the reuse of application utilities. In fact, the scale-based reuse addressed here and scope-based reuse discussed later are almost indistinguishable.

Internal Economies of Scope

Standardization. Several, although somewhat tenuous, areas of economies of scope are nevertheless found within the application and application utilities layers. Most are either standard features of ASP applications or standard interfaces to application utilities. Some examples of such standard UIs are search engines; e-commerce's shopping carts and credit card entry screens; personal preferences screens; and EDI forms.

Technology Reuse. As was indicated before, scope economies' reuse is virtually indistinguishable from the same for economy of scale.

Knowledge Reuse. Pure-play's knowledge reuse stems from two sources: knowledge of application domain and knowledge of particular products. The efficiency of requirements definition, configuration, deployment, and management for repeatable customer installations results in considerable scope economies due to such knowledge reuse.

Internal Economies of Learning

Anything that is done repeatedly can potentially be improved. This is the essence of learning. Pure-plays' learning flows from the repeated installations of applications involving varied phases of application life cycles. In fact, learning leads to life cycle methodologies that provide for implementation efficiencies.

External Economies of Focus and Logistics

All the logic used to highlight the importance and value of pursuing focus and logistics-based strategies described for AIPs equally applies to the pure-plays. Note that pure-plays' suppliers (see similar paragraph for AIP) imply more than just ISVs but also SIs and, possibly, VARs.

Pure-Play's Value Propositions

Table 9.4 highlights the pure-play's value propositions.

Table 9.4   *Pure-Play's Value Propositions*

Category	*True Benefits to Customer Usable as VPs*
Strategic	Best-of-breed application functionality for less Expedited access to sophisticated application functionality helps core business
TCO	Savings on the acquisition of application licenses Application switching requires no new licenses Reduced personnel for application development and runtime integration and management Expensed rental fees cover the use of runtime middleware
Peace-of-Mind	Timely upgrades to all of the aforementioned Access to proven implementation skills
Qualities	Proven reliability of application code Potentially, sophisticated application management for enhanced availability, manageability, and security
Support	See AIP
Miscellaneous	See AIP

Summary

This chapter provided a comprehensive analysis of ASP's competitive advantages. It used an authoritative outline by Michael Porter for the sources of such competitive advantages: low cost and differentiation. Porter's frameworks for low costs are based on the analysis of the business and its industry's value chains. It is believed, though, that Michael Porter's approach better applies to mature industries, which ASP is not. Hence, a more generic framework for analyzing the ASP costs—ASP Economics from Chapter 4—was also applied to the different ASP types. The analysis of ASP's differentiation-based competitive advantages, however, remained pure Michael Porter.

These analyses, however comprehensive and insightful, only helped recognize ASP's major competitive advantage. To realize them requires ASP management decisions in the areas of:

- Business strategy
- Technology choices
- Business processes

Understanding the potential for differentiation or cost savings is but the first step toward realizing ASP's competitive advantages. The only way, however, to achieve these advantages is to translate their paper descriptions into actionable items and then actively manage the processes of delivering them in order to gain larger market share, increase revenues, and develop a stronger good will. The need for action simply cannot be overemphasized. It is therefore this author's timid hope that some frameworks and ideas developed here will be accepted for considerations by, or at least serve as mind teasers to, some existing or future ASP entrepreneurs. If it happens at least once, this book's purpose will have been served well.

Chapter 10

ASP Enabling: Requirements and Fulfillment

The growing interest in ASP among businesses, entrepreneurs, and investors has spurred many established vendors as well as young entrepreneurial companies to enter the race for ASP products and services. At the time of this writing, the industry for ASP enablement was just about coming of age—some innovative ideas had already been developed, and new products created and introduced to the market. To understand the major issues of ASP enablement, this chapter's objectives are as follows:

- Define the requirements for ASP functionality and see what existing (and, perhaps future) products can support it; and

- Define the requirements for ASP service management and see what products are available today to implement it.

What is ASP Enabling and Why Do it?

What is ASP enabling and why do it? A quick overview of this book may help answer these questions. First, here is a rehash of the basic ASP definition given in Chapter 1. An ASP is required to (1) deliver services over the network (2) to multiple customers (3) who are charged usage-based fees and (4) are provided customer-specific service guarantees according to their SLAs.

Next, another question: Did the previous chapters address *all* the aspects of this ASP definition? The answer is, "no, they did not." They largely discussed (1) service delivery (2) to multiple customers. None truly dealt with the challenges of (3) usage-based fees and (4) customer-specific service guarantees according to their SLAs. These remaining issues make up the subject of this chapter, which thus brings the discussion back to ASP enabling.

Without any further argumentation, here is a simple postulate: The network-computing infrastructure should be called ASP-enabled when it is:

- Effectively leveraged (shared) across multiple customers
- Carefully managed for efficient utilization
- Accurately measured (metered) to derive a basis for charging customers usage-based fees

A little further refining results in three new technology-focused requirements for ASP enablement:

1. *Shared Resources* in support of multiple customers
2. *Manageable Systemic Qualities* to meet customer SLAs
3. *Measurable Resource Usage* for accounting, billing, and business planning

Where do these requirements apply? Figure 10.1 offers a familiar view of the two ASP domains: ASP infrastructure on the right, and ASP management on the left. The ASP enablement requirements apply differently to these domains.

- The infrastructure technologies *must possess* the ASP enabling properties described in the three requirements mentioned before. This means that these technologies must be shareable, manageable (for qualities), and measurable.
- The ASP management technologies *must manage* the ASP enabling properties of the ASP infrastructure. That is, they must be able to control sharing, manage qualities, and measure and meter resource usage.

For the infrastructure domain, many technologies meeting the enabling requirements already exist. Examples are UNIX SMP[1] servers with dynamic domain management; distributed application component platforms and frameworks, like Sun Microsystems' J2EE or Microsoft's COM/DCOM for hosting multiple applications; the popular SAN and NAS storage technologies, which can be totally indifferent to the ownership of data; newer network switching, routing, and signaling technologies capable of bandwidth shaping; and many others.

---

1. SMP stands for Symmetric Multiprocessing Systems.

For the ASP management domain, many new ASP-specific management technologies have been created and introduced to the market. These technologies include, but are not limited to, service modeling and definitions, customer procurement and provisioning, usage metering, accounting, and billing; dynamic resource monitoring and configuration per customer SLAs; needs analyses and future capacity planning, and so on.

The material in this chapter first examines the ASP-enabling technologies for the ASP hosting infrastructure domain (the stack on the right in Figure 10.1) followed by a discussion of ASP service management (shaded area in the left stack in Figure 10.1). For all practical purposes, this chapter is a reality check of the most salient ASP-enabling technologies at the time of this writing.

As was stated earlier, naming and discussing the vendors and products exemplifying the most applicable ASP enabling technologies does not constitute their endorsement by the author or the book.

Enabling Properties of ASP Infrastructure

This section provides brief descriptions of the technologies up and down the stack of the ASP infrastructure (right side in Figure 10.1) and the analyses of their enabling properties. The three aforementioned enabling requirements are applied to these technologies to derive their properties.

Figure 10.1 *Domains of ASP-enabling technologies.*

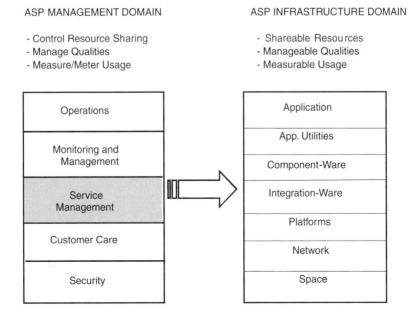

ASP MANAGEMENT DOMAIN

- Control Resource Sharing
- Manage Qualities
- Measure/Meter Usage

ASP INFRASTRUCTURE DOMAIN

- Shareable Resources
- Manageable Qualities
- Measurable Usage

| Operations |
| Monitoring and Management |
| Service Management |
| Customer Care |
| Security |

| Application |
| App. Utilities |
| Component-Ware |
| Integration-Ware |
| Platforms |
| Network |
| Space |

It would also be helpful to relate the technologies in the stack on the right in Figure 10.1 (while discussing their enabling properties) to the four types of ASP (co-lo, MIP, AIP, and pure-play) defined in Chapter 6. While this exercise is left to the reader, here is a simple "cheat-sheet:" This analysis should help identify the relative "power" of ASP enabling for each ASP type and reason about its intrinsic potential for economic leverage. Some conclusions would be quite obvious; others might not be so apparent. For example, it is clear that co-location ASPs offer shared space. At the same time, more insight would be required to analyze the management requirements of the shared application infrastructure.

Network Layer

Chapters 6 and 7 already discussed the ASP networks and network management, respectively, in considerable detail. What follows is a brief analysis of ASP-enabling properties specific to networks, in general, and IP networks, in particular.

Sharing. By definition, packet networks are shared. Even for dedicated networks required by some customers, IP is the most commonly used protocol.

Managing Networks' Systemic Qualities. The network is a vascular system and the main asset of any ASP. ASPs must always know how the network performs, how it is used, and what to do to maximize its utility to the customers. The basic systemic qualities of the network—performance, availability, scalability, manageability, and security—must therefore be carefully planned and managed. Fortunately, network management is a mature discipline that is comprehensive enough to address the complete spectrum of a network's systemic qualities.

It should be noted that there exists a major conceptual difference between phone networks and IP networks. On phone networks, there is an upper bound to the number of users who can use them at once and therefore a lower bound on network systemic qualities. IP networks, in turn, have no upper bound on the number of users who can use them and therefore no lower bound on qualities. Bandwidth sharing is, therefore, an important consideration for IP networks but one that doesn't apply to phone networks.

Metering. Traditional phone companies are known for sophisticated abilities to measure and meter services rendered to their customers. By leveraging their experiences, IP networking developed its own IP network-metering capabilities. While the phone companies use the so-called call message detail record (CMDR) for call accounting, IP networking developed a similar concept, the IPDR, for internet protocol detail record. Recognizing the importance of IPDR for the future of IP networking, a group of industry participants launched an IPDR initiative—IPDR.org—tasked with the development of IPDR interoperability standards. More specifically, the charter of IPDR.org is "to define the essential elements of data exchange between network elements, operation support systems, and business support systems. It will provide the foundation for open, carrier-grade IP-based support systems that enable next-generation service providers to operate efficiently and cost effectively."[2]

Platform Layer—Computing

SMP and Dynamic System Domains

The first thing that comes to mind when speaking of multiple customers running their applications on one computer is traditional time-sharing on a mainframe. In the world of the mainframes, each application used to get an allotment of resources (memory, CPU, etc.) and ran as though it had a dedicated machine. Sophisticated mainframe software (e.g., MVS, CICS) also made sharing possible by creating independent customer or application partitions. Similar capabilities could be accomplished on other systems, such as those on the UNIX-based "boxes."

Figure 10.2   *Sun's Starfire dynamic system domains.*

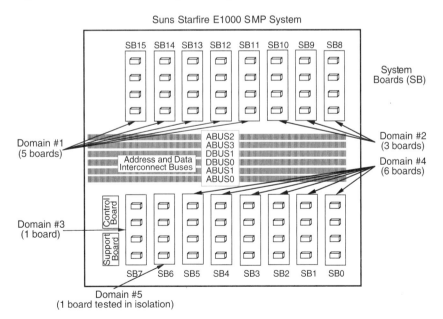

Although UNIX does multiprogramming well in and of itself, it doesn't provide for partitions like the mainframe. Yet the symmetric

2. See www.ipdr.org/about/index.htm.

multiprocessing (SMP) UNIX systems may make such partitions (or *domains* as they are called in UNIX) possible. Many vendors produce UNIX SMP systems—for example, Sun Microsystems, IBM, Silicon Graphics, Hewlett Packard—and some support dynamic systems domains in which resources are dynamically allocated among applications (and customers) similarly to the mainframe. One such implementation, on a Sun Microsystems' Starfire, is described here.

Sun's Starfire is a modular system consisting of multiple processor boards (each with four processors), memory modules, and I/O modules, all attached to four high-speed address buses. As Figure 10.2 illustrates, a "fully loaded" E10000 has 16 system boards (with memory and four I/O modules each) for a total of 64 processors. The E10000 can be subdivided into multiple SMP computers, each consisting of one or several system boards. Each domain runs its own copy of Sun's Solaris OS and has its own disk storage, network links, and a boot disk. Special hardware bit masks identify the systems boards to each domain and define the intradomain and interdomain memory-based networking.

Administering Starfire requires a systems service processor (SSP)—a Sun SPARC workstation that runs a standard Solaris OS and a suite of administrative and diagnostic tools. The SSP is connected to Starfire's control board via Ethernet and can perform various administration functions such as:

- Assign system boards to configure system domains;
- Switch system boards dynamically among domains (hence *dynamic* system domains), adding or deleting them as needed;
- Modify domains and interconnect masks for varying inter- and intradomain networking; and
- Remove system boards (e.g., for repair) from the domains and then reintroduce them back without interrupting Starfire's operations.

Benefits from SMP and Dynamic Domains

These flexibilities of dynamic system domains should appeal to ASPs. Here is a brief rundown of what an ASP can do with them:

- <u>Consolidation</u>. Different customers' applications can run in different domains. Resources can be shifted quickly among the domains to meet customers' changing requirements to ensure performance, availability, and scalability per customer SLAs.
- <u>Multiple Applications</u>. Customers may use separate domains to run different applications or to perform different life-cycle activities such as development, testing, and production—all on

the same system—with exceptional ease of application and data sharing and interdomain transfers.

- Special Functions. A domain can be dedicated to perform a certain unique function in support of one or multiple customers—such as providing access to tape devices for backup; furnishing access to high-speed networks; hosting an ASP management module for fault monitoring and usage tracking, metering, and reporting.

- Accounting. A system board is a convenient unit of usage-based pricing. Customers can be charged, along with other metrics, by the number of system boards they use.

These are unique economies of SMP systems vis-à-vis multiple UNIX systems. Note how consistent they are with the MIP generic economies described earlier in Chapter 9.

- First, every UNIX box, even by the same vendor, has its own technology, packaging, and management idiosyncrasies. For a system like Starfire, ASP personnel must be trained on only *one* system rather than on many (hence, specialization).

- Next, by consolidating many smaller systems into a large one, ASPs create the economies of scale due to substitution. Indeed, the price-performance metrics[3] of Starfire's total cost of ownership (TCO) are more attractive than those on multiple smaller systems.

- Further, overhead savings exist due to Starfire's smaller footprint, less external wiring, less power consumption, and fewer support personnel, just to name a few factors. These benefits can translate both into an economy of scale's overhead and an economy of scope's reuse.

- Additionally, many systemic qualities inherent in Starfire can be translated into cost savings, such as faster failover for improved availability, and dynamic scalability.

- And finally, costs advantages can accrue from clever choices of vendors (e.g., focus-based economies) and persistent logistics activities, as was described in Chapter 9.

ASP Enabling Properties of SMP and Dynamic Domains

The SMP and dynamic systems domains are capable of providing for all enabling properties as per the three enabling requirements mentioned before.

---

3. Alan Charlesworth, "Starfire: Extending the SMP Envelope," *IEEE Micro*, January/February 1998.

Sharing. Resource sharing is the essence of multiprocessing systems; the cabinets, buses, storage systems, and management tools are but a few examples. Yet, the shared pool of system boards—allocated (even dynamically) among applications and customers—is the major shared resource.

Qualities. The management versatility of SMP helps achieve performance, availability, and scalability as was already mentioned for consolidation.

Metering. Finally, while SMP doesn't directly assist metering, its granular nature (e.g., processors and boards for each domain running an application) makes accounting for resources used more obvious and easy.

Platform Layer—Storage

In 2000, Forrester Research predicted that companies' online storage would increase ten fold over the next five years. It also stated that if companies' storage costs amounted to about 5% of IT budgets today, they would reach 17% by 2003. Despite the costs of storage systems falling (see "Colossal Upset" in Chapter 3), companies are overwhelmed with the growing complexities of planning, acquiring, and managing them. This has attracted many providers, vendors, and ASPs (or, more precisely, storage service providers or SSPs) alike into the storage provisioning market. It should be noted also that the business outlook for storage provisioning is very promising. Dataquest researchers estimated that U.S. companies would "spend about $6 billion on storage utilities" in 2003. Another research firm, Enterprise Storage, was also very optimistic, predicting costs of $11.2 billion in 2004 alone.

SAN and NAS

There are many storage management technologies capable of supporting multiple customers while offering options for varied ASP economies. The two most prominent, and very popular as of this writing, are NAS and SAN.

Technically, both SAN and NAS offer a means for building storage infrastructures external to the computing systems while drastically simplifying storage management and providing for increased scalability and availability. SAN and NAS have different uses, support different systemic qualities differently, and offer potentially different ASP economies.

SAN is data-centric. It is an extension of a traditional computing model, a storage bus off the computer's back plane. Figure 10.3 shows how SAN can be logically derived from a standard server direct-attach storage solution. In a typical SAN, a computer continues to use its storage access protocol (e.g., Small Computer Systems

Figure 10.3   *Standard direct-attached storage solutions and SAN*

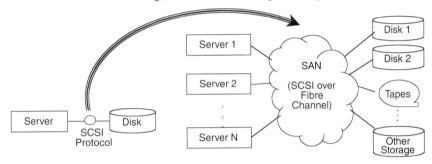

A fast network is "inserted" between servers and storage disks.
It wraps SCSI data transfer blocks into Fibre Channel protocol.
The network is transparent to the server. Multiple servers can share
the same SAN over a distance of 6 miles for near-local secure data
storage. SANs key features are:

- Isolated from business LAN traffic
- Storage is independent from computing
- Higher scalability and availability
- Centralized management & operations (e.g., backup)
- Data copy sharing among heterogeneous systems only
- Server-to-storage, server-to-server, storage-to-storage transfers

Interface or SCSI) except that SCSI block transfers are wrapped in a
fast LAN-like protocol implemented using Fibre Channel. Other
storage access protocols can also be used on SAN such as Enterprise
Systems Connection (ESCON), Serial Storage Architecture (SSA),
High Performance Parallel Interface (HIPPI), and others. Fibre[4]
Channel has been chosen via industry consensus to be SAN's architecture. Since Fibre Channel is a shared medium, SAN can attach to
multiple computers and storage systems. Yet, SAN is an OS-oriented
solution. Each computer manages its own I/Os using its own OS.
SAN is a fast storage access medium due to Fibre Channel currently
running 1.7 GBPS (that is gigabits per second!). SAN may employ
routers, switches, gateways, hubs, bridges, and other data movement
devices to enable it to handle traffic on behalf of heterogeneous servers, storage devices, interfaces, and storage formats.

Some of the key advantages of SAN are:

- Separation from a business LAN. SAN is dedicated to storage
  access only and is not encumbered by business traffic. SAN can
  be local or near-local, up to six miles away according to Fibre
  Channel's architectural limitations

---

4. The term *Fibre Channel* uses French spelling for *fiber*. Some authors state
this is to indicate that copper wires may also be used in lieu of fiber optics to implement Fibre Channel architecture and protocols.

- Improved application availability and scalability by off-loading storage processing
- Consolidated storage with simplified management and scalability with faster upgrades
- Enhanced physical security—near-remote storage can be vaulted for controlled access and disaster protection

Back in August 1999, IBM Corporation published the White Paper,[5] "Introduction to Storage Area Network, SAN" in which it described the various types of data sharing. Since sharing, per se, is critical to ASP, the following excerpt is provided:

> SANs enable storage to be externalized from the server and centralized, and in so doing, allow data to be shared among multiple host servers without impacting system performance. The term *data sharing* describes the access of common data for processing by multiple computer platforms or servers. Data sharing can be between platforms that are similar or different; this is also referred to as homogeneous and heterogeneous data sharing.
>
> - **Storage Sharing.** With storage sharing, two or more homogeneous or heterogeneous servers share a single storage subsystem whose capacity has been physically partitioned so that each attached server can access only the units allocated to it. Multiple servers can own the same partition, but this is possible only with homogeneous servers.
> - **Data-Copy Sharing.** Data-copy sharing allows different platforms to access the same data by sending a copy of the data from one platform to the other.
> - **"True" Data Sharing.** In true data sharing, only one copy of the data is accessed by multiple platforms, whether homogeneous or heterogeneous. Every platform attached has read and write access to the single copy of data.

This terminology is essential to understanding the types of sharing SAN and NAS support.

NAS is file system-centric. NAS is a LAN-attached file server optimized for storage operations and management as a high-performance, high-speed, dedicated network device. It uses its own operating system for storage operations. Figure 10.4 shows a simple view of NAS. NAS works with distributed file systems such as NFS for UNIX, Common Internet File System (CIFS) for Microsoft Windows, and others. It utilizes TCP/IP for data transport and networking and Ethernet (preferably gigabit Ethernet) for media access. It may also use fast media (e.g., ATM over the Internet). In lieu of distributed file systems, NAS may also use higher TCP/IP stack protocols such as HTTP or FTP.

---

5. Ravi Kumar Khattar, Mark S. Murphy, Giulio John Tarella, Kjell E. Nystrom, "Introduction to Storage Area Network, SAN," White Paper, IBM Corporation, www.redbooks.ibm.com, document SG24-5470-00, August 1999.

Figure 10.4   *Network attached service.*

Storage is "outsourced" to NAS server(s), anywhere over the network. The network can carry NFS, CIFS, and other file systems, over TCP/IP, over Ethernet, or other media access. NASs key features are:

- Dedicated high-speed, high-performance file servers
- File servers may link many networks & multiple message protocols
- Data copy sharing between heterogeneous systems
- Data sharing between heterogeneous systems

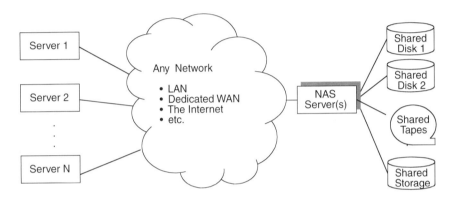

NAS is an "equal opportunity" storage access system in that it services data access requests from multiple clients (e.g., computing systems) and can share data (not only storage and data copies) among them regardless of their OS and/or file systems. With an explosion of different media—video, audio, graphics—easy sharing among different systems or customers is a welcome capability. A simple example could be advertising banners ASPs may want to place selectively on their customers' Web pages. Key benefits of NAS are:

- It relieves servers' computing cycles from storage management tasks, making computing and storage access independent and, hence, more predictable.

- It allows for faster time-to-market for storage scaling. Computing servers need not be taken down for adding/changing storage devices; upgrading can be done faster on NAS servers optimized for these functions. Some newer NAS devices allow for hot-swapping and upgrades without interrupting operations.

- Like in SAN, data storage vaulting can ensure higher physical security.

- It allows for easier and more reliable operations such as backups and restores, and disaster recovery.

Using SAN and NAS

In the early days of SAN and NAS their uses differed. For traditional data service with multiple customers accessing the same data, such as Web content, NAS was the preferred choice. It was also used successfully for managing email and other messaging systems (whose nature was mostly read-intensive) that could survive "reasonable" high latencies and communications delays.

SAN, on the other hand, was considered more appropriate for low latency applications with equally intense read and write operations. Examples were online transaction processing systems (OLTP), especially those with unpredictable loads, decision support systems (e.g., data warehousing or data mining), or other applications required to process very large volumes of data.

What explained this functional segregation? The answer was simple—network and processing speeds. The early versions of NAS used Ethernet (10 and 100 MBPS), which was also burdened by business traffic. For that reason, faith in NAS performance was quite low. However, all of this changed by the time of this writing. Many new technologies defied the conventional wisdoms about slow LAN and server processing speeds that used to limit NAS and SAN performance. The former ones have now been replaced by multigigabit Ethernet and 1.7 GBPS Fibre Channel, and the latter, by the emerging wave of "silicon servers of the optical age."[6] Here is what George Gilder writes about these servers, pioneered by the technologies from such young companies as BlueArc:

> ... BlueArc's Silicon Server architecture separates and pipelines the four key server functions into four parallel processing modules. Designed more like a switch or a router than like an ordinary server, the BlueArc device blasts open the bottleneck between users and storage by putting the TCP/IP stack, the file servers, and storage protocols, with all their hundreds of lookup tables, directories, and connection lists, in hardware. One of the parallel modules contains the world's fastest all-hardware TCP/IP networking subsystem. Another holds the world's fastest fibre channel controller. Sandwiched in the middle are diverse protocol translation units and file subsystems that perform all the key storewidth functions–SAN, NAS, you name it–of delivering data from storage to the Web.

> BlueArc initially offers a single box with throughput of 2.5 gigabits per second between gigabit Ethernet at one end and gigabit Fibre Channel at the other. Scaling up to 200 terabytes of storage through a single Ethernet connection, BlueArc blows away the sixteen terabyte limit of current NAS and SAN devices. Consuming nearly half the power and scaling to tens of thousands of simultaneous users, BlueArc pulverizes the current server limits of less than two hun-

---

6. George Gilder, "The Storewidth Warp," Gilder Technology Report, February 2001.

dred. For 20 percent of the capital costs, this architecture offers five times the bandwidth for streaming applications, 10 times the bandwidth for traditional file transfers, 30 times the amount of accessible storage, and a hundred times the number of simultaneous user connectivity, all with five-9s of solid-state reliability. It is a "Silicon Server for the optical age.

It is without a shadow of a doubt that all these developments epitomized by BlueArc (with many other companies to follow suit) will enhance the scale, scope, and capabilities of storage technologies. While these advances will surely help end users, service providers will be their major beneficiaries, where larger scale and higher-performing products will lead to more express economies and further evolution of ASP/SSP business.

Economies of SAN and NAS

Despite some conceptual differences, NAS and SAN seem to offer very similar cost economies. The most obvious of such economies are listed here.

- **Specialization for Economies of Scale:** Work efficiencies of NAS/SAN personnel that are involved in technology acquisition, packaging, servicing, and selling increase when the operational scale increases and the number of vendors/products decreases.

- **Substitution for Economies of Scale:** Larger, more powerful NAS servers can be shared among multiple customers or customer applications (homogeneity is implied for SAN), all leading to concrete economies of scale due to substitution.

- **Overhead for Economies of Scale**: NAS and SAN may cost less in fixed costs and overhead—real estate, wiring, and power consumption, support personnel—than the total costs of attached storage on multiple servers for multiple customers. Also, labor to support and manage shared storage on behalf of multiple customers costs less than the sum of similar services rendered separately. This creates payroll savings that can be passed on to the customers.

- **Rules of Geometry for Economies of Scale**: Since disk and tape devices are physical three-dimensional entities, the economies of scale due to geometry also work in favor of NAS/SAN. Large volume disks might be the same size as smaller ones; the same analogy also applies to tapes, and so forth. While these advantages may appear negligible, on the scale of large ASP (or SSP) facilities, resultant savings may be sizable.

- **Technology Reuse for Economies of Scope**: Technology reuse is present in NAS/SAN by definition. There are numerous common costs in management processes and tools.

- **Knowledge Reuse for Economies of Scope:** Examples of knowledge reuse in regards to NAS/SAN are common algorithms for storage capacity planning, allocation, performance, and so on.

- **Economies of Learning, Focus and Logistics.** Most generic economies from Chapter 9 for MIP apply here.

ASP Enabling Properties of SAN and NAS

SAN and NAS successfully meet the three requirements for ASP enabling.

Sharing. While nothing prevents a single application or customer to use dedicated SAN or NAS, the real purposes for both technologies are to centralize and share the high-speed, high-volume, and low-latency storage facilities.

Qualities. SAN and NAS provide storage access priorities (for performance), redundant designs (for availability), and the ability to add storage when needed (for scalability)—all covered by sophisticated security.

Metering. Both native SAN and NAS operating systems as well as add-on products provide for usage metering.

Integration and Component Layers

Component-Based Application Infrastructures

Integration-Ware and Component-Ware are the domains of AIP ASPs. Therefore, the following material applies mostly to AIPs.

Enterprise-level NC solutions require robust yet flexible computing platforms. Over the years, through the collaborative work of numerous companies and individuals, the component-based platform has admittedly become the most promising method for designing the NC (and ASP) computing architectures. Two competing component-based platforms are J2EE, authored by Sun Microsystems, and COM/DCOM created by Microsoft. This section describes the J2EE platform, focusing on its abilities to meet the three criteria outlined at the start of this chapter. A brief description of J2EE follows.

J2EE defines a collection of Java extensions in the form of Application Program Interfaces (APIs). The most critical API is EJB, which defines the server-side component model for applications. The J2EE runtime environment consists of two major parts: *Application Components* and *Containers*, as seen in Figure 10.5.

Figure 10.5 *J2EE Application components and containers.*

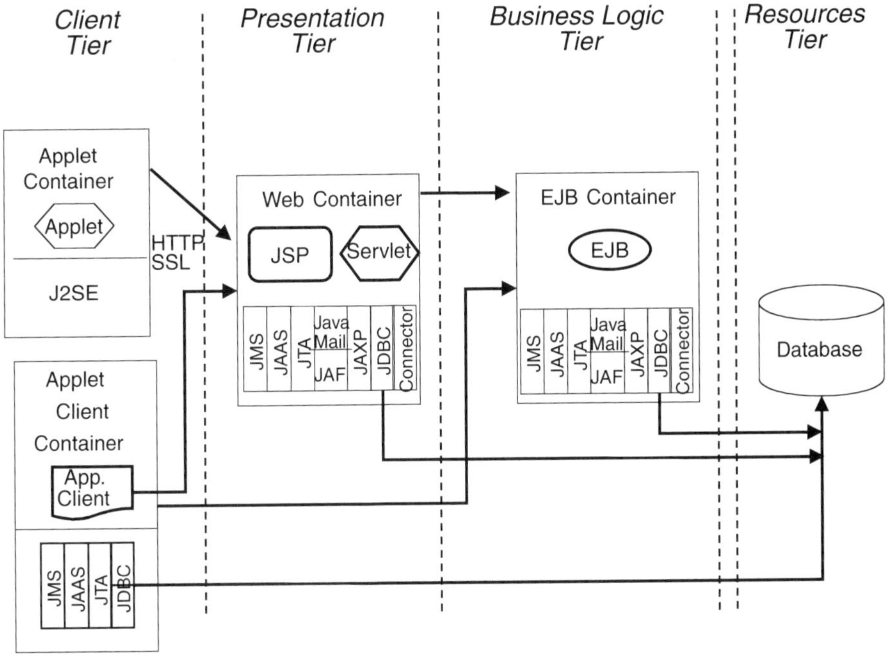

Application Components. The best way to describe application components is to quote Sun Microsystems' public document on J2EE:[7]

> Application clients are Java programming language programs that are typically GUI programs that execute on a desktop computer. Application clients offer a user experience similar to that of native applications, and have access to all of the facilities of the J2EE middle tier;

> Applets are GUI components that typically execute in a web browser, but can execute in a variety of other applications or devices that support the applet programming model. Applets can be used to provide a powerful user interface for J2EE applications (simple HTML pages can also be used to provide a more limited user interface for J2EE applications);

> Servlets and Java Server Pages (JSP) typically execute on a web server and respond to HTTP requests from web clients. Servlets and JSP pages may be used to generate HTML pages that are an application's user interface. They may also be used to generate XML or other formats of data that is consumed by other application components. Servlets, and pages created with JavaServer Pages™ technology, are often referred to collectively in this speci-

---

7. Java™ 2 Enterprise Edition, v1.3 Public Draft (Sun Microsystems, Inc.).

fication as "web components." Web application are composed of web components and other data such as HTML pages;

Enterprise JavaBeans™ (EJB) components execute in a managed environment that supports transactions. Enterprise beans typically contain the business logic for a 2EE application.

J2EE Containers. The J2EE containers provide the runtime environment and management support to the application components described before. The containers represent the view of the world to these components, meaning that they provide a federated (combined) view of all the APIs supported within the given J2EE implementation.

When a J2EE vendor produces a J2EE compliant product, this product typically includes multiple containers for all four types of application components described earlier. Also borrowed from the same Sun Microsystems' public J2EE document quoted before, Figure 10.5 shows examples of such containers:

- **a Web Container** that hosts Web components (Java servlets and JSP)
- **an EJB Container** that hosts the EJBs that represent business application logic
- **an Applet Container** that hosts presentation applets
- **an Applet Client Container** that provides a runtime environment for applets on the client machine.

Selectively, these containers support multiple services and APIs (a nonexhaustive list):

- HTTP, HTTPS
- JMS, for Java Messaging
- JAAS, for Java Authentication and Authorization Service
- JTA, for Java Transaction API
- JAF, for JavaBeans™ Activation Framework
- JNDI, for Java Naming and Directory Services
- JavaMail™, for Java-based mail extensions allowing component–based applications to exchange Internet mail
- JAXP, an API for XML parsing
- RMI-IIOP: RMI is used for Remote Method Invocation style of programming and IIOP is used for access to CORBA services
- JDBC, Java Database Connectivity
- Connector Architecture SPI, a Service Provider Interface for building adapters for access to other information systems this J2EE environment must interface

More detailed descriptions of these APIs can be found in the afore-mentioned Sun Microsystems' public document or many other sources from the truly vast body of available J2EE literature. J2EE is not limited to the API mentioned here. Many new ones can, and inevitably will be, added in the future.

The topology of J2EE containers in Figure 10.5 is reminiscent of 3DF tiers. The vertical lines show the tiers' boundaries. Even the terminology is similar. One tier, Integration, is visibly missing. Yet, the various J2EE APIs offer abstractions to support the missing Integration tier's functionality. Chief among them are JDBC and Connector SPI.

Economies of J2EE

There are many possible ways to leverage J2EE to create ASP econo-mies. Using the J2EE products for multiple customers leads to increased work efficiencies of the AIP ASP personnel who specify, build, test, and operate customers' application infrastructures. Also, the fewer different J2EE products AIP ASPs use, the higher the additional benefits of *Specialization*.

AIP ASPs may also uncover and recognize some savings due to a *Shared Overhead* of using the same J2EE products and APIs across multiple customer implementations. The savings come mostly from purchase discounts (for products, services, and maintenance) and reduced labor and other resources used for handling the application code, simplified configuration management, and so on. The most crit-ical economic benefit of J2EE, *Technology Reuse*, arises from:

- Multiple containers using the same APIs, which are in turn used by multiple applications and customers

- Reusable development tools

- Reusable services (such as directory and messaging) based on J2EE

- Reusable servlets, applets, JSP pages, and EJBs

Incidentally, the last two bullets are the most critical consider-ations behind the EJB philosophy. Similarly, *Knowledge Reuse* flows from the accrued experiences and realized efficiencies of working with familiar J2EE containers and APIs.

Finally, the economies of *Learning, Focus, and Logistics* are all related to *Specialization*. "Sticking" with a limited number of J2EE vendors and products results in many additional efficiencies and economies, such as broader and richer knowledge bases, joint fea-ture/function developments, and improved application integration tools and techniques.

ASP Enabling Properties of J2EE

Using J2EE helps meet the three requirements for creating ASP enabling properties.

Sharing. Since J2EE containers can run multiple applications, they can run multiple customers' applications, or multiple applications by the same customer, spelling different forms of resource sharing.

Qualities. J2EE containers allow administration of many parameters, such as the quantity of processing threads, pools of database connections, communications sessions, and others. At times, pools and threads may be administered per application, such as for setting initial performance characteristics. But this may not be necessary as it is possible to run multiple containers. Concurrently, many implementations of J2EE containers (e.g., Web and application servers) support clustering and automatic failovers, the former helping scalability, the latter—availability. As for the security, most containers implement the concepts of security realms, which are sufficient for application access control, authentication, authorization, and other forms of user credentialing.

Metering. Many J2EE containers can monitor threads and other resources. This is exactly the information that is needed for metering.

Application Layer(s)

This section focuses on ASP-enabling of hosted applications themselves. Ideally, ASPs should be able to run a single instance of an application for multiple customers. Some ASPs are doing it today for such applications as personal productivity tools, office space reservation systems, time and attendance systems, some B2B procurement systems, some analytical tools, training software, and so forth.

Enabling the applications to support multiple customers depends on the platforms these applications run on and their own complexity. Application complexity, in this context, is not about an application's logic but its external interfaces, for example, access to databases, directories, transaction middleware and communications. Managing these interfaces to avoid conflicts and locks-ups is a major challenge for ASPs.

Up until recently it had not been clear how to ASP-enable the applications themselves. One theme of ASP enablement is about optimizing applications for the Web. This theme has inspired several ASPs, and other members of the ASP ecosystem, to found the Internet Business Services Initiative[8] (IBSi) in December 1999 "as a

---

8. See www.ibusinessservices.org/.

mutual benefit, non-profit corporation formed to assist companies in providing better software solutions to the marketplace... The primary business of an IBSi is to develop, host, and service business-to-business applications designed from the ground up for deployment over the Web." IBSi was chartered to enable its members to "work together to develop technical standards, create industry net-working-opportunities, and educate the market on the benefits of the one-to-many IBS business model." IBSi clearly recognized the challenge of *one-to-many* (support multiple customers), calling for ASP-enabling of future Web applications. An example of a J2EE based application is used below to demonstrate the issues related to, and possibilities of, a single instance of an application supporting multiple customers.

One Application Copy Supports Multiple Customers

By definition, most J2EE-based containers can run multiple applications. The BEA's WebLogic or iPlanet's iAS 6.0 application servers are good examples of such containers.

Next, applications driven by metadata (e.g., policy) may run in multiple threads themselves and thus support multiple customers too. The BEA's WebLogic Application Server maintains such policies, the so-called property files, on behalf of all applications it runs. These policies include:

- J2EE security realms (defining where the application gets policy information from for user authentication as well as other user and application metadata)
- Databases for applications to access
- Resource pools (connection, databases, threads, etc.)
- Other configuration information

How would a single J2EE container support multiple customers? Here is an example:

- A user from a customer dials the ASP Web site.
- The user is authenticated by accessing directory database or another data store for policy information.
- The retrieved policy describes the unique application processing requirements for this customer's users:
  - Databases they store data in
  - Unique workflows (if any)

- Unique interfaces, addresses, URLs, and so on
- Unique look and feel

This flow should apply to multiple users from multiple customers running the same application. Each customer's users will run in their own container threads and, short of a few exceptions outlined in the policies, will also share the same EJBs, JSPs, and APIs. This approach ensures the ability to share one instance of an application among multiple customers.

ASP Enabling Properties of Application Sharing

Some issues and caveats related to ASP-enabling of application are described here.

Sharing. The aforementioned materials spoke sufficiently to the issues of enabling ASP applications for shared use. The applications that are policy driven are the best candidates for sharing. More research, however, into the options and technologies enabling application sharing is still required.

Qualities. There are several issues and caveats related to ensuring manageable qualities for ASP applications.

- Configuration information for each J2EE container must be designed carefully to accommodate the requirements of multiple customers. Limitations in flexibilities required for accommodating multiple customers must be well understood and properly managed. For example, the property files for WebLogic Application Server 5.1 from BEA can specify only one J2EE security realm, which must therefore apply to all customers. For some customers, this common realm may not be good enough, for others, it may be overkill.

- Policy data schemas for each customer stored in an LDAP database (or any other form) must be carefully designed and coordinated with the design of application logic. The tools to manage policy data must have high enough security privileges to prevent unintended or malicious changes.

- Database schemas used by shared applications may need to be examined for any changes due to their ownership by different customers.

- Application security is a big issue, both in reality and customer perception. Security is determined via J2EE realm, with one realm for all.

- Because configuration information is frequently provided for the entire container, individual customer performance and availability guarantees may be hard, if not impossible, to ensure.

Metering. Some resources used by customer application, for example, storage and network transactions, can be measured directly. These measures are needed for ASP's accounting of its internal costs. The use of shared applications by different customers requires prorating. This can be done indirectly by measuring an application's memory footprint, or its CPU consumption patterns, or by measuring each customer's transactions and inputting them to the CPU and memory. These numbers are needed for reconciling application software license costs with the ISVs.

ASP Service Management

The ASP service management process was defined in detail in Chapter 7. Figure 10.6 is borrowed from Figure 7.4 to serve as a reminder of the ASP service management process and its functions.

The objectives of this section are to identify the *foundation* technologies used to enable the ASP service management functions and discover the products (and vendors) that make the use of these enabling technologies practical.

Figure 10.6   *ASP service management process and functions—the "wheel."*

Here is a brief review of the ASP service management process and its functions.

- **Business Planning** is a business-related implementation function used for planning investments, services, and facilities; recurring analyses of changing ASP requirements; and continuous reviews and adjustments of customer management.

- **Service Definition** is also an implementation function used to define and then deploy the real services, such as applications, hosting infrastructure, management functions, and customer care.

- **Customer Provisioning and Allocations.** These functions are used to subscribe customers and provision for them the application services previously mentioned.

- **Metering and Accounting** are operational functions used to collect usage and performance data for subsequent accounting, billing, and making operational and strategic management decisions.

- **Dynamic Configuration and Management**—an operational function—uses the data collected by metering to run sophisticated algorithms for managing and reconfiguring the elements of ASP's operational infrastructure to meet customers' SLAs.

- **Reporting and Billing** runs reports, helps compute invoices according to pricing plans, renders customer bills, and analyzes usage and growth trends.

Enabling ASP Service Management Functions

The analysis of existing service management products resulted in the identification of four *foundation* technologies (disciplines) enabling the ASP service management:

1. Agent Technologies
2. Directory Services
3. Data Warehouses (along with data mining tools and methods)
4. Mathematical and Statistical Models

These technologies and disciplines are implemented within, and used by, the various functions of the "wheel" process. Their brief definitions and benefits are provided next.

Agent Technologies for ASP Service Management

It is more reliable to use the words of experts. A simple definition of *agent technologies* is: "agents represent an exciting and promising new approach to building a wide range of software applications.

Agents are autonomous problem-solving entities that are able to flexibly solve problems in complex, dynamic environments, without receiving permanent guidance from the user."[9]

The next quote explains why to use the agents: "The dynamic and distributed nature of both data and applications require that software not merely respond to requests for information but intelligently anticipate, adapt, and actively seek ways to support users. Not only must these systems assist in coordinating tasks among humans, they must also help manage cooperation among distributed programs... In response to these requirements, the efforts of researchers from several different fields have begun to coalesce around a common broad agenda: the development of software agents."[10]

These definitions accurately describe the use of agents for ASP. Agents developed and used for ASP service management are independent—even nomadic—entities collecting multifaceted data from the managed infrastructure's elements (servers, networks, applications, etc.) The agents send so-collected data to designated central authorities, which may rule agents' functions and activities and use them to exert control over the managed elements.

An example is a performance-monitoring agent that may run on various Web servers and collectively control the behavior of a load balancer to redirect traffic based on load, response time, server health, and end-to-end availability of the applications accessed from the Web servers.

Directory Services for ASP Service Management

Giga Group estimated that by the end of 2001 about 90% of all enterprises would employ some type of *directory* services. Why use directories? Directory is a centralized repository of data about various entities—users, systems, and so forth—in the managed infrastructure. Directories provide the following benefits (by categories):

- **Data Management**: Improve data management and increases data integrity.

- **Administration**: Simplify and reduce redundancies of administration by making it possible to manage all entities remotely and from a central location; additionally, delegated administration enables user self-service.

- **Security:** Consolidate authentication and authorization in one secure place.

---

9. Michael J. Wooldridge and Nick R. Jennings (Eds.), *Agent Technology: Foundations, Applications, and Markets*, New York, NY: Springer-Verlag, February 1998.

10. Jeffrey M. Bradshaw, Ed., *Software Agents*, Menlo Park, CA: AAAI/MIT Press, 1997.

- **Development**: Ensure software design independence from single vendor solutions and systems platform and reduces application development time by eliminating the need to build metadata repositories for each application.

- **Costs:** Ultimately, directories help lower the Total Cost of Ownership (TCO) for all infrastructure's managed systems.

In short, directories help manage identities, relationships, and business risks. LDAP, which stands for Lightweight Directory Access Protocol, is a standard many companies opt to use for their directory needs. While the following quote addresses LDAP in particular, it might as well apply to any other type of directory protocol in support of the overall directory concept:

> An Internet service provider, for example, might create an LDAP directory that contains information about all its subscribers and the special add-on services it may have purchased. The directory can be consulted each time the user wants to access a given service. If the user has appropriate permissions, as registered in the directory, the application grants the user access; otherwise, access is denied. Management of all the value-added services is handled by updating the directory.[11]

This quote adequately explains the importance of directories to ASP. For this, and many other reasons, the various service management products rely on the capabilities of directory services.

Data Warehousing for ASP Service Management

A *data warehouse* is a collection of data used for making management decisions. *Data warehousing* is the process of creating, populating, and then using the warehouse's data for decision-making. The business of data warehouses and warehousing encompass numerous markets, methodologies, technologies, and tools used for building, using, and managing the data warehouses.

Not all ASP service management vendors refer to their databases used for collecting and processing data as data warehouses. Yet the moniker can be safely applied. The recognized "father" of the data warehouse, Bill Inmon, stated in many books and articles that a data warehouse is "a subject-oriented, integrated, time-variant, non-volatile collection of data in support of management's decision making process."[12] However long and seemingly complex, this definition perfectly fits the purposes of using the data warehouses for ASP. Indeed,

---

11. Tim Howes, Mark Smith, Gordon Good, *Understanding and Deploying LDAP Directory Services*, chapter 3, London: Macmillan Technical Publishing, January 1999.

12. One such book is *Building the Data Warehouse* by W.H. Inmon, New York, NY: John Wiley & Sons, 1996.

the data is focused on service management (*subject-oriented), integrated f*rom multiple sources, accumulated over a period of time (hence, *time-variant*), and must not be changed once collected (*non-volatile*). The data collected from many sources represents a comprehensive picture of the managed systems' conditions in real- or near-real time required for making informed ASP service management decisions. These decisions are either operational, such as those for reconfiguring the environment when the dynamic conditions change, or strategic, such as those for planning future investments in systems, people, and processes.

Statistics and Math for ASP Service Management

Statistical modeling is an effective technique to analyze traffic and resource data to extract growth and distribution patterns. Other techniques—expert systems, knowledge management systems, data mining, and so forth—are also found in the arsenal of vendors building the service management products. For example, for dynamic infrastructure configuration changes, complex algorithms are frequently used to anticipate the capabilities of the infrastructure and reconfigure it to better meet the requirements of customers' SLAs.

Although the least developed, formal modeling is perhaps the most crucial among the management tools. Without it, budgeting, scheduling, and planning cannot be adequately performed, and the management of an ASP can be severely hampered.

ASP Service Management's Conceptual Architecture

Figure 10.7 depicts the *conceptual architecture* of ASP service management and shows how the aforementioned foundation technologies work together.

Agents are located throughout the data centers and network nodes (big cloud at the bottom) installed on various devices, attached to applications and middleware and tasked with gathering (Arrow 1) data on performance, resource usage, and faults. Some intelligent agents can also exert control over different devices. They either do so independently when their monitored devices act inconsistently with prescribed policies, or when instructed from the Operational Service Management Center (Arrow 4).

Data Warehouse is where the data collected by the agents is stored (Arrow 2) in formats required by virtually all of the functions of the "wheel" controlled from the management console (Arrow 5).

Directory (e.g., LDAP based) is where all relevant customer information and systems configuration information is stored. It is mostly updated by Service Definition and Provisioning and Allocation functions (Arrow 3) but is also accessed by other "wheel" functions as well.

Service Management Center is the brain of the entire ASP service management environment.

- It supports the Definition and Customer Provisioning and Allocations functions for setting up application services and customers.

- It runs, during the runtime, the Metering and Accounting and Dynamic Configuration and Management functions for processing collected data for further analyses, reporting, and display and for the dynamic management of resources to meet customer SLAs, respectively.

- It executes Reporting and Billing functions to generate reports (by customers, by service, by SLA, etc.) and generate invoices, according to whatever pricing schemes the customer used for billing

- Finally, it runs all the required data processing (e.g., data mining, statistics) on behalf of Business Planning to make service, market, and investment decisions from the historical data.

Management Console is used for the display and management of the entire ASP service management environment (Arrow 5).

Figure 10.7 *Conceptual view of ASP service management enablement.*

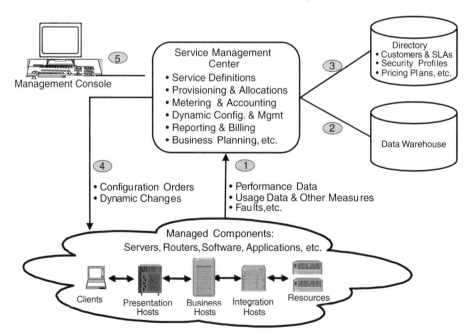

ASP Service Management Products

It is generally not advisable to even attempt to offer product overviews in a book like this, especially when everything related to the subject of discussion—ASP—is changing so fast. On the other hand, this is the only way to validate claims already made and models drawn to explain the nascent technical and business phenomena associated with ASP. While the danger of drastically changed conditions is always looming, this brief note should be considered a disclaimer of this author's efforts to drive home the salient points of this book.

So, there are many service management products already on the market that may selectively support the various functions of the "wheel" (Figure 10.6). Some vendors claim their products are point products (e.g., focused on security only), others assert they publish integrated suites. While the overall nomenclature (categories) and terminology used by many vendors differ from the "wheel," it is still possible to assemble a list of product categories and product/vendor references that collectively support all the functions of the "wheel." This is exactly what is done below. Here are the chosen product categories:

- Performance and Availability Monitoring and Management
- (Dynamic) Network Optimization
- IP Network QoS Management
- Trend Analysis
- Usage Accounting and Chargeback
- User Credentialing
- Service Management Platforms

Most service management products are implemented as nonintrusive add-ons (or are based on agent technology) and therefore can be tested before being implemented.

However, in practice, building a comprehensive service management environment would inevitably require an integration of products from different vendors. Fortunately, numerous interface technologies and techniques exist, the most notable being XML, which facilitate the process but don't make it completely painless and cheap.

The following sections describe several point and suite products and then map their capabilities against the functions of the "wheel."

Performance and Availability Monitoring and Management

ASPs must provide managed performance and availability. Deploying agent technology-based tools to monitor, compute, report, and manage service qualities on a per-customer basis (actually, the

SLAs) does the job. By using these tools ASPs guarantee systemic qualities by customer, by application, or both.

Performance and availability monitoring helps manage traffic distribution according to the dynamic capacities and availabilities of the facilities processing this traffic. Thus, performance and availability tools can distribute traffic among multiple servers based on such criteria as availability, message type and priority, and message content (e.g., application).

Performance monitoring and management tools may support three (of five) processes of ASP service management: metering and accounting, dynamic configuration and management, and reporting and billing. Examples follow:

Example 1: **ProactiveNet**[13] publishes software products with extensive capabilities for monitoring and management of distributed systems performance and availability. It uses its own agents and service management center software. It performs the following activities:

- Sets intelligent thresholds for normal ranges of infrastructures' performance and availability for all monitored elements

- Monitors and tracks performance and availability levels and logs and displays the real-time and/or historical views

- Takes action when the levels exceed the thresholds, the actions being logging traffic abnormalities for future analyses, ringing alarms, or even executing changes in the computing and networking environment to bring the levels into the normal range again

- Uses collected data for computing and reporting customer SLAs.

The data ProactiveNet collects can be used to compute user interface SLAs.

Example 2: **Peakstone**[14] products serve a similar purpose to ProactiveNet's but with the use of statistical methods.

- Peakstone applies traffic pattern detection technology to dynamically learn, build, and adaptively modify (on an as-needed basis) the capacity and resource utilization models within the ASP's infrastructure. It does so using dynamic real-time information culled from the traffic itself.

- Peakstone agents "reside" between the application protocols and application layers in order to collect information from user messages at the session and application request level.

---

13. See www.ProactiveNet.com.
14. See www.ProactiveNet.com.

- Peakstone can integrate with other performance monitoring and management systems like server load balancers, dynamic caches, bandwidth managers, and others. It can then fine-tune those products' policies and configuration parameters to adjust to changing conditions in order to better serve customer performance requirements.

- Peakstone can also enforce and manage dynamic resource provisioning.

To sum up, Peakstone provides differentiated levels of performance and resource usage based on the dynamic behavior of Web-based infrastructure and according to the policy of each customer (e.g., SLAs).

Example 3: Resonate[15] is a company offering a suite of capabilities to support diverse forms of load balancing. Resonate product CentralDispatch™ performs service level monitoring and service level control too. Key features are:

- Multitier resource monitoring—across the tiers of Web, application and databases—extending application and resource awareness across all tiers of a network-based application.

- Sophisticated policies-based event translation system, logging, and notification.

- Real-time, automated control–sophisticated traffic management technology and control of (integration with) third-party traffic management products, system and application process control.

- Real-time performance measurement, historical charting, threshold event generation, and management.

- Works well in combination with content delivery networks (e.g., Inktomi, Akamai).

  - Caching stores frequently requested content close to the end user for optimized performance and reduced bandwidth utilization.

  - When traffic increases, content distribution replicates, distributes, and synchronizes content among multiple sites. This distributed approach ensures the availability of the freshest content and minimizes access latencies.

  - Content management enables real-time, centralized monitoring and control of the distributed content and application components.

  - Service level management provides the control necessary to deliver highly available services to end users.

15.See www.Resonate.com.

Central dispatch can assess all information in a TCP packet to differentiate incoming traffic requests and match those requests to appropriate resources. It will also improve an end user's on-line experience by using outbound data stream processing to look for application error codes and then take corrective action before the error message reaches the end user.

Central dispatch will also provide enhanced protection against denial of service attacks by allowing regular traffic to proceed even when a site is flooded with SYN requests or by slowing down outbound transfers of large files when numerous large file requests occur.

Dynamic Network Optimization

Dynamic network optimization is based on a few simple premises: observe and measure the network performance, identify trouble spots, and then route customer traffic around these spots per traffic management requirements and customer priorities. This way, the use of network optimization systems could help ASP avoid network congestions, bypass the points of packet loss and higher latency, and minimize the impact of other problems not always addressed by conventional network management technologies.

Example: A company called **InterNAP**[16] offers a family of sophisticated network optimization products. InterNAP provides the P-NAP® network facilities and ASsimilator™ technology that jointly coordinate the routing of data over the network faster, more reliably, and in a better managed fashion than over the network without InterNAP's products. InterNAP's major customers are services providers, ISPs, co-location providers, and others.

IP Network QoS Management

The IP network QoS management is based on the collection of IP detail records (IPDR)[17] from a variety of network elements:

- Traffic statistics from IP routers
- Firewall logs
- Intrusion detection systems (IDS) logs
- Server OS and other systems logs
- Access control server user access logs
- LDAP databases
- DNS server

Once collected, these data are processed (filtered, sorted, sometimes reduced) and then fed into a variety of business support sys-

---

16. See www.internap.com.
17. IPDR is similar to Telco's CMDR records.

tems (BSS) and operational support systems (OSS), such as bill rendering systems for usage-based bill generation, traffic flow analysis systems for better network planning, and network management systems, for dynamic network performance optimization.

Example: A company called **XACCT** is an active player in this IP QoS space (otherwise frequently called "network mediation"), enabling the collection and processing of IPDR. With its product XACCTusage™ it collects IPDR from a wide variety of network elements (see the aforementioned list) and subsequently feeds this data into multiple BSS/OSS (similar to the ones mentioned before). More than half of XACCT's customers use IPDR to support usage-based network services and billing.

Trend Analysis

In the core of trend analysis lie powerful databases, sophisticated agent technologies, plus reporting and data mining tools. Typically, trend analysis requires these components:

- <u>Agents</u> collecting data from virtually all elements of the NC or ASP infrastructure including Web and application servers, firewalls, storage, load managers, caches, bandwidth managers, applications, components of application hosting infrastructure, and Web pages.

- A <u>Management System</u>, where agents send collected data and which hosts databases, report creation and generation tools, and trend analysis applications.

- A Management <u>Console(s)</u> for displaying real-time data and conducting on-line management of the infrastructure's performance and availability.

Most trend analysis tools offer both real-time and deferred capabilities. A comprehensive set of real-time capabilities may include the following:

- Collecting performance and availability data from all components monitored by distributed agents

- Viewing the entire monitored environment's health on a management console

- Generating and processing alerts to performance and availability problems

- Running diagnostic tools to pinpoint performance problems

- On-line managing of policies for monitoring, collecting, and logging of data; by agents, by components, by customers

- Logging of data to the Management System's central data warehouse

- Interfacing other systems such as pricing and billing
- Running and printing performance, availability, and many other reports

In addition to computer and network data, trend analysis tools can also interface with and collect systems logs, router logs, security logs (e.g., IDS), phone usage logs, specific ISV applications' logs, and so forth. The deferred capabilities are:

- Data mining of recorded data to understand statistical and historical trends for services, resource usage, and demand distribution
- Generating reports

Example 1: A company called Appliant[18] offers a product called Lateral Line supporting many of the aforementioned features. To understand how comprehensive trend analysis report portfolios can be, here is a roster of reports obtained from Appliant's marketing literature: client page stop trends, HTTP error components by URL, HTTP error trends by component, server page request trends by servers, network latency by server, client render latency distribution, client render latency trends by URL, client response time by URL, client page stops by URL, client page stops by server, client response time distribution, server page requests by server, server latency by server, server HTTP errors by server, network latency trends, client dwell time distribution, client render latency trends by server, server page requests by URL, and so on. A pretty comprehensive collection, is it not?

Example 2: SAS Institute offers the IT ServiceVision™ product, which brings the diverse data collected by various monitoring systems (SAS interfaces to many) into a comprehensive data warehousing structure and offers many of the aforementioned trend analysis capabilities.

Usage Accounting and Chargeback

Some usage accounting and chargeback systems are implemented as add-ons to data collection and warehousing operations (Example 1). They work off the warehoused data to analyze resource usage and costs applying the metadata of pricing plans, rate models, billing rules, and so forth.

In other cases, usage accounting and chargeback processes are components of comprehensive service provider (e.g., ASP) deployment and management platforms (Example 2 and next section). There, these capabilities are integrated with customer care, user

---

18. See www.Appliant.com.

management and self-administration, security, service management and provisioning, pricing engines and metadata, and so forth.

Example 1: SAS Institute, Inc.'s IT ChargeManager™ is an add-on to aforementioned IT Service Vision. It brings the capabilities of Online Analytical Processing (OLAP) to the data warehouse to analyze and report on resource usage and costs. It can "generate customized Actual vs Budget reports, simulate changes in rate models, produce invoices, and export data to general ledger applications."[19]

Example 2. Solect Technology Group, Inc.'s[20] product IAF Horizon—with IAF standing for Internet Administration Framework—is a billing system which includes service management, customer care and self-care, a rule-based rating engine, and provisioning data collector (PDC) plug-ins.

User Credentialing Technologies

This section doesn't invent new security technologies to support ASP service management but briefly shows how the existing ones are packaged. Most security point solutions offer what is called *secure subscription models* with some of the following capabilities:

- Comprehensive management of controlled access to applications and information
- Facilities and techniques for customer self-subscription and self-care
- Complex organizational security models (workgroups, individuals, roles, etc.)
- Subscription and usage-based pricing plans

Example 1: Netegrity Inc.'s popular Site Minder™ product actively uses the central repository as "a platform of shared services enabling single sign-on, authentication management, entitlement management, distributed administration and affiliate services."[21]

Example 2: SevenMountain Software, Inc. products 7M Integrate and 7M Aspire offer administration of application access and "singular subscription and profiling functionality... with easy access to internal applications and information via a universal thin client interface."[22]

Service Management Platforms

The service management platform vendors focus their products on the first three processes of the ASP service management cycle: service modeling, provisioning and allocations, and metering and

---

19. See www.sas.com/products/itchargemgr/index.html.
20. See www.solect.com.
21. see www.netegrity.com/products/siteminder.html.
22. See www.sevenmountains.com/html/products.htm.

accounting. They also feed the last process of reporting and billing. However, for the latter, they frequently only provide collected data in agreed-upon formats, development kits, and APIs.

Example 1: Xevo Corporation[23] is a representative of vendors of service management platforms. Since ASP customer needs for application packages may vary, XevoLogic™ offers a data model, which manages packaging of applications and services by defining features and dependencies for applications. This accomplishes service modeling by creating customized packages and effecting customer change when needed. For provisioning and allocation, Xevo automates the activation of new customers, manages changes in customer information, and offers quick access to services. For metering, it uses metering agents to record usage and resource consumption within the context of the original sales order. It collects, consolidates, and organizes the data received from the metering agents for subsequent submission to other systems for reporting and billing. This may include: billing, customer service and support, vendor (e.g., ISV) license reconciliation, and capacity planning and resource allocation.

Example 2: Another example of a service management platform is offered by Solect. Briefly put, Solect's IAF Horizon product suite for ASPs "enables application provisioning, account and user management, usage data collection, and billing for hosted applications."[24]

Example 3: Ensim Corporation is a third and very unique service management platform vendor. Ensim's ServerExchange™ allows a customer to create a truly virtual environment—a private server—from an arbitrary collection of server resources, for example, multiple processors in an SMP system or a slice of a small processor. All will appear to the customers as an individual computer that will handle its own resources, security, management, and faults independently of others. ServerXchange™ offers capabilities to:

- Start out as a small ASP and quickly grow; manage from 25 to 25,000 hosting application plans and from 25 to 250,000 customers

- Control all hosting operations from a single administrative interface

- Manage multiple physical and private server domains and customers

- Quickly and easily provision new customers and automate key hosting operations

- Handle mass application upgrades across multiple servers

23. See www.xevo.com.
24. See www.solect.com.

- Quickly roll out new hosting plans for new applications, e-commerce, intranet collaboration, and streaming

- Provide an intuitive set of control tools for administrators, customers, and users

To summarize, Ensim offers a hosting technology to maximize the use of hosting platforms combined with the very sophisticated capabilities in support of service modeling, provisioning and allocations, and dynamic configuration and management.

Mapping Terminology and Service Management Functions

Table 10.1 maps the various product categories against the service management processes defined before.

Table 10.1 *Service Management Products and Functions*

Product Categories	Vendors	Functions					
		Service Modeling	*Provisioning & Allocation*	*Metering & Accounting*	*Dynamic Mgmt & Configuration*	*Reporting & Billing*	*Planning*
Performance and Availability Monitoring and Management	Proac-tiveNet Peakstone Resonate			X X X	X	X X	
Dynamic Network Optimization	InterNAP			X (network only)	X (network only)		
IP Network QoS Management	XACCT			X (network only)			
Usage Accounting and Chargeback	Solect SAS						X X
Customer/User Credentialing·	Netegrity Seven-Mountains		X X				
Service Mgmt Platforms	Xevo Solect Ensim	X X X	X X X	X X	X	X	
Trend Analysis	Appliant SAS					X X	X X

Many of the companies in Table 10.1 have integrated their products with other companies' products to provide for comprehensive sets of service management capabilities. Some companies listed are integrated among themselves, for example, Solect works closely with XACCT, and so on.

Summary

The structure of this chapter is similar to that of many others: It introduces the frameworks and taxonomies, explains their components and interrelationships, and finally applies them, as much as possible, to the real world of ASP. Perhaps the most significant result of this chapter is the distinction between the two types of technologies in the ASP domain:

- Those that enable the ASP infrastructure (e.g., SMP, SAN/NAS, J2EE)

- Those that manage it (e.g., the agents, directories, data warehousing, statistics and math and all the products using them).

The first type assumes enabling of ASP's resource sharing, managed qualities, and measurable usage. Incidentally, these capabilities were not invented for ASP, and were present in the NC. Yet, some products already exhibited the properties applicable to ASP, as was shown in this chapter. Recognizing this, many hardware and software vendors may be expected to design more ASP-enabled products in the future.

The second type is about the capabilities to control this resource sharing, to effectively manage infrastructure qualities, and to accurately measure resources usage. These capabilities are not new either, as some network and systems management technologies had already addressed similar management challenges in the past. Still, the advent of ASP dramatically increased the pace and quantity of new product introductions, and greatly enhanced their sophistication.

The framework defined in this chapter is the "wheel" of the process of ASP service management (Figure 10.6). It consists of operational and implementation functions (three each) built on four *foundation* technologies—agents, directories, data warehousing, and statistics and math. The conceptual view of these *foundation* technologies working together is shown in Figure 10.7.

Finally, a survey of ASP service management products reveals that there truly exist products, at the time of this writing, which may collectively support the ASP service management functions.

Chapter 11

The Future of ASP

This is the last chapter of the book. It attempts to visualize the future of ASP using a very prosaic approach—asking questions. The questions are about who the future ASP customers will be, the kinds of services ASPs will offer these customers, the ASP industry and its evolution, the technologies these ASPs will use, and finally, the impact of all of this on the other members of the ASP ecosystem.

To "peek" into the future requires a choice of a predictive analysis. The analysis used here assumes that the development of ASP may be similar to that of the IT industry. Surprisingly, as the material shows, this assumption works well as it turns out that most up-to-date ASP developments truly resemble the events in the history of IT, although they are occurring at a faster pace. From there, it is easier to draw parallels for the future.

Finally, the summary at the end of the chapter is just an optimistic note proclaiming this author's strong confidence in the bright future of ASP. The author also timidly hopes that this conviction of his becomes contagious.

The ASP Industry's Formative Stage

From its very inception, ASP looked attractive to the entire ASP ecosystem (see Figures 3.1 and 11.1). It promised new and expanded markets to ISVs, large sales to hardware vendors, more networking to NSPs, novel ideas and new clients to SIs, VIs, and consultants, and potentially major economic benefits to end users. The future demand for ASP also seemed huge, perhaps bigger than the entire IT industry, as it potentially hinted at a total substitution of ASP for incumbent IT along with the massive expansion of services in the future.

As a result, many companies from different camps rushed into the ASP space with a variety of products and services. No one could allege, though, to completely understand the structure and future of the new industry. The new industry was and still is forming and shaping, shaking-out and consolidating, while also offering major opportunities to all the players to potentially become ASP industry's thought leaders, first-mover brands, and hopefully financial successes. Due to the ASP industry's shakeout and consolidation, fast under way at the time of this writing, the future of the industry and markets should inevitably look different from its early inception period. Indeed, in the three years of ASP history, almost 2,000 companies have claimed to offer ASP services. Yet only about half of them could be qualified as ASPs based on the assertions of major market analysts. In one of its statements, at a conference in March 2001, Gartner Group representatives said the following:[1]

> The current ASP market could see a consolidation of about 60 percent by the end of this year. There are between 700 and 1,000 ASPs today, and that number could diminish to about 20 within the next five years.

Despite all these growth pains, many ASPs continue to persist. Those who understand the history of economic evolution truly believe in the objective inevitability of ASP (Chapters 1 and 2) and stay the course, notwithstanding how trying, complex, or disruptive their journey to the future might be.

Analyzing ASP Industry

Samuel Goldwyn of MGM[2] fame once said, "It is very dangerous to make predictions... especially about the future." In the world of IT, and now the Internet, this holds especially true. Many business

---

1. *Computer Reseller News*, www.cmp.com, Manhasset, NY: CMP Media, LLC, March 3, 2001.
2. MGM—Metro Goldwyn Meyer, a major Hollywood movie studio.

ideas (technologies, products, services, etc.) frequently arrive on the scene just to enjoy their "15 minutes of fame" and then fade away. Many events, frequently considered momentous, soon turn out to be fleeting and irrelevant. For these reasons this chapter doesn't make predictions on the basis of short-term technology and business trends. Instead, it elects to take cues from the history of IT, which reflects how user needs evolved, how vendors responded, and how the entire IT industry was shaped over time. Thus, analyzing IT and its history should provide insights into how ASP should evolve.

IT has been around for more than 50 years, but truly exploded in the last 15 to 20. During its illustrious history, IT has endured many critical transformations—from an occupation of military scientists in the late 1940s to a mature and powerful business responsible for massive investments, vibrant commerce, and a sizable share of, and impact on, many a national GNP.

The last 20 years, as noted, have also been critical, as they heralded major changes in the nature and uses of IT. Table 11.1 lists some key developments in IT during those years that are relevant to the subject matter of this chapter, ASP.

Some of the definitions from the IT transformation are used here for analyzing ASP and its future.

Table 11.1 *IT Industry's Transformation From Early Initial To Modern Mature State*

Earlier & Initial State	*Modern & Mature State*
1. Home-grown custom solutions	Application packages
2. Single-function/purpose systems	Application suites
3. Detached, unconnected designs	Networked, distributed systems
4. Long, multiyear development cycles	Short, few-month-long application assembly and customization projects
5. General purpose solutions	Specialized solutions, by functionality, industry, user size, application, and so forth
6. Rigid systems and application architectures	Modular and component-based designs that are easy to modify, customize, and extend
7. Budget-driven IT	IT as an investment
8. In-house development organizations	SWAT-style temporary professional development teams
9. IT practitioners: scientists, business people, and engineers	Bona-fide IT departments become middlemen between user and suppliers

ASP Markets—Future Customers and Their Needs

Initially, ASPs targeted SMBs. They believed (quite prophetically) that the global markets and the Internet had put SMBs on an equal footing with their larger competitors for access to suppliers and customers. Now, they continued to reason, SMBs wanted the same sophisticated application functionality their larger competitors enjoyed. Yet, SMBs could not afford those applications. The answer to the puzzle was obvious, "applications as service," that is, ASP!

What came next was totally unexpected, but welcome. Numerous large enterprises opted for ASP as well. Motivated by the same logic incorporated in the generic value propositions in Chapter 9, they wanted to "rescue" capital from IT, reduce variable costs, go faster to market, gain higher ROI, and improve QoS via formal SLAs. But their most important reason was a desire to finally focus on their own core competencies in lieu of tending to their bloated and demanding corporate ITs.

All this came as a big surprise to many commercial ASPs (and market observers), but it further reassured their commitments to their young business and drew many other important parties into the ASP ecosystem. Overall, these early experiences showed that any size enterprises could be ASP customers.

As for the end consumers, ASP was not novel to them at all. They had already used it for a while without, perhaps, suspecting it. Indeed, as was mentioned earlier, by signing up with an ISP—whether a giant AOL or a ma-and-pa local shop—the consumer effectively rented access to Internet applications and paid monthly fees for using them. These applications included the Web, email, chat, and others. Similarly, by using auction sites, the consumer was gaining access to a market exchange for fees from executed transactions. Or, going to a portal, the consumer was accessing news and views by paying with personal time for being exposed to advertising banners.

In addition to size, customers started coming to ASP as they began to see diversified application services: value chain functionality, vertical (industry) specific services, sophisticated data processing features, and analytical applications.

Did the development of ASP markets resemble that of IT? Yes, it did. Over time, more and more customers began to recognize the following benefits:

- Value of renting packaged solutions in lieu of developing and running their home-grown systems (Item 1 in Table 11.1)
- Efficiencies of integrated suites replacing single function applications (Item 2)
- Major operational and strategic advantages of distributed systems (Item 3)

Further, the development of ASP markets is consistent with Item 5 in Table 11.1, connoting a transition from the use of general-purpose applications to specialized solutions—by functionality, industry, customer size, application type, or any combination thereof.

Finally, instead of counting costs for equipment, software, and support, ASP customers could study and compare ROIs from dealing with different ASPs. This would stimulate and precipitate a cultural changeover from viewing IT as a cost to treating it as investment (Item 7 from Table 11.1).

ASP Industry – Future ASPs and Their Services

Chapter 6 described the ASP taxonomy as consisting of four basic types: co-location, MIP, AIP, and pure-play ASPs. The recent developments in ASP markets are proving the validity of this classification.

Co-Location. Most NSPs are building physically and geographically expansive data center facilities aiming to stake out the co-location business early, once and for all. This is quite similar to what these companies always did for their traditional telecom business by seeking the rights-of-way for terrestrial networks, buying out cable companies for broadband, and paying top dollar to the government for wireless bandwidth. Examples of their involvement in building co-location plant are numerous:

> Some of the biggest investors in data center expansion will be telecommunications providers. QWEST opened a 15th U.S. data center last month in Dallas and plans to open nine more by year's end. AT&T said it will add eight U.S. data centers this year, more than doubling its domestic data center capacity, and Sprint said it will spend almost $2 billion to 11 U.S. data centers by the end of 2002.[3]

Data centers are not just where the customers host their systems. They are also network nodes. At each data center, NSPs build powerful POPs and ensure diverse public and private peering. Most NSPs position themselves to serve not only the end-user customers but also the numerous *other* ASPs (MIP, AIP, pure-play ASPs) that offer higher layer services (see following) and therefore need to co-locate.

MIP. In real life, many ASPs package their offerings for managed and fully managed co-location services, perfectly fitting the definition of MIP from Chapter 6. These managed and fully managed co-location ASPs own, supply, and manage most of the computing, storage, and network equipment as well as systems software, ultimately ensuring comprehensive infrastructure hosting for their customers and higher services ASPs that feature application infrastructure (AIP) and application hosting (pure-plays). At the same time, many

---

3. From a Tier 1 Research report, March 12, 2001.

co-location ASPs have begun to move up the stack and expand into the roles of managed and fully managed co-location services. A good example is Exodus Communications, which has successfully repositioned itself into this role from being initially a traditional co-location provider.

AIP. The higher services ASPs are what Chapter 6 called AIPs. As of the time of this writing, AIPs are becoming very popular. Loud-Cloud, already mentioned in previous chapters, could be considered the epitome of AIP, even though LoadCloud was not the first to invent and embrace the concept.

Pure-Play ASPs. Pure-Play ASP offerings are exploding beyond the wildest dreams of most optimistic ASP proponents. While Chapter 6 attempted, albeit somewhat tentatively, to list a few pure-play ASP types and services, it requires a truly untamed imagination to fathom the real scale and scope of their expansion. Here are a few remarkable examples of pure-play ASPs. All are real companies and can be easily found on the Web.

- **hotelBANK** supports *hospitality industry's e-commerce*; it connects hotels, customer corporations, and travel suppliers and portals, assisting them to carry out travel industry related e-commerce.

- **IntraLinks** offers new *digital collaboration workspace* enabling intercompany collaboration, improved communications, and workflow implementation.

- **Mymaincontrol.com** provides solutions for *e-infrastructure inventory management*. It offers "proven role- and process-based e-infrastructure management solutions" with access right on the browser.

- **GroupSystems** is a *collaborative reasoning service* that enables customer companies' creative life cycle. GroupSystems online software features tools, best practices, and processes to "help organizations make sense of information and act upon it more effectively... Its unique group dynamics and goal attainment methods allow organizations to narrow in on key issues, generate ideas, organize information, prioritize alternatives, build consensus and ready themselves for action."

- **AgilQuest's** solutions enable organizations to manage *workspace utilization* in flexible field office arrangements. In addition to supporting mobile workers to reserving and allocation assets, AgilQuest's software helps corporate management analyze utilization and allocation of resources for the entire distributed enterprise.

- **CyberShift.com** features online services for *time and attendance tracking and management* to help customers track and manage their workforce.

- **gForce Central** delivers a sophisticated *eLearning platform* helping its customers create, manage, and deliver personnel training programs by building so-called *Knowledge Exchange Portals*.

- **eRoom** helps distributed project teams create a *virtual project space* on the Web. eRoom manages all major elements of team communications and collaboration by bringing together project documents, schedules, meeting agenda and minutes, issues, roles and responsibilities, and other forms of project management collateral essential for project success. "eRoom leverages an enterprise's infrastructure and integrates with all desktop and eBusiness applications to deliver an easy, fast solution to improve project success and timeliness. eRoom is differentiated by its speed of implementation, cross-organizational approach and enterprise integration."

In summary, the real market segmentation of commercial ASPs that started in 2000 and is still continuing into 2001 vividly confirms the architectural layering and ASP type definitions given in Chapter 6. Notwithstanding their labels or definitions, many commercial ASPs are beginning to understand their positions on the stack of NC layers (See Chapters 5 and 6) and make business decisions based on that knowledge. These ASPs are beginning to reinvent and reposition themselves to leverage their incumbent competencies and relationships with other members of the ASP ecosystem in order to enable services which they believe would lead them all to success.

The future of the ASP industry is also related to Item 6 in Table 11.1. Modularization, componentization, and other "divide-and-conquer" approaches have always been good for systems and applications. By minimizing design rigidities, they help champion specialization, promote innovation, encourage linkages and relationships, and help ASPs pursue numerous operational and management economies.

ASP Services—Qualities and Diversity

Services that customers expect to receive from their ASPs will be of higher quality (QoS), cheaper, and delivered faster than with their own IT organizations in the past. The two requirements—faster and better—are directly related to items 4 and 8 in Table 11.1. Indeed, if the service is an ISV product, it is assumed to have built-in quality and can be delivered immediately. If a customer's application requirements are unique, new technologies (SMP servers, component platforms, etc.) and professional services are brought to bear to help deliver quality applications and host them faster, in the Internet time. The third requirement—cheaper—implies that some ASPs will eventually learn how to wring costs out of their hosting infrastructure and processes and eventually pass those savings on to their customers.

Similar to the history of IT, future ASPs will also prefer hosting integrated application suites to single-purpose applications (Item 2 in Table 11.1). This will make many customers with distributed enterprises happy and enable ASPs themselves to enjoy the economies of scope inherent in these application suites.

Since many ASP customers will be distributed enterprises, ASPs will continue leveraging their own distributed architectures to support them. This echoes back to the support for distributed applications by IT (Item 3 in Table 11.1).

Finally, the role of ASP professional services will also continue to grow. As one moves up the ASP stack, from co-location to pure-play, the diversity of services for customers (and ASPs) increases while the potential for services commoditization decreases. The higher up the stack, the more relevant professional services become for implementing and supporting ASP operations and management and helping with customers' application life cycle, bringing new customers through a customer pipeline, continuous support, customizations, M&M, operations, security, and so forth.

ASP Technologies—Enablement of ASPs

Chapter 10 covered the enabling technologies for the whole ASP architecture. It described in detail the enabling technologies for the ASP hosting infrastructure, applications, and management, the latter emphasizing service management in particular. At the moment of this writing, the ASP industry is fast at work developing the standards for ASP enablement. For example, the abovementioned IBSi targeted the following recommendations for standards to be introduced in 2000 and 2001:[4]

1. Common look and feel
2. Common reporting key data integration, including financial information
3. Policy integration
4. Single customer sign-on
5. Data extraction and backup methodologies
6. Coordinated session management
7. Account provisioning
8. Consolidated billing
9. Workflow integration

While many ideas for ASP-enabling overlap, it is still possible to differentiate among them and argue that some recommendations from the list aim at applications (Items 1, 2, and 3), others at the ASP hosting infrastructure (Items 4, 5, and 6), and still others at ASP management (Items 7, 8, and 9). More recommendations and standards are needed, though, and can be introduced at any time now.

The enabling technologies and standards can be compared to the history of the IT industry. Here are the parallels:

- ASP application deployment, management, and operations (also spoken to by IBSi) are similar to what the IT industry did to enable application interfaces to their runtime environments, management tools, and operations (Item 1).

- ASP application integration (also addressed by IBSi) can be compared to the IT industry's challenges in building application suites (Item 2, Table 11.1).

- ASP Web-enabling is analogous to IT's network-enabling of applications (Item 3, Table 11.1) to support SNMP for management; CORBA and RMI for distribution; SNA or TCP/IP for networking, to name a few.

Over time, the ASP-enabling technologies will grow and morph and begin to enjoy the economic benefits of standardization. Standardization is good news for ASP as it promotes its future. Once started, standardization never stops.

---

4. IBSi press release, October 24, 2000; www.ibusinessservices.org/releases/ibsi001024.html.

ASP Ecosystem—Others Affected by the ASP

Figure 11.1 clearly shows a possible proxy role ASPs could play for other members of the ASP ecosystem.

While already a reality for many ASPs, it is difficult to say whether this proxy role will result in the ASPs' commandeering customer account control, fully or partially, from their traditional owners—technology vendors, ISVs, SIs, consultants, and others. While there are indications that this proxy role will persist and increase in relevance, there are also reasonable expectations of strong resistance from current account owners. Regardless of who will eventually prevail, it is clear that many members of the ASP ecosystem will need to review and possibly revise their own business models, strategies, and behaviors. Following is a brief review of what that might mean.

Customer Data. ASPs will be the first point of contact and the first line of support for their customers. Because of this, ASPs will be in the best position to collect data on customer perceptions about their services. For example, they will quickly know the types of SLAs customers really care about and how to provide for them.

Figure 11.1 *ASP's proxy role.*

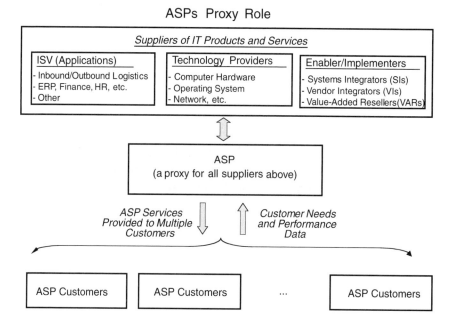

ISV Applications. ASPs will be the first to know what ISV applications and what features and functions customers really want.

Network Services. ASPs will be the first to learn of new network services that customers are interested in, such as roaming-access support, wireless links, more geographical POPs, and so forth.

Infrastructure Systems. Additionally, ASPs themselves will be accruing valuable data in lieu of their customers. This means that what the customers used to collect themselves will now become the privilege of ASPs. ASPs will collect vendor equipment performance statistics for servers, storage systems, routers, switches, firewalls, and so forth. They will also measure the functionality of infrastructure software: OSs, middleware, component platforms, security, service management software, and others. This data will be extremely valuable to other members of the ASP ecosystem and, hence, will have to be handled as such.

Ownership of this customer and performance data will further boost ASPs' ability to control customer accounts. But it will also require ASPs to make investments in the technologies and processes to gather, process, and deliver this data to others. No matter what dispensation, reciprocation, or remuneration (this data can be a source of ASP revenue), other members of the ASP ecosystem will need to take good notice of ASPs' newly acquired power.

- The ISVs will need to listen to ASPs regarding the features, functions, integration options, and ASP enablement requirements of their application systems and other software.

- Hardware and infrastructure software vendors will need to get closer to ASPs and their major sources of actual field-test data, which should be collected continuously, on a large-scale, and in an organized fashion.

- Likewise, SIs, VIs, and various consultants will need to seek work through ASPs, which should explain the flurry of alliances being announced in professional and business press releases virtually every day between ASPs (large and small) and a broad range of professional services organizations.

- Finally, business and investment analysts and market researchers will need to be very "nice" to ASPs who will possess a wealth of information about customers, products, services, qualities, and market trends.

The proxy role of ASPs is similar to the role of mature IT departments which, when they came of age, became real middlemen between the enterprise's users and all technology vendors, ISVs, SIs, and consultants (Item 9 in Table 11.1).

ASP Education—Public Learning of ASPs

Every new industry's first movers always pay an extra price for educating the markets. Hopefully, their first mover positions should translate into longer term business success and brand identity. Common industry bodies, such as IBSi or an ASP Consortium, play an important role in propagating general knowledge and education about ASP.

Additionally, though, many new subjects must be taught specifically. This includes the knowledge about ASP contracts, SLAs, ASP specific security and privacy concerns, systemic qualities, legal issues, and so forth. Most of these subjects are the domains of ASPs themselves, delivering training to their customers. However, it is also reasonable to expect the traditional education and training companies to enter the space which, besides offering professional education and training services, will also legitimize these services in the eyes of the ASP ecosystem, end customers, and the business community at large.

Summary

The overfranchised, but nonetheless humorous, adage "may you live in the interesting times" has an amazing relevance to the age of ASP. To witness and participate in this remarkable socio-economic paradigm shift associated with one of the most complex disciplines ever invented by a human mind—computing—is a challenge, a privilege, and an exhilarating experience.

Those who believe in the laws of economics may impute the concepts of specialization to information technology and reason that ASP is preordained. Even while others may resist and rally against it, they are fighting a lost cause. Whatever the objections, the transition to the ASP has already begun and ASPs are here to stay.

It is possible to try to envision ASPs of the future (as the material of this chapter attempts), their influence on their own ecosystem (virtually everyone who's anyone in IT and networking industries), and the impact on society at large. But the real scenarios of the future are hard and "dangerous" to come by.

One thing, though, is absolutely clear. "The interesting times" are here and more are still to come. And many readers of this book stand a great chance to take an active part in, and hopefully benefit from, the forthcoming ASP revolution.

Index

A

access control management, 222
access diversity, 110
accessibility, 79
accounting, 288
accuracy, 181
acronyms, list of service provider, 105–106
age discrimination in hiring practices, 40
agent technologies, 288–289
agents, 291
agreement between ASP and customer,
    SLA as, 179–181
AIP
    Application Component, 139
    Application Integration Broker
        Component, 140
    Application Integration Brokers, 137–138
    application integration challenge, 136
    application servers, 134–135
    Application Utilities Component, 139
    availability, 134–135
    communication middleware, 133
    competitive advantages. *See* AIP competitive
        advantages
    component based services, 129
    computing middleware, 133
    Content Services Component, 140
    cost economies. *See* AIP cost economies
    Database Component, 139
    database middleware, 134
    developing and hosting customer
        applications, 131–135

    Development Component, 141
    Directory Component, 140
    Disaster Recovery Component, 141
    distributed file systems, 133
    enterprise application integration, 136–138
    future issues, 308
    high performance, 134
    hosting customer applications, 130–131
    Management Component, 140
    Messaging Component, 140
    middleware, 132–134
    overview, 128–130
    QA Testing Component, 141
    scalability, 134
    Security Component, 140
    service components, 139–141
    Staging Component, 141
    Storage Management Component, 141
    Transaction Middleware Component, 140
    value propositions, 257–258
    Web Component, 139
    Web servers, 135
AIP competitive advantages
    differentiators, 250–254
    functional focus, 254
    implementation skills, 252
    industry focus, 254
    industry-leading suppliers, 251–252
    products/service quality, 252–253
    proprietary integration technologies, 253
    SLAs, 253
    technology focus, 253–254
    timeliness, 252

315

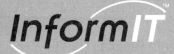

PRENTICE HALL

Professional Technical Reference

Tomorrow's Solutions for Today's Professionals.

Keep Up-to-Date with
PH PTR Online!

We strive to stay on the cutting edge of what's happening in professional computer science and engineering. Here's a bit of what you'll find when you stop by **www.phptr.com**:

@ Special interest areas offering our latest books, book series, software, features of the month, related links and other useful information to help you get the job done.

Deals, deals, deals! Come to our promotions section for the latest bargains offered to you exclusively from our retailers.

$ Need to find a bookstore? Chances are, there's a bookseller near you that carries a broad selection of PTR titles. Locate a Magnet bookstore near you at www.phptr.com.

! What's new at PH PTR? We don't just publish books for the professional community, we're a part of it. Check out our convention schedule, join an author chat, get the latest reviews and press releases on topics of interest to you.

✉ Subscribe today! Join PH PTR's monthly email newsletter!

Want to be kept up-to-date on your area of interest? Choose a targeted category on our website, and we'll keep you informed of the latest PH PTR products, author events, reviews and conferences in your interest area.

Visit our mailroom to subscribe today! **http://www.phptr.com/mail_lists**

www.phptr.com